1978

CHILD ABUSE

CHILD ABUSE
PREDICTION, PREVENTION AND FOLLOW UP

*Papers presented by the Tunbridge Wells
Study Group on Child Abuse at their
Farnham meeting*

Edited by

Alfred White Franklin, M.B., F.R.C.P.

CHURCHILL LIVINGSTONE
EDINBURGH LONDON AND NEW YORK
1977

CHURCHILL LIVINGSTONE

Medical Division of Longman Group Limited

Distributed in the United States of America by
Longman Inc., 19 West 44th Street, New York,
N.Y. 10036 and by associated companies,
branches and representatives throughout
the world.

ISBN 0 443 01641 0

British Library Cataloguing in Publication Data

Child abuse.
    1. Child abuse – Great Britain – Congresses
    I. Franklin, Alfred White
    362.7'1   HV751.A6   77-30322

Printed in Great Britain by Lowe & Brydone,
Thetford, England.

Authors and Participants

Mary Anderson, MB, FRCOG Consultant Obstetrician and Gynaecologist, Lewisham Hospital, London SE13

Sally Beer, Senior Medical Social Worker, representing the British Association of Social Workers

Keith Beswick, FFARCS, MRCGP General Practitioner, Didcot Health Centre

Jessica Blooman, Chief Probation Officer

Raymond L. Castle Executive Head, NSPCC National Advisory Centre on the Battered Child

Winifred Cavenagh, PhD, JP Lately Professor of Social Administration and Criminology, University of Birmingham

D.R. Chambers, MB, BS, LLB, AKC Barrister, H.M. Coroner

Christine Cooper, OBE, MD, FRCP Paediatrician, Department of Child Health, University of Newcastle upon Tyne, British Paediatric Association

Joan Court, SRN, SCN, HV Cert. Department of Health and Social Security

Jean M. Davies, SRN, SCM, HV Cert. Area Nurse Specialist (Child Health), Wiltshire AHA, Chairman, Health Visitors Association

Carol Dukes Health Visitor

Anthony C. Fairbairn Consultant Child Psychiatrist, Bristol and Bath

Alfred White Franklin, MB, BCh, FRCP Paediatrician, British Paediatric Association

Roger D. Freeman, MD Associate Professor of Psychiatry, University of British Columbia

Jean Graham Hall, LM (Lond.) Circuit Judge

Ruth Hanson, BA Lately Senior Research Psychologist Associate, Department of Psychiatry, University of Birmingham

E.C. Higgins, OBE Director of Social Services, London Borough of Wandsworth

Pamela Howat, RGN, SCM Research Sister, Neonatal Unit, John Radcliffe Hospital, Oxford

Beti Jones, BA Chief Adviser, Social Work Services Group (Scottish Office)

Carolyn Okell Jones Formerly Research Officer, Battered Child Research Department, NSPCC, Part-time Project Leader, National Children's Bureau and Tutor in Applied Social Studies, Bedford College, University of London

Daphne Learmont, SRN, SCM, HV Cert. Nursing Officer, Department of Health and Social Security.

Geoffrey Lupton Principal, Department of Health and Social Security

Margaret A. Lynch, MRCP, DCH Research Paediatrician, Human Development Research Unit, Park Hospital for Children, Headington, Oxford

Ronald Mac Keith, MD, FRCP Paediatrician, Director, Medical Education and Information Unit, The Spastics Society

Harold P. Martin, MD Associate Professor of Paediatrics, University of Colorado Medical School, Associate Director, JFK Child Development Center, University of Colorado

J.J. Pietersee, MD Paediatrician, Rotterdam

Cynthia Reynolds, MA(Ed) Advisory Teacher, Inner London Education Authority

R.W. Speirs Deputy Chief Probation Inspector, Home Office

Richard Stone, BM, MRCGP General Practitioner, Paddington, W

Mary Wedlake, MBE Chief Superintendent, Community Relations Branch, New Scotland Yard

Richard A.H. White, L1B Senior Assistant Solicitor, London Borough of Camden

Kulsum Winship, MRCP, HSCM, DCH, Senior Medical Officer, Department of Health and Social Security

CO-AUTHORS (not present)

Susan A. Hartley Senior Secretary and Assistant, Social Work Research Unit, University of Bradford

C. Henry Kempe, MD Professor of Paediatrics and Microbiology, University of Colorado Medical School

J.W. McCulloch, AAPSW, MSc, PhD Director, Social Work Research Unit, University of Bradford

Jacqueline Roberts, MA, MSc Research Social Worker, Human Development Research Unit, Park Hospital for Children, Headington, Oxford

Contents *treatment prevention*

Part 5. Proposals and resolutions

Introduction

A very large amount of work and of attention has been devoted to the subject of Child Abuse since 1973. Evidence exists that the number of murdered babies and children has since diminished while public knowledge of the subject has patently increased. The demands on helping agencies, notably the social service departments, have grown also and to a size which threatens the discharging of their other vitally important responsibilities. The time seemed ripe, therefore, for another residential discussion meeting, to be concerned chiefly with practicalities and the definition of areas for improvement in methods, for study and research.

When the original study group first met in Tunbridge Wells, from which we derived the group's title, we were hoping to increase both professional and public awareness of the existence and the nature of that type of child abuse which was then changing its name from the battering of babies and children to non-accidental injury to children (NAIC). The emphasis was properly on the medical and social aspects of recognition with reference also to police and legal elements in management. A set of resolutions was agreed which followed and enlarged upon plans then being encouraged by the DHSS and the British Paediatric Association and aimed at greater co-operation between the various involved professions.

The members of the study group left Tunbridge Wells feeling inspired and hopeful that something of value had been achieved. The publication and circulation by the DHSS of our report and resolutions in October 1973 seemed to justify our hopes. That the publication of the papers read at the meeting with reports of our discussions would provide a useful reference book for professional workers seemed a reasonable ambition but publishers could not be found to take the risk. It needs to be recorded that the Inquiry into the death of Maria Colwell was what focused public and publisher's interests on the subject. Churchill Livingstone decided that the risk was a proper one to take and *Concerning Child Abuse* appeared early in 1975. The use of the term 'child abuse' showed that our concern was wider than physical injury.

In the Introduction to that book the Working Party of the Tunbridge Wells Study Group was reported to be 'engaged in planning a residential meeting for 1975 when educational and preventive aspects of the subject will be discussed' (p.viii). Through the generosity, once again, of the Medical and Information Unit of the Spastics Society and with the active help of its Director, Dr. Ronald MacKeith ably assisted by Mrs. Eve Kelly, this meeting has now been held at Moor Park College, Farnham, Surrey, October 18 - 21, 1976. Once more the Study Group's gratitude must be recorded to the Spastics Society. Dr. MacKeith and Mrs. Kelly.

The wisdom of attempting a sequel to a successful venture is always in doubt. In the event, the Farnham meeting generated the same enthusiasm and our hope is that this new volume, which attempts to define the present position and which draws attention to many current problems, will be received as a second volume to *'Concerning Child Abuse'*. The composition of the study group is not the same. The organisers believe firmly that thirty is the maximum number for really useful group discussions. Some of the original members, who were not actively engaged in prediction, prevention or follow-up, generously agreed to stand down, but enough original members came to Farnham to provide continuity. Among the newcomers two general practitioners, an obstetrician and a probation officer filled some obvious gaps. For prediction and prevention, the group relied heavily on Ruth Hanson's further studies from Birmingham (Ch. 5) and naturally on work in progress in Oxford under the inspiration of Christopher Ounsted, both in The Park Hospital for Children and the Neonatal Unit at the John Radcliffe Hospital (see Ch. 3 and 4) The key figures in follow-up were Harold Martin who was fortunately able to accept an invitation to fly over from Denver (Ch. 2) and Carolyn Okell Jones reporting from the Battered Child Research project of the NSPCC (Ch. 7). The importance of Martin's paper is recognised by its position in the book. At Farnham, Martin and Jones occupied almost a whole morning. The discussion, one of the most valuable parts of the meeting, is reported at some length after Chapter 7 (see page 67).

The general plan of the previous meeting was followed. Papers were precirculated and the authors each allowed a short time in which to stress the main points. Most of the time was spent in discussions. The convenor and two reporters appointed for each of the eleven sessions made the notes from which the editor has produced the reports scattered through the book. The order of the papers has been changed and, with authors seeming to be more self-conscious this time, many have been revised for publication.

The meeting began with the showing of two films, *Breaking point,* introduced by Margaret Mawer and Henry Kempe's *Mothers' reactions to their newborn babies* introduced by Christine Cooper. Kempe's own introduction to this film forms Chapter 9 and serves as a prelude to Part 2, called 'The educational element', in which the topics, include relevant teaching in the schools and the maternity departments.

In Part 3, 'Current views from the professions', many of the problems of practice are discussed and in Part 4, legal aspects include the preparation of evidence in care proceeding, wardship jurisdiction, some of the effects of the new Children Act 1975 and the controversial statutory removal of a newborn baby.

At a meeting in London in March 1977, some changes in the original Tunbridge Wells' Resolutions were agreed (see Ch. 27) and a number of fresh ones approved (see Ch. 29). These concern fairly broad subjects or activities. Many matters of detail, of no less importance than those more widely applicable, were suggested. The editor has incorporated these as proposals into Chapter 28. About these three chapters the original warning note must be repeated from the introduction to the Report and Resolutions of the Tunbridge Wells Study Group on non-accidental injury to children 1973.

'Not every participant agrees with every detail and no participant could commit the body which he represented or of which he was a member. Nevertheless the greatest care has been taken to achieve wording most of which satisfies most of those who took part'.

The Tunbridge Wells Study Group on Child Abuse and Neglect, not now limited to non-accidental injury, and with some sixty names on its roll will, with its Working Party, continue in being and will meet again. Whether amid the torrent of books and articles springing from this sad subject the group will publish a third volume remains for the future. Meanwhile the group has taken responsibility for promoting the Second International Congress on Child Abuse and Neglect to be held in London in September 1978.

Acknowledgements to the Spastics Society, Dr. Ronald MacKeith and Mrs. Eve Kelly have already been made. We are grateful to Mr. Powell, Warden of Moor Park College and his staff for tending our creature comforts so well during the meeting. The Editor wishes to express his personal thanks to the members of the Study Group for their friendly co-operation and especially to the four DHSS participants under whose kindly but exacting eyes most of the really controversial matters have passed. His thanks are due also to his secretary, Mrs. Dorey, and to Miss Carmen Rodrigues for typing the manuscript and finally to the publishers, Messrs Churchill Livingstone for once more agreeing to publish.

1. Present pre-occupations

ALFRED WHITE FRANKLIN

Many mysteries still surround child abuse and the question remains unanswered, is it possible in a human society to stop it? We have learned how to recognise it, and, perhaps too well, how and when to suspect it. In the following pages are described some of the circumstances and the clusters of circumstances that lead up to it. We are on the way to making predictions about it and to being able to recognise when a baby or a child is at risk within the *milieu* of a vulnerable 'family'.

Methods of prediction are forms of screening tests, sharing with them deficiencies as well as value. The screening test has another problem apart from those of false positives and false negatives; the test only gives an answer to the question asked. We must therefore look as critically at the questions as we do at the answers. What exactly are we predicting? As the antenatal and perinatal questionnaire gains popularity, that question is assuming more importance. We know that we can now identify at least some women who are likely to find mothering this particular child difficult. Not all such mothers abuse their children. So we are led to ask two more questions. What differentiates them and does her difficulty really matter in the absence of abuse, whether to her, the baby's father or the baby itself? Instinctively we answer 'yes'.

To support this affirmative, important observations are being made by ethologists, who are moving from the animal laboratories to the human scene. What they tell us and what we can discern in our predictive studies provide the basis for recognising the biological needs of human beings from the time of birth if not from the time of conception, needs whose fulfilling allows - what? Is the right adjective 'normal' or 'proper' or 'correct' or 'complete' growth and development into a mature adjusted and adaptable adult? Insight into 'normal' emotional needs widens the subject from child abuse to the whole question of optimal routine care.

When the new baby lacks optimal care, and when the handling is bad enough to justify the use of words like neglect and abuse, we can find in follow-up studies some precise disabilities.

Experience as well as ethological observation supports our affirmative answer: harm does result. There are degrees of harm ranging from death or physical injury leading to permanent handicap, all the way to stunted growth and to distortion of the developing personality and the 'cycle of abuse'. When the environment is less hostile, can damage, while less obvious or less dramatic, still be very serious? Does the child have any defences? Some certainly seem to provoke attack. The contribution of the father or of the caretaking consort must not be overlooked. When a helping agent intervenes, this too must carry weight in the assessment.

Screening tests carry another warning. General application to a population must await preventive treatment. Merely to predict trouble and then be powerless to prevent it can do more harm than good. Many therapeutic measures and systems have been described. We need to compare results and to refine decisions about which is the preferred method for a given family. Even more pressing, while we await answers we need to survey in each area what can be provided and what can not. We must ensure also that resources are sufficient for treatment as well as for the comprehensive assessment of the results of treatment.

The system of case conferences and area review committes taxes resources. Professional time spent here is taken from other work, so that the system requires periodic examination. To this end some method of evaluation is urgently wanted. The monitors themselves need monitoring.

Society's part, played by the courts with contributions from the police, continues to be a pre-occupation with all those who work with child abuse. Current anxieties and some positive proposals are described in the book and throughout runs the plea for education, education of professional workers of every kind, of lawyers, of expectant and parturient mothers and not least of the children who will be the parents of the future. As to the education of Society itself, the media do their routine work, bringing to public notice the dramas and the tragedies. The 'set-piece', the Public Tribunal of Inquiry, has probably ceased to be useful. It may now be even harmful, since it insists on a scapegoat when, by the nature of the problem one person alone can never be at fault. The possibility of such an enquiry should things go wrong does not help a worker to make wise decisions, but it can warp judgement.

Two important subjects, which were only mentioned at Farnham, remain for future deliberation. Service families are not immune from abusing their children. Failure to appreciate the true position and hasty posting abroad, when an investigation begins, are helpful in the long run neither to the abusing parents nor to the children.

The second subject is that of sexual abuse including incest.

Fifteen years ago the thalidomide tragedy drew attention to handicapped children. Since then we have a better understanding of the needs of all the handicapped and we have translated this understanding into practical methods of help. The study of child abuse, by its dramatic focusing of attention on the basic biological needs of babies and children in the context of family life, may bring about a much needed general improvement in their care.

PART 1

Techniques and studies

2. A child-oriented approach to prevention of abuse

HAROLD MARTIN

Introduction

This Study Group has gathered to discuss identification and prevention of abuse and neglect of children. The participants in this conference come with different experiences, priorities, and conceptual frameworks regarding abused children. It is expected that there will be some overlap of ideas and views, and just as clearly, there shall be differences in opinion as to where the most important priorities lie. I should like to address three components of identification and prevention, all of which may well be elaborated on by others (Martin, 1976a). I choose these three aspects of prevention because I feel they have not received the attention they should elicit.

The first issue to be discussed is the need not only to prevent abuse, but to prevent *abusive parenting*. I shall be discussing the characteristics of the abusive home, apart from the physical abuse, which needs our attention. The second area to be considered is the *early identification* of the parent-child dyad which as at high risk for abuse. In this area, I wish to emphasise the factors in the child which increase the potential for physical abuse to occur. Finally, I should like to address the issue of *primary* prevention - the task of breaking the cycle where abused children grow up to become abusive parents. Ultimately, in my opinion, a significant reduction in the incidence of child abuse must require our preventing abused children from repeating the 'sins of their fathers'.

Prevention of abusive and neglectful parenting

The title of this section was chosen rather carefully to emphasise the task of trying to change patterns of parenting rather than to prevent solely abuse and neglect. Abusive and neglectful parenting connotes more than physical trauma or ignoring the child and his needs. For the purposes of this paper, I shall be addressing child abuse, while it should be clear that most of the pertinent points are germane to child neglect as well.

The abused child not only lives in a family where he is at risk for physical attack; he is usually in a family where the entire fabric of parenting is deviant and counterproductive to healthy growth and development. Many clinicians and

*Parts of this work were made possible by Maternal-Child Health Grant 926 and The Grant Foundation.

researchers have studied the characteristics of abusive parents and that ground shall not be covered here in any detail. However, I should like to direct the reader to Table 2.1, which lists characteristics common to abusive parents, which Brandt Steele has discussed in a recent U.S. government publication (Steele, 1975).

Table 2.1

1	Immature and dependent
2	Social isolation
3	Poor self-esteem
4	Difficulty seeking or obtaining pleasure
5	Distorted perceptions of the child
	Often role-reversal
6	Fear of spoiling the child
7	Belief in the value of punishment
8	Impaired ability to empathize with the child's needs and respond appropriately

When a child has been identified as abused, in addition to treating the medical and psychological wounds of the child, the primary goal of professionals and social agencies is to prevent abuse from recurring. I put to you that there is another important goal which should have priority, and that is to prevent the continuation of the whole abusive style of parenting. The wounds to the child are not only secondary to the physical trauma *per se*, but stem just as importantly from the overall type of parenting to which he has been exposed.

For example, colleagues and I have found in follow-up studies of abused children that physical abuse aside, a number of symptoms in the children were related to the quality of parenting that they experienced, whether in biologic, adoptive or foster homes (Martin & Beezley, 1977). The severity of psychiatric symptoms correlated most highly (0.001) with the child's perception of the impermanence of his home. The stability of his family and the number of home changes after abuse was recognised and were also correlated with the degree of psychological pathology. Psychiatric symptoms and developmental delays did not correlate with the type of injury or the age of the injury.

Neurologic integrity was, of course, correlated with significant injury to the cranium of the child. However, in one study (Martin *et al*, 1974), we looked at those children who had no history of head trauma and whose neurologic examination had not revealed any significant pathology. We were interested in seeing what factors in the child's environment might be affecting the child's learning and intelligence, which are neurologic functions of special social significance. In this subgroup of abused children, where there was no evidence of traumatic injury to the nervous system, impaired intellectual performance was related to such factors as disorganisation of the family, frequent unemployment, high geographic mobility, and chaotic structure and function of the family. It was also noted, that even though the children were not being physically abused at follow-up, poor intellectual performance was related to the degree to which parents used punishment, especially physical punishment, to control these children.

The point I want to emphasise is that the abusive home has a number of characteristics which are detrimental to the development of the child. Our goal then is not only to prevent abuse from recurring, but to identify characteristics of the abusive family which are harmful to the child and to attempt to modify and change those environmental factors. The task, then, is two-fold, to prevent physical abuse *and* to prevent abusive parenting.

One of the tasks we have before us in preventing abusive parenting is to consider what the relevance of various characteristics of the abusive home is to the child (Martin, 1976b). For instance, what is the relevance to the child if we find that few parents have telephones with listed numbers? The fact in itself is of minimal interest to the child. However, it may indicate that the child is being raised in a home where there is a mistrust of strangers, minimal contact with people outside the nuclear family, and without modelling for the child in how to find enjoyment and gratifica-tion from social contact with others. Similarly, the religious affiliation of the abusive parents is a superficial piece of information to the child developmentalist, unless we can draw inferences from such datum to understand the flexibility or rigidity of the parent and some insight into parental superegos which will affect the growing child. Let us look again then at Table 2.1 and consider what these parental traits may mean to the growing child.

The abused child is quite apt to be born to a woman who has excessive and quite distorted expectations of the baby. Often, the mother is looking to the child for need gratification, fantasising that the baby's love for her will make up for a life-long pattern of being unloved and uncared about. The child will not find that his parents are pleased when he is happy, but will be pleased with him when he minds and obeys, when he 'acts his age' and when he tends to the physical and emotional needs of his parents. He will receive the message time and again that he is a bad child and a disappointment to his parents. He will be in an environment where he has no value as an individual, as a child; but rather, where his value is related to his willingness to be good and to stay out of trouble. His curiosity and investigativeness will be discouraged or punished. He is not expected to have fun; indeed, his home is a sombre place where he will see little joy and happiness. He may be ignored and his basic needs neglected. His parents will probably be erratic and unpredictable. For example, a specific behaviour may at times be ignored, at other times reinforced, and still at other times met with disapproval and physical punishment. His parent will sometimes respond to his needs, while just as often, they will ignore them or get angry at his demands.

If one translates characteristics of the abusive home into their impact on the development of a child, then it becomes ever so much clearer why it is important not only to prevent physical abuse from occurring, but to intervene and change those characeristics which are part of the abusive environment. The rationale for changing abusive-parenting styles stems from two factors. The first and most immediately pertinent issue is to attempt to bind up the psychological and developmental wounds that the child has suffered in the abusive environment. The developmental delays, psychiatric symptoms and neurologic dysfunction which the child may suffer from living in an abusive environment are unlikely to improve without a change in the family environment. The second rationale for changing the abusive environment is its relevance to primary prevention of abuse which will be discussed below.

Early identification of the high risk parent-child dyad

When hoping to anticipate child abuse, it would be prudent to remind ourselves that there are three factors which make up abuse. Helfer and Kempe pointed this out in 1972. These ingredients include:
1.   A certain type of adult, the abusogenic parent
2.   Stress, both chronic and in acute crises
3.   A special child, i.e. a child who has some qualities making him different or special to the parent.

Now most of the attention in prediction has centred on the first two factors. Characteristics and profiles of abusive parents have been used to formulate questionnaires or checklists for predicting what parent is at higher risk of abusing a child than the average parent. This approach aims at identification of personality characteristics of the abusing parent. It may take the form of identifying historical events in the lives of most abusing parents which are felt to be related to their subsequent abusive behaviour. It may take the form of identifying behaviours of abusive parents which are reflective of their personality. Or, it may take the form of collecting intrapsychic data on abusive parents. Regardless of the approach, the common thread is the hope that one might identify those adults who represent a high-risk group for abusive parenting (Kempe & Helfer 1976). Once that is done, a variety of approaches may be attempted to intervene and prevent abuse from occurring. One of the most recent and exciting pieces of work in this area has been reported by Gray and her colleagues (Gray, Cutler, Dean & Kempe, 1977).

There is another school of thought which primarily emphasises the social stresses which are believed to be the primary etiological factors in abuse. Gil., (1970, 1975), Gelles (1973), and to some degree Neuberger (1974) have emphasised the futility of preventing or reducing the incidence of abuse unless one takes a sociological view. Such a view leads to suggested remedies which primarily stress changes in social policy and societal mores. Chase's recent book (1975) outlines just such an approach to prevention of abuse through such social programmes. While my own experience and professional bias lead me to believe that such sociological programmes are not adequate to identify or prevent child abuse, nonetheless, one cannot help but be impressed with the importance of such sociological data. Abusive parents often are under chronic stress. It is also true that acute crises often seem to ignite the abusive incident. Certainly, when the clinician is working with an individual family, the social stresses of poverty, child-rearing, social isolation, inadequate housing, etc. should be addressed if one truly hopes to help the family and reduce the probability of recurrent physical abuse.

The third component of child abuse has received much too little attention, that is the role that the child plays in increasing the probability of abuse (Martin, 1976c). Lynch (1976) from England has been one of the pioneers in this field, although limiting her current work to factors in the parent-child dyad which may intrude into optimal bonding and attachment.

I put to you the thesis that the role of the child in contributing to the abusive incident must be explored and considered for us to give us the best chance to identify and predict those families where abuse is likely to occur. We have recently been impressed with the tremendous capacity the child has to influence and modify the behaviour of his parent. Lewis and Rosenblum's book (1974) *The Effect of the Infant on its Caregiver,* explores this issue in some detail. Brazelton's work (1973; Brazelton *et al.,* 1974) has heightened our awareness of individual differences in children from infancy, differences which do impact on the type of parenting that the child is apt to elicit.

I am suggesting that we consider all parents as having the capacity to attack their children physically. This potential for abusing children varies in intensity. Given a parent with a higher than usual potential to abuse a child, and given certain life stresses which might increase that potential, some characteristic or attribute of the child may be just enough to tip the scale. Something about the child may be just that ingredient necessary to ignite the act of physical abuse. What are some of the factors in the child, then, that may increase the chances of physical attack?

We know that premature children are overrepresented in any group of abused children (Klein & Stern, 1971; Martin, 1976c; Martin *et al.,* 1977). While my own studies do not confirm the finding, Smith and Hanson (1974) and others feel that mentally retarded and physically handicapped children are at greater risk of abuse. Klaus and Kennel (1976) and Klein and Smith (1971), suggest that any factor which interrupts the early attachment process places the child at greater risk of abuse. Lynch's findings (1975) also suggest that perhaps medical illness is a contributing factor. My own experience suggests that mild neurologic immaturity in a child increases the difficulty in establishing good parenting patterns. This all suggests that the following factors increase the chances of physical abuse, given a parent with a high valency for becoming an abusive parent:

1. Any factors which intrude into the early bonding and attachment of mother to child, such as prematurity, separation of mother and newborn.
2. Characteristics of a child which make him a less gratifying child; a child for whom it is more difficult to care and who gives less reinforcement for good parenting. This may be a normal child who is more difficult to feed or soothe than most babies. It may be a child with mild neurologic immaturity or dysfunction who typically is less gratifying and more difficult to care for
3. Any child who does not meet the expectations of the parents. This may be as simple as the child being of the wrong sex, or more often, a normal child who does not measure up because the parents' expectations are so unrealistic and and distorted. Perhaps the imperfect newborn with anomalies or illness represents such a disappointment.
4. The developmental level of the child may present special stresses to a specific parent. There are some children who are only abused during the toddler stage, or preschool age, or during latency or teenage years. The marginal parent may be able to parent the child at other ages adequately, but the normal behaviours of a specific developmental stage may elicit physical attack. For almost all parents find some developmental stages more stressful than others. Some of us do not find the dependencies of the infant easy to meet, while others find

the inquisitive, talkative preschooler difficult, and yet others deal badly with the tempestuous teenager.

5.   The child invites abuse. We have seen a number of abused children who seem deliberately to invite or provoke abuse, knowingly behaving in a provocative manner, or expecting and inviting physical punishment. This may be the child's only way of obtaining attention from the parent, as if equating punishment with love. In some children, the provocative and often aggressive behaviour seems to be an identification with the abusive parent.

It would appear to me that identifying such factors within the child could increase our chances of identifying the parent-child dyad at risk for abuse. When an adult is identified as having a greater than average capacity to abuse, we should intensify our preventive efforts when, in addition, the child has any of those attributes noted above, such as prematurity, medical illness, being difficult to care for, or having little capacity to reinforce good parenting.

It seems to me that this is an area which needs considerably more study and research. We know very little about the child's role in abuse and neglect. We *do* know that the victim is not entirely blameless.

Primary prevention

Child abuse tends to be self-perpetuating in many families. We have seen a number of families where abuse has been documented in three or more generations. As Steele points out (1976), 'Repeatedly, we have found the most common element in their lives to be the history of having been significantly deprived or neglected, with or without physical abuse, in their own earliest years'. What, then, are the effects of abuse and neglect which result in a child growing up to mistreat his own children?

Unfortunately, there are no prospective longitudinal studies of abused and neglected children which can answer our question. However, what we can do is to look at what we do know about the effects of the abusive environment on children. Ironically, many of the characteristics of abused children are quite similar to pathological traits of their parents. Follow-up studies of abused children by myself and colleagues (Martin, 1976a) have resulted in highlighting several personality traits and neurological impairments which are overrepresented.

Intellectual deficits

At least one in three of abused children will have intellectural deficits of significance. Sometimes this is reflecting difficulties in *performance*, rather than in intellectual *potential*. It is related both to central nervous system damage, as well as to psychosocial factors which curb the child's attentiveness, investigativeness and cognitive experimentation.

Learning disabilities

Learning disabilities are thought to be greatly increased in abused and neglected children. Kline (1977) reported on this phenomenon at the Geneva First International

Congress on Child Abuse and Neglect. At least 50 per cent of abused children will have significant deficiencies in speech and language, perceptual motor development or other cognitive problems which interfere with learning (Blager & Martin, 1976; Martin, 1976d; Martin & Miller, 1976; Martin & Rodeheffer, 1976; Mirandy, 1976).

Poor self-concept

Poor self-concept has been a significant finding in over 50 per cent of abused and neglected children I have seen over the past 10 years. It should not surprise us since children are usually raised in families who are chronically dissatisfied with the child's behaviour.

Lack of joy and play ability

The most impressive characteristic of most abused children is their rather sombre and joyless demeanour. These children have little ability to enjoy themselves. Indeed, in the Pre-school at the National Center in Denver, we find that many of these children need to be taught *how to play*, (Mahler *et al.,* 1975). The play activity one does see is often obsessive-compulsive, and engaged in to please the teacher or examiner. Pleasure is found from meeting the adults' expectations rather than stemming from the child's own enjoyment.

Poor sense of self

The abused child often seems to have little sense of self, and expends a great deal of energy in scrutinising his environment for clues as to what is going to happen next. The child has learned to ignore his own inner wishes and impulses, and instead he adapts and modifies his behaviour to meet what he believes others want from him. This may take the form of role-reversal, where he literally cares for the physical and emotional needs of adults. It may be seen in quick obedience and acquiescence in early life. It is highlighted by the keen ability many abused children have in searching their environment, hyperalert to minimal cues from adults, so as to stay out of harm's way.

Deviant object-relations

Perhaps the most distressing characteristic of most abused children is found in their deviant object-relations There truly seems no sense of trust in people. Object-constancy as described by Mahler (Mahler *et al.,* 1970, 1975) is essentially non-existent. We so often see abused children, who are indiscrimately friendly with people, acting inappropriately affectionate with strangers; they have no sense of some people being more important to them than others. Investment in other people stems primarily from the adults' capacity to give to them, rather than any inherent qualities in the adult. Social and peer isolation is the rule. These traits seem amazingly similar to the abusive parent who is socially isolated, trusts no one, has few if any friends, and judges people primarily in terms of their capacity for need-gratification.

While we must consider how these children have been affected by the abusive environment, we must also consider the iatrogenic effects of our well-meaning treatment plans. Far too often, our treatment plans have added more stress for the child to cope with. What happens when physical abuse is recognised? We hospitalise the child even though there may be no medical indications, and the child must cope with the deleterious effects of the hospital environment. We separate the child from his parents, parents who, even though abusive, do represent caring people to the child. Foster placement often means repeated changes in homes for the child, as many foster parents cannot tolerate their behaviour and so repeated loss of parent surrogates becomes another impediment to the child's tenuous sense of trust. We discourage adequate contact between biologic parent and child when the child is in foster care, so that attachment between child and parent is unduly weakened by our social policies. This is but an incomplete listing of stresses to normal development of the child which we, the professionals, have imposed. To this I must add our reluctance to provide treatment to the child for his psychological wounds.

When we first became aware and concerned about the magnitude of mistreated children some 15 years ago, our first priority was mortality; to treat the medical wounds of the child. To assure that battering would not recur, we recommended placement of the child in the supposedly safe environment of an institution, or a foster home. It is time now to recognise the many developmental and psychological wounds that the abused child has. We have now come to a point where we need actively to provide treatment for those less obvious and less dramatic wounds. For it is just these psychological and developmental consequences which must be treated if we have any hope of breaking the cycle of abuse. If an abused child is mistrusting, has a poor self-concept, has little capacity to relate in a healthy way with other children and with adults, and is handicapped by developmental delays or disabilities, there is every reason to expect that that child has a great chance of growing up to be much like his abusing parent. There is every reason to expect that that child will be at very great risk for becoming an abusive parent in adulthood. If the abusive environment results in traits in children which increase the chances of that child growing up to be an aggressive, delinquent, or abusive adult, then primary prevention must take the form of preventing those personality characteristics from becoming an immutable part of the growing child's psyche.

One form of primary prevention is to provide treatment for the child, directed at those developmental and psychological problems which augur poorly for the future. In our experience at the National Center in Denver, we have found therapeutic pre-schools to be a most helpful treatment modality (Mirandy, 1976). Deficiencies in speech and language, learning, motor-coordination and perceptual ability can all be addressed in such a therapeutic setting. Just as importantly, psychological issues can be dealt with by a staff, which is sensitive to personality development.

Some abused children will require more formal types of specific treatment, including psychotherapy (Beezley, *et al.*, 1976, a,b) either individually or in groups. It seems clear to me that when a non-abused child presents with many of the traits we usually find in abused children, such a child is more apt to be recognised and have therapy prescribed. I believe that we operate on the premise that the *abused child* has these personality traits because he has had inadequate or bad parenting, and that then we go on to assume that if we remove that child from this malevolent environment, the consequences of such an environment will go away. It is just not so. If the child is anxious, fearful, untrusting, oppositional, or depressed, he needs some form of psychotherapeutic intervention. Similarly, many abused children really do require speech and language therapy (Blager & Martin, 1976), physical or occupational therapy, (Martin & Miller, 1976), or special educational help (Mirandy, 1976).

At every child abuse team conference, the members should routinely ask themselves, what is the developmental and psychological status of this child? What types of treatment modalities should we consider to help this child with the developmental probelms he exhibits? With such a routine, it would be hoped that adequate treatment for the abused child might be offered. And more, that there will be a greater chance that this abused child will not grow up to be an unhappy adult who is apt to abuse his children physically.

Finally, as addressed above, primary prevention will include our efforts to prevent not only abuse from recurring, but to alter and change the pattern of parenting to which the abused child is exposed. This may involve various types of efforts to help abusive parents change their patterns of child-rearing. I am truly not sure what approaches will work best with which parents. Psychotherapy, social case-work, parents groups and more didactic educational efforts to change child-rearing practices have all had some limited success with various abusive parents. Recently, several staff at the National Center in Denver have attempted direct efforts at working with abusive parents around child-rearing with some optimistic results. Regardless of the approach I want to stress the importance of changing abusive parenting. Abusive parents can attend psychotherapy sessions and obtain considerable help for themselves *without* any demonstrable changes in the parents' feelings or behaviours toward their children. Those working with the abusive adult must include in their therapeutic goals a major thrust towards improving the parents' attitudes, feelings and behaviours towards their children.

Summary

My own experience in the field of child abuse and neglect has been that of a paediatrician who works in a child development centre. I have been involved in testing, examining and trying to understand children who have been abused. I am particularly sensitive to the enormous price these children pay, the morbidity of child abuse. I am troubled by the developmental and psychological wounds that these children have. When I am faced with the knowledge that most abusive parents were abused and/or seriously deprived in their own childhoods, it seems to me a fortuitous opportunity to suggest that primary prevention of abuse and neglect might be accomplished by ensuring that abused children will not grow up to be abusive parents. It gives me a forum to plead for greatly increased interest and efforts in providing help and treatment to the abused child, for his medical wounds and for his developmental and psychological wounds.

I have also pointed out that the child brings something to the abusive incident of his own. I have suggested that the surest way to identify those parent-child dyads in which abuse is highly likely, is to include factors within the child, which increase the risk, given an abusogenic parent and a stressful social climate. By including the traits of the child which increase the risk of abuse, our predictive and preventive efforts should be more accurate.

I have also taken this opportunity to ask that we not only consider ways to prevent abuse from occurring or recurring, but that we broaden that concept to consider ways to prevent abusive and neglectful *parenting*. The abused child is not only exposed to episodic physical trauma, but is exposed unrelentingly to a type and style of parenting which impedes his physical, mental and emotional growth and development. We not only should want to prevent abuse, but also we should hope to change the abusive environment, which also impacts upon the child.

My comments and my interests are quite child-centred. They do not derive from interest in the law, nor interest in abusive parents, nor interest in social policy. They derive from interest in children, in this case children who have been mistreated. It seems to me that this should be the primary perspective for those interested in preventing child abuse.

The discussion of this Chapter begins on page 67.

References

Beezley, P., Martin, H.P. & Kempe, R. (1976a) Psychotherapy, In Martin, H.P. (1976a) Ch. 16, pp. 201-214.

Beezley, P., Martin, H.P. & Alexander, H. (1976b) Comprehensive family oriented therapy, In Kempe & Helfer (1976).

Blager, F. & Martin, H.P. (1976) Speech and language of abused children. In Martin, H.P. (1976a), Ch. 7, pp. 83-92.

Brazelton, T.B. (1973) Neonatal behavioural assessment scale. *Clinics in Developmental Medicine,* **50,** Philadelphia: J.B. Lippincott.

Brazelton, T.B., Koslowski, B. & Main, M. (1974) The origins of reciprocity: the early mother-infant interaction. In Lewis & Rosenblum (1974).

Chase, N.F. (1975) *A Child is Being Beaten,* New York: Holt, Rinehart & Winston.

Gelles, R.J. (1973) Child abuse as psychopathology: a sociological critique and reformulation. *American Journal of Orthopsychiatry,* **43,** 611-621, July 1973.

Gil, D.G. (1970) *Violence Against Children: Physical Child Abuse in the United States.* Cambridge, Mass., Harvard University Press.

Gil, D.G. (1975) Unravelling child abuse. *American Journal of Orthopsychiatry,* **45,** 346-356.

Gray, J., Cutler, C., Dean, J. & Kempe, C.H. (1977) Prediction and Prevention of child abuse and neglect. *International Journal of Child Abuse and Neglect,* Oxford: Pergamon Press. In press.

Kempe, C.H. & Helfer, R.E. (1972) *Helping the Battered Child and His Family,* xiv-xv. Philadelphia, J.B. Lippincott.

Kempe, C.H. & Helfer, R.E. (1976) *Child Abuse and Neglect: The Family and the Community.* Cambridge, Mass: Ballinger. See Ch. 18, Basic issues concerning prediction, Helfer, p. 363; Ch. 19, Perinatal assessment of mother-baby interaction, Gray, Cutler, Dean, Kempe, p. 377; Ch. 20, A predictive screening questionnaire for potential problems in mother-child interaction, Schneider, Hoffmeister, Helfer, p. 393.

Klaus, M.H. & Kennel, J.H. (1976) *Maternal-Infant Bonding: The Impact of Early Separation or Loss on Family Development.* St. Louis: C.V. Mosby.

Klein, M. & Stern, L. (1971) Low birthweight and the battered child syndrome *American Journal of Diseases of Children,* **122,** 15-18.

Kline, D.F. (1977) Educational and psychological problems of abused children. *Child Abuse and Neglect: an International Journal,* **1,** 301-307, Pergamon.

Lewis, M. & Rosenblum, L.A. (1974) *The Effect of the Infant on its Caretaker.* New York: John Wiley & Sons.

Lynch, M. (1975) Ill health and child abuse. *Lancet,* **2,** 317-319.

Lynch, M. (1976) Risk factors in the child: a study of abused children and their siblings. In Martin, H.P. (1976), Ch. 4, pp. 43-56.

Mahler, M.S., Pine, F. & Bergman, A. (1970) The mother's reaction to her toddler's drive for individuation. *In Parenthood: Psychology and Psychopathology,* Anthony and Benedek (Eds), Ch. 11, pp. 257-274, Boston: Little, Brown.

Mahler, M.S. et al., (1975) *The Psychological Birth of the Infant: Symbiosis and Individuation,* New York: Basic Books, 1975.

Martin, H.P. (1976a) (Ed) *The Abused Child: A Multidisciplinary Approach to Development Issues and Treatment.* Cambridge, Mass: Ballinger.

Martin, H.P. (1976b) The environment of the abused child. In Martin, H.P. (1976a), Ch. 2, pp. 11-26.

Martin, H.P. (1976c) Which children get abused: high risk factors in the child. In Martin, H.P. (1976a), Ch. 3, pp. 27-42.

Martin, H.P. (1976d) Neurologic status of abused children. Ch. 6, pp. 67-82.

Martin, H.P. & Beezley, P. (1976) Foster placement. In Martin, H.P. (1976a), Ch. 15, pp. 189-200.

Martin, H.P. & Beezley, P. (1977) Psycho-social factors related to abused children. *Developmental Medicine and Child Neurology.* In press.

Martin, H.P., Beezley, P., Conway, E. & Kempe, C.H. (1974) The development of abused children, Part I: A review of the literature; Part II: Physical, neurologic, and intellectual outcome. *Advances in Pediatrics,* **21,** 25-73.

Martin, H.P. & Miller, T. (1976) Treatment of specific delays and deficits. In Martin, H.P. (1976a), Ch. 14, pp. 179-188.

Martin, H.P. & Rodeheffer, M. (1976) Learning and intelligence. In Martin, H.P. (1976a), Ch. 8, pp. 93-104.

Mirandy, J. (1976) Pre-school for abused children. In Martin, H.P. (1976a), Ch. 17, pp. 215-224.

Neuberger, E.H. (1974) The myth of the battered child syndrome. *Annual Progress in Child Psychiatry and Child Development,* Chess & Thomas (Eds). New York: Brunner/Mazel, pp. 569-574.

Smith, S.M. & Hanson, R. (1974) 134 battered children: a medical and psychological study. *British Medical Journal,* **3,** 666-670.

Steele, B. (1975) Working with Abusive Parents: from a Psychiatric Point of View. *U.S. Dept. of Health, Education and Welfare,* Office of Child Development, OHO75-70.

Steele, B. (1976) In Kempe & Helfer (1976), pp. 13-14.

3. A nurse's observations on mothers and babies in a Special Care Baby Unit

PAMELA HOWAT

Neonatal separation is one of the factors identified in families where there has been child abuse, (Lynch, 1975; Lynch, Roberts & Gordon, 1976).

In a study by Dr Lynch at Oxford of a group of children and their non-abused siblings 40 per cent of the proband had been in the Special Care Baby Unit whereas only 6 per cent of the sibling controls had been in the Unit. In a further study of 50 abused children and their matched controls 42 per cent of the abused children had been in the Special Care Baby Unit but only 10 per cent of the controls had been in the Unit. Observations made inside such a nursery may have predictive value and could lead to the adoption of methods by which some aspects of this problem might be modified.

A study of thirty mothers

In Oxford, children suspected of being neglected or physically abused are generally referred to the Park Hospital for Children. Over the period 1972-1975, 30 babies, all of whom had been through the Special Care Baby Unit at the John Radcliffe Hospital Maternity Hospital in Oxford, were referred to the Park Hospital, where most of them and their familites were seen by Dr Lynch in the Human Development Research Unit. The reasons for referral were, in 13 cases, physical abuse, and in four cases, neglect. Thirteen cases were considered to be at risk, perhaps an unrepresentative proportion owing to our accessibility to the Park Hospital.

As a Research Nurse in the Special Care Baby Unit in the Maternity Hospital, I have been through the neonatal nursing records of these 30 index babies to see whether there were any common features which might have caused us to be concerned about the mother's ability to care for her infant. To form a matched control group of babies, I took the first baby admitted to the Unit after the index baby, matching for parity of mother, sex of baby, 500gm weight group, and as near as possible the length of stay of the baby on the Unit.

Table 3.1 shows the distribution of the gestation period of the index group, Table 3.2 the length of stay of the index group in the Unit and Table 3.3 the distribution of the weight of the index group.

Tables 3.4 - 3.9 show the results of comparing the neglected, the at risk, the abused and the total index groups with the control groups.

Table 3.1 Gestation of Index Group

Weeks		30	30-32	33-35	36-38	39+
Neglected	4	-	-	1	3	-
At Risk	13	-	3	-	7	3
Abused	13	-	-	5	5	3

Table 3.2 Length of stay on the unit of Index Group

		less than 48 hours	2 - 7 days	8 - 14 days	14 - 28 days	over 28 days
Neglected	4	-	-	1	2	1
At Risk	13	2	4	2	1	4
Abused	13	-	1	-	8	4

Table 3.3 Weight of Index Group

Gm		1000 - 1500	1501 - 2000	2001 - 2500	2501 - 3000	over 3001
Neglected	4	-	2	1	1	-
At Risk	13	1	2	6	3	1
Abused	13	-	3	4	3	3

Table 3.4 Known to MSW before delivery

		Known	Not known
Neglected	4	2	2
At Risk	13	3	10
Abused	13	6	7
All Index	30	11	19
Controls	30	4	26

p 0.05

Table 3.5 Mode of Delivery

		Caesarean Section	Forceps	Spontaneous Vertex Delivery
Neglected	4	0	3	1
At Risk	13	1	6	6
Abused	13	8	3	2
All Index	30	9	12	9
Controls	30	8	14	8

not significant

Table 3.6 Degree of illness

		Ventilatory Support given	Ventilatory Support not given
Neglected	4	-	4
At Risk	13	3	10
Abused	13	4	9
All Index	30	7	23
Controls	30	3	27

not significant

Table 3.7 Initial feeding choice

		Breast	Bottle
Neglected	4	-	4
At Risk	13	5	8
Abused	13	5	8
All Index	30	10	20
Controls	30	10	20

not significant

Table 3.8 Visiting pattern

		Poor infrequent	Good fairly frequent
Neglected	4	1	3
At Risk	13	2	11
Abused	13	3	10
All Index	30	6	24
Controls	30	none stated	30

p 0.05

Table 3.9 Concern at mothering

		Concern	No concern
Neglected	4	4	-
At Risk	13	6	7
Abused	13	10	3
All Index	30	20	10
Controls	30	2	28

p 0.001

The data studied, were the mode of delivery, the initial feeding choice and the degree of illness. None of these showed significant differences. On reflection it might have been of greater importance to look at the type of delivery in relation to what analgesia or anaesthetic had been given. Significant differences were shown when the mother was known to the medical social worker before delivery, when the mother showed concern at mothering and when the visiting patterns in the unit were compared with the control group. Concern at mothering was assessed retrospectively from records made by the nurses who were unaware that we would be looking at them from this aspect.

Measuring maternal feelings

All of these represent objective characteristics. An attempt has been made to measure the feelings of mothers while their babies are in the unit, in the hope that such measurements may prove useful prospectively in identifying the mother and baby at risk. These observations were not available for the index mothers who were studied restrospectively.

It is obviously a near impossible task to define normal behaviour, to define the reactions to a unique situation. In this study we try to get an overall picture of the mother's mood, perhaps, even to elicit an abnormal pattern in this mood.

Using a visual analogue scale questionnaire, a subjective assessment was made by the mother of her feelings
1. About entering the unit,
2. About her baby's condition,
3. About handling her baby,
4. And about her feeling of closeness to her baby.

The mother was asked to mark a position on a 10 cm line corresponding to her feelings at one particular visit. We could thus calculate a score which, expressed as a percentage, was plotted on a graph against post-natal age of the infant. Events were noted in relation to a noticeable rise or fall in the score. The lower score represents a higher degree of maternal anxiety. The maximum period of anxiety was in the immediate post-natal period. Subsequently there were rises and falls in this score and we believe that these reflect appropriate changes in the mother's feelings with a change in the clinical condition of her baby. It can also reflect such changes as when the baby is removed from an overhead radiant heater to the older-fashioned all-enclosed incubator. While this is seen by the medical staff as an improvement in the baby's clinical condition, from the mother's point of view it isolates the baby from her. This system of assessment gives a global score rather than defining individual features, but it may identify the mother, whose consistently low score, despite the baby's well being, perhaps mirrors unconsciously her true attitude to the whole event. Does this predict a child at risk?

A ward diary

Another more diffuse but still important means of collecting information about the parents with a view to identifying the child at risk is the use of a ward diary in which we record the visiting pattern and the telephone calls the parents make to the unit. We can, at a glance, note any irregularities in communication and try to find out why the parents do not contact us. Very often the reasons are justified.

Possible preventive techniques

It should be possible to predict some of the families at risk. Are there ways in which these families can be helped in the period of neonatal care? It must be stated that these ideas, based on our experience in Oxford, have not yet been proved to prevent child abuse.

Can we cut down the number of babies admitted to the Unit? This histogram

(Fig. 3.1) indicates the pattern of change of the type of baby admitted to our Unit over the last three years, showing the trend towards fewer big babies in 1975. The reasons associated with this fall are that we no longer routinely admit all babies of Rhesus negative or diabetic mothers, of all babies weighing less than 2500 gm. This reverses the old idea of taking the baby to the Unit for observation and then, if all is well, to his mother. Now the mother is involved and she is the observer. The baby goes to the Unit only after medical concern. The frequent reason for separation of the bigger baby from his mother is for phototherapy in the treatment of jaundice. It is hoped that some babies can stay with the mothers and the phototherapy go to them. Mothers do not all react in the same way and we should listen to their opinions, for some mothers prefer the baby to be admitted to the Unit for this type of treatment. The obvious answer would be a mother-baby unit, but this is not always possible.

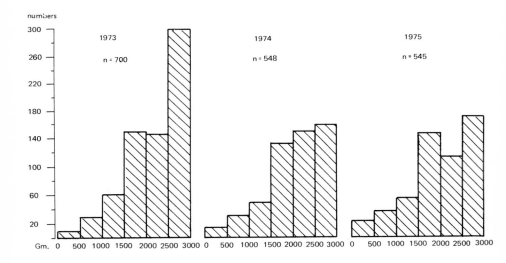

Fig. 3.1 admissions to special care baby unit by weight.

In the case of the mother who had delivered a seriously ill or preterm infant some degree of separation from the mother is necessary. This is the time of bonding, so difficult for many mothers to achieve in unpleasant or unfamiliar surroundings, and we should do all we can to mitigate the effects of this separation. We freqently resuscitate the sick baby in the delivery room where the mother was delivered. This has the disadvantage that it may intensify her anxiety, but it may help her to realise that although she has not got her baby in her arms it truly is her child. This is when bonding begins. We like every mother to handle her baby before he is taken away after delivery to the Nursery and she can usually do this, even when the baby is extremely immature or when an umbilical catheter has been inserted.

For those mothers whose babies must be admitted to the Unit a polaroid photograph of the baby is taken which, while no substitute for the actual presence of her baby, does confirm the reality of his existence, and certainly seems to bring the mother some degree of comfort. Siblings are encouraged to visit; although they do not come into the nursery, they can see the baby through the glass window. When the mother visits after her discharge, this solves the baby-minding problem, as she can bring the child, or children, with her and begin to think of the new baby as an integral part of the entire family.

Today, in our culture, it is felt that the mother should be fully involved. Should we share the care of the baby with her more? We have started to teach the mothers and fathers to tube-feed their babies. One way the mother does feel totally involved is when her own breast milk is given to her baby and not just pooled with other mothers' milk.

Can part of the nursery be made less clinical? The walls are bare, the linen white. Should we introduce attractive pictures, coloured cot covers or brightly painted rocking chairs? In the family already under social strain, the mother may resent the child who puts her into an environment that she may dislike intensely. It would be invaluable to have someone acutely aware of the baby's clinical condition continually available to the mothers. The course of this event could be eased by someone to mother the mother. I should like to stress the importance of teaching the nurses to do this; so often the nursing staff is too much occupied in emergency work to spend *adequate* time with the parents when they do visit the Unit.

All families leaving the nursery are referred to the liaison health visitor for the hospital, as well as to the health visitor for the area from which the mother comes. It is she who has access to the home. A discharge letter is sent to the general practitioner and comment made if there is concern. Because the mothers, about whom we are anxious, may not be highly motivated in seeking out help, it might be to their advantage to put them in contact with a mother who had similar problems with her child and who could provde a self-help life-line.

A medical social worker, solely employed for the Unit, now sees all the mothers and is available to any mother seeking advice on home problems. She can alert us to the families with problems. However, it is the nurse in the nursery who is in an unique situation to observe the mother actually learning to be a mother. It is during this time, that a nurse can observe a lack of responsiveness in the mother, so that we can intervene and provide her with additional support.

Conclusion

There are several things that the nurse can do herself in conjunction with all the members of the paediatric team to try to help these mothers.

Prediction

1.   Get information from the medical social work department,

2.   Make objective observations, have an ongoing record of visiting,
3.   Obtain a subjective assessment of the mother's feelings.

Prevention

1.   Avoid unnecessary separation,
2.   Share the care of the child with mother,
3.   Mother the mother,
4.   Cooperate closely with the medical social worker and with the health visitor.
        The nursing staff on the special care baby unit are in the best position to
collect information and to make observations on the mothers. Given the knowledge of
the subsequent course of events of those children under their care who were later
ill-treated, I believe that the nursing staff would become more highly motivated to
observe the mothers from this aspect. Much good could follow their indirect involvement in the longer term care of their patients.
        All involved are now aware that when a baby who has been born very early or
has been very ill in the neonatal period is discharge from the unit with every prospect
of good physical and mental health, there still remain potential hazards.
        My thanks are due to Professor J.P.M. Tizard for his help and advice.

References

Lynch, M.A. (1975) Ill-health and child abuse. *Lancet,* 2, 317.
Lynch, M.A., Roberts, J. & Gordon, M., (1976) Early warning of child abuse in the
        maternity hospital. *Developmental Medicine and Child Neurology,* 18, 759.

Discussion

The group expressed great interest in the practical value of organised labour ward
observations in the selection of mothers who were likely to need special care and
help over mothering their babies. These observations depended, for accuracy as well
as completeness, upon being given a value. They might then be more helpful than
prenatal and historical data. Some confusion of function was suspected between the
sister and her midwife pupils in the antenatal department, the hospital medical social
worker and the health visitor with the community midwife coming later into the
picture, all with different points of view and different functions. There is room for
discussion about both overlaps and gaps. The group supported the suggestion that
the health visitor should be notified of all maternity department bookings. General
practitioner attachment helps the gathering of information about families, all of
which should be communicated to the hospital.
        After delivery the mother and her baby should be kept together unless there is
a strong reason to part them for some special treatment. Some mothers themselves
need to be mothered at this time, problems, especially emotional ones, and feelings

of depression need to be identified and handled with sympathy, and mothers should be given appropriate responsibilites and treated like adults, not like silly children.

4. Early alerting signs

MARGARET LYNCH AND JACQUELINE ROBERTS

Introduction

The aim of our recent research in Oxford has been to increase our understanding of the process that leads to abuse in order to identify factors and circumstances in a child's biography that increase the risk of battering.

A case history as a flow-diagram

In every case of child abuse a series of interrelated events has led up to the final cata-strophe. These events can be laid out in the form of a flow-diagram or critical path. Figure 4.1 shows the case history of Rachel and her family presented in this way. At the age of 11 weeks, Rachel was admitted, fitting and moribund, to the hospital; she had bilateral subdural and fundal haemorrhages. A skeletal survey showed a recent fracture of one femur, and an old fracture of a radius. When this young family came with their child for admission, initially they seemed much the same as many of our local families. Father was polite and well-dressed and was earning good money at a local factory. The mother was young and attractive and naturally in tears. They were accompanied by their boy toddler, who was obviously thriving and much loved by his parents. They were living in a smart new council house. However, when we draw out a critical path for this family, we begin to understand why the parents did not bond to Rachel, and why ultimately, the child was abused. We can also see how alerting signals were given by the family, but were not recognised.

The father had an ordinary upbringing, but the mother, the dominant partner, came from a notorious problem family. Indeed, she had been known to the social services department for most of her life. There was evidence that she herself, had been physically, emotionally and sexually abused by her own father. When her parents finally separated in her early teens, she became the cinderella of the house-hold, having to stay home from school to look after her young siblings. She met her future husband when she was only fifteen years old. She changed her job many times and indeed encouraged her boyfriend to give up his apprenticeship for a better paid job without prospects. After a courtship of two and a half years they married and a pregnancy quickly followed. They were, at this time, living amid hostility in the future maternal grandmother's house. Mother was well during the pregnancy, and the baby, when born, was the boy they wanted, physically fit, happy and contented. While he was still very young, they moved to a distant town in the north. Mother

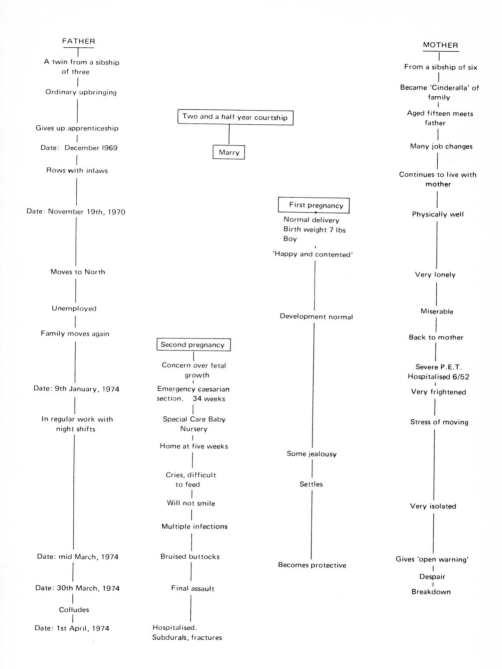

FATHER

A twin from a sibship
of three

Ordinary upbringing

Gives up apprenticeship

Date: December 1969

Rows with inlaws

Date: November 19th, 1970

Moves to North

Unemployed

Family moves again

Date: 9th January, 1974

In regular work with
night shifts

Date: mid March, 1974

Date: 30th March, 1974

Colludes

Date: 1st April, 1974

Two and a half year courtship

Marry

First pregnancy
Normal delivery
Birth weight 7 lbs
Boy
'Happy and contented'

Development normal

Some jealousy

Settles

Becomes protective

Second pregnancy
Concern over fetal
growth
Emergency caesarian
section.   34 weeks

Special Care Baby
Nursery

Home at five weeks

Cries, difficult
to feed

Will not smile

Multiple infections

Bruised buttocks

Final assault

Hospitalised.
Subdurals, fractures

MOTHER

From a sibship of six

Became 'Cinderalla' of
family

Aged fifteen meets
father

Many job changes

Continues to live with
mother

Physically well

Very lonely

Miserable

Back to mother

Severe P.E.T.
Hospitalised 6/52

Very frightened

Stress of moving

Very isolated

Gives 'open warning'

Despair

Breakdown

Fig. 4.1 Critical Path of Rachel's family

Reprinted with permission from *The Abused Child* : A Multidisciplinary Approach to
Developmental Issues and Treatment by Harold P. Martin. Copyright 1976, Ballinger
Publishing Company.

became very lonely and depressed and the father could not find a job. For this reason the family soon moved back to the home of the maternal grandmother.

A second pregnancy occurred. On this occasion, mother became very ill with raised blood pressure and was in hospital for six weeks before delivery, which she resented very much and blamed on her unborn child. The obstetricians were anxious over the fetal growth rate. Many investigations were carried out, culminating at 34 weeks in an amniocentesis, during which the umbilical cord was pierced. An emergency caesarian section was necessary to save the baby's life. Mother was naturally very frightened. The baby, Rachel, weighed 5lb 6 oz. She developed respiratory distress and had to remain in the special care nursery for five weeks. Mother felt strongly that this baby did not belong to her - 'just flesh and bone with wires hanging out everywhere'. Ten days after leaving the hospital without her baby, the mother had the additional stress of moving to her own home for the first time. Her husband was in regular work, but often on the night shift. They found it difficult to visit their baby, and spent little time with her.

When Rachel did come home, there was no bond between her and the parents. She was difficult to feed, cried all the time, and always seemed to have a cold. Her smile appeared late, and was difficult to elicit. Her brothers became jealous of the attention she was receiving. Any help offered by neighbours or the health visitor was regarded as interference by this very defensive mother, who became more and more isolated. Two and a half weeks before Rachel's admission to hospital mother hit her during a feeding battle and bruised her buttocks. She immediately called the family doctor. Unfortunately this open warning was not read. Mother received reassurance that the injuries were not severe and was given some tranquillizers for herself. Father was aware that all was not well, but as happens in so many cases, he colluded with the mother's abuse of the child. The final outburst soon came. Mother attacked the child violently. Forty eight hours later Rachel was admitted, almost dead, to the hospital.

There was in Rachel's family an increased potential for abuse even before she was born, because of mother's upbringing and the parents' social circumstances. They had, however, begun to rear Rachel's elder brother successfully. Rachel was the product of a difficult pregnancy and an operative delivery, spending five weeks in the special care nursery. The parents found themselves unable to bond to her. She turned out to be a sickly and 'unsatisfactory' baby, and her brother's behavioural disturbance was blamed on her. As tension in the family increased Rachel became the target for resentment, and finally abuse.

Our experience with families like Rachel's led to the research studies to be described in this paper. The first study, by both authors on identification in the maternity hospital, shows that children like Rachel can be identified in the maternity hospital. The second study (by M.A. Lynch only), on identification within the family, demonstrates how one child within a family comes to be singled out for abuse.

Identification in the maternity hospital (Lynch and Roberts, 1977)

Pregnancy and delivery inevitably bring families into contact with the medical services when basic information is recorded on all mothers and infants. The aim of this study (Lynch & Roberts, 1977) was to see if such data could be used to aid the busy maternity hospital staff to identify families in need of extra help in bonding to their baby.

Fifty children referred to the Park Hospital for actual or threatened abuse were compared with 50 controls born at the same maternity hospital. The controls were obtained by taking the next live child to be born after each index child. Enquiries were made to ascertain whether any of the children in the control group had been abused, neglected or considered 'at risk'. Only one was considered to be 'at risk' by his family doctor. No child in the control group appeared on a social services 'at risk' register nor had the possibility of abuse been raised on any hospital referral. The maternity hsopital obstetric, paediatric, nursing and social work notes were consulted. All our data were therefore, obtained from information recorded before abuse occurred and were readily available in the maternity notes.

All socio-economic groups were represented, although there were more social class IV and V families, unemployed fathers and unsupported mothers in the abused group. There was no significant difference in the number of primiparous women in the two groups. This would indicated that previous experience of motherhood does not necessarily protect against bonding failure. Four previous children from abusing families had died, compared with two in the control group. Six previous children from the abused group had been adopted or placed in long term foster care. No such placements were reported in the control group. 54 per cent of the abusing mothers and 40 per cent of the control group mothers required hospital admission during their pregnancy. 44 per cent of the abusing and 34 per cent of the control mothers had complications of labour and/or delivery. These differences are not statistically significant.

There were five factors which clearly differentiated the abused group from the control group (Table 4.1).

1   More abusing mothers were under 20 years when they had their first children: 50 per cent compared with 16 per cent
2   Abusing mothers were more likely to have signs of emotional disturbance recorded in the maternity notes: 46 per cent compared with 14 per cent
3   More abusing parents were referred to the maternity hospital social worker: 58 per cent compared with 6 per cent
4   The abused babies were more likely to have been admitted to the special care baby nursery: 42 per cent compared with 10 per cent
5   The abusing mothers more often evoked concern over their mothering capacity: 44 per cent compared with 6 per cent

All these factors highlight characteristics frequently observed in abusing families..

Table 4.1 Maternity hospital identification

	Under 20 at first child's birth	Recorded emotional disturbance	Referred to social worker	Admitted to SCBU	Recorded concern over mothering
Park Group n = 50	50%	46%	58%	42%	44%
	(25)	(23)	(29)	(21)	(22)
Control Group n = 50	16%	14%	6%	10%	6%
	(8)	(7)	(3)	(5)	(3)

Age at birth of first child

Many abusing parents are, in actual, and emotional age, too young for parenthood. (Lynch, 1975; Lynch & Ounsted, 1976; NSPCC, 1975; Ounsted & Lynch, 1976; Smith *et al.,* 1975). The first pregnancy may well have been planned in an effort to escape from a harsh and rigid home. Such young, deprived parents expect the child to provide them with the love they have never had and their expectations of his behaviour and development are likely to be totally unrealistic.

Recorded emotional disturbance

Abusing parents are likely to have an increased incidence of emotional and relation-ship problems extending back into their childhood (Pollock *et al.,* 1972; Baher *et al.,* 1976). A few will have well-defined psychiatric illness and it is important that the psychotic mother be recognised. In this study we found that an opportunity is pro-vided in the maternity notes for the mothers 'psychiatric history' to be recorded Most of the entries made describe emotional disturbances rather than well-defined psychiatric illnesses. Examples of such entries are: suicide attempts, nervous break-downs, drug addiction, contact with child or adolescent psychiatrists, being a runaway and educational subnormality.

Referral to social worker

Referral to the social worker around the time the child is born is a sign of the inter-related emotional and practical difficulties besetting these families (Baher *et al.,* 1976). It is the diffuse nature of their problems that distinguishes these mothers from the majority of women seeking social work help (Lynch *et al.,* 1976). Frequently the family has accumulated a whole range of interlocking problems affecting every aspect of their lives: the marriage, housing, financial matters and employment (Ounsted, *et al.,* 1976). While adverse social conditions can be found it is the severity of the relationship problems, which is most striking.

Baby admitted to Special Care Nursery

Admission of the baby to a Special Care Nursery because of extreme prematurity or illness causes distress and jeopardises the normal bonding process, and increases the risk of subsequent abuse (Klaus & Kennell, 1970; Lynch, 1975).

Recorded concern over mothering

It has been shown that certain parental attitudes and behaviour at the time of the child's birth are signals of possible bonding failure (Kempe, 1971; Helfer & Kempe, 1972; Fanaroff *et al.,* 1972. Gray *et al.,* 1976). In this study 44 per cent of the abused group mothers had evoked sufficient concern over their 'mothering' capacity for it to be recorded; for example, 'cannot stand her baby's cry', 'has not visited baby for more than a week', 'does not know how to respond to baby's need'. These reports of concern over mothering show that maternity staff are already recognising vulnerable mothers. Unfortunately recognition does not necessarily lead to appropriate action.

Table 4.2 shows the distribution of the adverse factors described in the two groups. None of these factors could be used in isolation to predict abuse. For example, not all women under 20 years old having their first baby should be seen as probable baby-batterers. There are many competent teenage mothers and in some subcultures, it would be unusual for a girl of twenty not to have had a baby. It was the progressive accumulation of interconnected medical and social problems that differentiated the abusing parents in this study from their controls. 70 per cent of the Park group had two or more adverse factors recorded while only 10 per cent of the control group had more than one adverse factor. Thus, if one offered extra help to that 10 per cent of the hospital population, with more than one adverse factor, 70 per cent of the subesequent abusers would be included. The events leading up to abuse in the other 30 per cent are being studied further. As abuse is never an isolated event, it is unlikely that warnings were not given.

Table 4.2 Maternity hospital identification - number of adverse factors

No. of factors	0	1	2	3	4	5	Total
Park Group n = 50	4	11	11	12	9	3	120
Control Group n = 50	31	14	3	2	0	0	26

This study shows that it is possible to identify a group of families in need of extra help using data already routinely collected by most obstetric departments.

Identification within the family (Lynch, 1975)

In families where only one child in a sibship is abused, the parents frequently claim that he is the child most difficult to rear. This was confirmed by the study in Oxford which compared 25 abused children with their 35 unbattered siblings, (Lynch, 1975). By using an internal control group, the parents' pedigrees, biographies and personalities remained constant, and the differences between the abused child and his unharmed siblings emerged with clarity.

The families studied did not come predominantly from any one social class. More of the unabused siblings were illegitimate, and it was claimed that more of the abused children were planned. There was no significant sex difference either in the abused or sibling groups. Half the abused children were under one year old when referred and could come anywhere in the sibship (Table 4.3).

All information, negative as well as positive, given by the parents about the pregnancies and early life of all the children was checked against obstetric, neonatal and paediatric records. Social work and family doctor records were also used.

Table 4.3 Identification within the family - Place in sibship n = 50

1/2	2/2	1/3	2/3	3/3	1/4	2/4	3/4	4/4
4	11	0	2	3	0	2	1	0
			+ 1 set of twins					

Six factors were shown to be highly significantly over-represented in the abused group as compared with the sibling group (Table 4.4). The abused child was more likely

1   To be the product of an abnormal pregnancy: 60 per cent compared with 20 per cent
2   To be the product of an abnormal labour/delivery: 48 per cent compared with 20 per cent
3   To have required separation in the neonatal period: 40 per cent compared with 6 per cent
4   To have had other separations from the mother in the first six months of life: 36 per cent compared with 6 per cent
5   To have been ill in the first year of life: 60 per cent compared with 9 per cent
6   To have had a sick mother in the first year of life: 48 per cent compared with 6 per cent

Table 4.4 Identification within family

	Abnormal Preg.	Abnormal Lab/Del.	Neonatal Separation	Other Separation	Child 1st year	Mother ill 1st year
Proband n = 25	60% (15)	48% (12)	40% (10)	36% (9)	60% (15)	48% (12)
Sibling n = 35	20% (7)	6% (2)	6% (2)	6% (2)	9% (3)	6% (2)

Pregnancy and delivery

In the previous study complications of pregnancy and abnormal labour and/or delivery did not distinguish between abused and non-abused. Within the family, however, it does differentiate between the abused child and his unharmed siblings.

Neonatal separation

Both studies show an increased incidence of neonatal separation. The neonatal separations in this second study lasted for 48 hours or more. Many of the subsequently abused infants suffered serious and lengthy illness, for example, the very preterm infant requiring assisted ventilation for respiratory distress.

Other separation

Even after the neonatal period the subsequently abused child continued to present more problems than his non-abused brother or sister. He was more likely to have been separated from his mother again in the first six months of life. The commonest cause of separation was the child's illness. Five abused children required hospitalisation compared with one sibling. Although hospitals in our area have facilities to admit mothers with their children, none of these mothers availed herself of the opportunity, probably because of her fear and hostility towards the hospital. The other separations were due to fosterings, or the child being left with friends or relatives while mother was away. In one instance, the mother was in jail and in the others she was in hospital. The effect that hospitalisation of a young mother can have on the mother/child relationship is easily over-looked. Such a separation, especially in a family without close friends or extended family can be as traumatic as a separation due to admission of the child himself.

Illness in child

An ill child is likely to be particularly distressing to parents with high potential to abuse (Steele *et al.*, 1968). The abused children in this study had an increased incidence of illness in the first year when compared with their unabused siblings. Both severe illness and recurrent minor health problems were included. There was a high incidence of ill-health among the abused group; pneumonia, bronchitis, viral carditis with heart failure, pyloric stenosis, severe cleft palate and hare lip, cerebellar ataxia and convulsions were all found, as were an abundance of minor but irritating health problems.

Illness in mother

The mother too was more likely to have been sick in the abused child's first year. Any parent who is ill is likely to have difficulties in relating to their baby. The illness included puerperal complications, physical ill-health and psychiatric breakdown. Three mothers had made suicide attempts in the abused child's first year of life.

This study clearly demonstrates the part that illness in the family can play in the process leading to abuse. In 84 per cent of the families either mother or child were sick in the abused child's first year of life.

Table 4.5 Identification within family - number of adverse factors

	0	1	2	3	4	5	6	Total
Proband n = 25	1	4	5	7	3	4	1	73
Sibling n = 35	23	8	2	2	-	-	-	18

It is easy to understand how any of the early events described in this study can interfere with the establishment of a healthy bond between parent and child. In the history of many abused children we find not one but a sequence of adverse medical events leading to the cataclysm of abuse. Indeed 60 per cent of the abused children in this study had three or more adverse factors in their early history, while 66 per cent of their siblings had none (Table 4.5).

Many families face such problems and only a very few will abuse their child. However, such factors can act as valuable warnings in families where parents' biographies and social pressure increase the potential for abuse. All the factors considered bring the family into contact with medical or social services, providing an opportunity for mutual recognition of potential child-rearing problems.

The siblings

The brothers and sisters of the abused children in this study were outstandingly healthy. Their admission rate to the Special Care Nursery was far below the expected and the incidence of subsequent illness was low. It would seem that the siblings' good health and development preserved them from physical harm. It must be remembered that, although free from apparent physical injury, these children were constantly exposed to abnormal child-rearing patterns.

Conclusion

Abuse is the result of a complex process with origins before the abused child's birth. These two studies reveal some of the important features often found in the critical path leading to abuse (Lynch, 1976), and highlight moments in a family's biography when intervention might prevent actual abuse occurring.

The use of data merely to draw up check lists and at risk registers can only lead to further frustration among those expected to work with these young families. Identification of families in need of extra help with child-rearing must lead to a comprehensive assessment of each family, followed by preventive action (Kempe & Helfer, 1972; Ounsted *et al.,* 1974; Beswick *et al.,* 1976).

Acknowledgements

The research was funded by Action Research for the Crippled Child. Jacqueline Roberts is seconded by Oxfordshire Social Services Department. Secretarial help was given by Miss Alison van Dedem Edwards, who is funded by the Oxford Regional Health Authority locally organised research scheme. We thank Dr C. Ounsted for his advice and encouragement.

References

Baher, E., Hyman, C., Jones, C., Jones, R., Kerr, A. & Mitchell, R. The Parents. (1976) In *At Risk: an Account of the work of the Battered Child Research Department,* NSPCC Ch. 5. London: Routledge & Kegan Paul.
Beswick, K., Lynch, M.A. & Roberts, J. (1976) Child abuse and general practice. *British Medical Journal,* 2, 800.

Fanaroff, A.A., Kennell, J.H. & Klaus, M.H. (1972) Follow-up of low birth weight infants - the predictive value of maternal visiting patterns. *Pediatrics,* **49,** 287.

Gray, J., Cutler, C., Dean, J. & Kempe, C.H. (1976) Perinatal observations. In Helfer, R.E. & Kempe, C.H. (Eds), *Child Abuse and Neglect. The Family and the Community,* Ch. 19. Cambridge, Mass: Ballinger.

Helfer, R.E. & Kempe, C.H. (1972) The child's need for early recognition, immediate care and protection. In Kempe, C.H. & Helfer, R.E. (Eds), *Helping the Battered Child and his Family,* Ch. 5. Philadelphia: J.B. Lippincott.

Kempe, C.H. (1971) Paediatric implications of the battered baby syndrome. *Archives of Disease in Childhood,* **46,** 28.

Kempe, C.H. & Helfer, R.E. (1972) Innovative Therapeutic Approaches. In Kempe, C.H. & Helfer, R.E. (Eds), *Helping the Battered Child and his Family,* Ch. 3. Philadelphia: J.B. Lippincott.

Klaus, M. & Kennell, J. (1970) Mothers separated from their newborn infants. *Pediatric Clinics N America,* **17,** 1016.

Lynch, M.A. (1975) Ill-health and child abuse. *Lancet,* **2,** 317.

Lynch, M.A. (1976) Child abuse - the critical path. *Journal of Maternal and Child Health.*

Lynch, M.A. & Ounsted, C. (1976) Residential therapy. A place of safety. In Helfer, R.E. & Kempe, C.H. (Eds), *Child Abuse and Neglect. The Family and the Community,* Ch. 11. Cambridge, Mass: Ballinger (In press).

Lynch, M.A. & Roberts, J. (1977) Prediction of child abuse — signs of bonding failure in the maternity hospital. *British Medical Journal,* **1,** 624.

Lynch, M.A., Roberts, J. & Gordon, M. (1976) Early warning of child abuse in the maternity hospital. *Developmental Medicine and Child Neurology,* **18,** 759.

NSPCC (1975) Registers of Suspected Non-accidental Injury. A report on registers maintained in Leeds and Manchester by NSPCC Special Units, 1975.

Ounsted, C. & Lynch, M.A. (1976) Family pathology as seen in England. In Helfer, R.E. & Kempe, C.H. (Ed), *Child Abuse and Neglect. The Family and the Community,* Ch. 4. Cambridge, Mass: Ballinger (In press).

Ounsted, C., Oppenheimer, R. & Lindsay, J. (1974) Aspects of bonding failure: the psychopathology and psychotherapeutic treatment of families of battered children. *Developmental Medicine & Child Neurology,* **16,** 447.

Pollock, C. & Steele, B. (1972) A therapeutic approach to the parents. In Kempe, C.H. & Helfer, R.E. (Eds) (1972) *Helping the Battered Child and His Family,* Ch. 1. Philadelphia: J.B. Lippincott.

Smith, S.M., Hanson, R. & Noble, S. (1975) Parents of battered children: a controlled study. In Franklin, A.W. (Ed) (1975) *Concerning Child Abuse,* Ch. 5, pp. 41-48. Edinburgh, London & New York: Churchill-Livingstone.

Steele, B. & Pollock, C. (1968) A psychiatric study of parents who abuse infants and small children. In Helfer, R.E. & Kempe, C.H. (Eds) *The Battered Child,* Ch. 5. Chicago: University of Chicago Press.

Discussion

The prediction of vulnerable families was generally accepted as one of the most important areas for study, because it is an essential pre-requisite of prevention, prevention in this sense being the secondary prevention of the abuse which is associated with breakdown of family relationships. Alerting signals are given but are often not read or not interpreted correctly. The presence of such signals shows the need for extra help, but it must be remembered that not all violent families automatically become abusers. One key is the absence of a healthy bond between mother and baby. Some observers look for causes at the mother or the family, some at the child and some, like Fontana, at social conditions. The flow diagram can reveal a great deal about the family and about the coming together of stressful events. Factors brought into the relationship by the child must not be overlooked, neurological abnormality, screaming, feeding difficulties and unmanageable behaviour among them.

Studies like those of Pam Howat and Margaret Lynch are identifying and sifting what data are important, but routinely collected information is of questionable value. Records are useless unless they lead to action. It was noted that abuse had occurred although 58 per cent of mothers had previously been referred for social problems (see p. 31).

What support entails needs identifying, as well as which programme and which worker can best provide it, social worker, health visitor or lay volunteer. Is the need for one person or for a team? In any system, the essential is that someone must always be at the end of the telephone. Information must be shared between the workers. For some families, in-patient care is the priority. The Park Hsopital type of care is expensive and inevitably restricted, but more of such residential facilities are urgently needed in other areas. For other families a crisis nursery, transport or social help are required. The long term help that can be given by social workers suffers from the constraints imposed by competition from other urgent priorities and by limited resources. Nothing happens when there are no resources.

5. Key characteristics of child abuse

RUTH HANSON, WALLACE MCCULLOCH AND SUSAN HARTLEY

The findings of the Birmingham Child Abuse Study have been published in a number of papers, of which many people have read only one or two. Because of this, findings have been open to fragmentary reporting and in a few instances we have been accused of oversimplification. The opportunity will be taken on this occasion to put the record straight by drawing all the findings together.

The list of variables found to distinguish Index from Control cases significantly, and given below, is of interest in itself. Many check-lists have been suggested for use with new cases of obvious or suspected child abuse. They vary in length and reliability. Some are speculative, being based on the observation of few cases and with inadequate controls. Others specify a few features and over-emphasise their importance at the expense of features not considered at all.

When the Birmingham study was designed it was thought necessary to encompass a wide range of factors, in recognition of the exploratory nature of the work. Seven years later, widespread concern for the management of cases sometimes gives the impression that research into aetiological factors is now redundant, but this is far from true. A *full-scale* assessment of the parents and child, which gives due emphasis to the various factors at work, is essential if prognosis and treatment are to be worthwhile.

Practitioners who have to deal with cases of child abuse often ask researchers about the inter-relationships between significant variables. Or they offer their own explanations of the co-existence of two findings within a single sample, which are of course not necessarily correct since these features may co-exist but not correlate. It is all too easy to speak of such 'correlations' as if they were established and most studies, including the Birmingham study, have fallen into this trap.

Because of the quantity of data to be analysed and published from Birmingham, it has not, hitherto, been possible to explore the inter-relations between the significant variables. The dominant ones are described below in the hope that they will give some foundation to current discussions about the processes underlying child abuse.

Distinguishing characteristics

Of all the variables on which it made sense to compare the Index and Control samples, 67 differentiated between them to a significant degree after both age and class had been taken into account, and these are listed below.

First impressions from the study (Smith, Hanson and Noble, 1973 and Smith, Honigsberger and Smith, 1973)

Mother under 20 years old at birth of first child
Mother has psychiatric diagnosis of neuroticism
Mother has high neuroticism score on Eysenck Personality Inventory
Mother has psychiatric diagnosis of personality disorder
Father has psychiatric diagnosis of personality disorder
Mother has borderline or subnormal intelligence on a short form of the Wechsler Adult Intelligence Scale
Father has manual occupation
Mother has a criminal record
Father has a criminal record
Mother has a high General Health Questionnaire score
Mother has an abnormal EEG
Father has an abnormal EEG

Social characteristics of the families (Smith, Hanson and Noble, 1974)

Child's natural father absent from the home
Mother unmarried
Parents acquainted less than 6 months before marriage
Mother considers the marriage unsatisfactory
Mother conceived pre-maritally
Battered child illegitimate
Mother thinks her partner rejects the child
Mother says there is no discussion about child-rearing
Mother considers self the decision-maker in the house
Child lacks his own room
Accommodation lacks one or more basic amenities
Mother rarely sees her parents
Mother rarely sees any relatives
Mother has no opportunities for breaks from child
Mother has no social activities
Mother has no friends
Mother considers her allowance inadequate
Mother is generally dissatisfied with her situation

Interpersonal relations (Smith and Hanson, 1975)

Mother was unhappy in childhood
Mother recalls two or more childhood neurotic symptoms
Mother thinks she was a poor scholar
Mother got on badly with her parents as a child

Mother's mother scolded her as a chief means of punishment
Mother gets on badly with her parents now
Mother had bad relations with siblings as a child
Mother gets on badly with siblings now
Father's mother was unreasonable in discipline
Father's father was unreasonable in disclipline
Mother's mother was unreasonable in discipline
Mother's father was unreasonable in discipline
Mother has a high 'lie' score in the Eysenck Personality Inventory
Mother scores high on criticism of others, Paranoid hostility and guilt on the hostility
    and direction of hostility questionnaire
Father scores high on guilt

Child-rearing practices (as above)

Mother is abnormal (very quick or very slow) in responsiveness to the child's crying
Mother becomes emotional over feeding problems
Mother is not very demonstrative towards the child
Mother is abnormal in her enjoyment of the child (says she finds no pleasure in him
    or he is 'her life')
Infrequent surveillance of child's well-being or whereabouts
Obedience expected at second or third request
Mother physically punishes frequently
Father physically punishes frequently
Mother withholds love as a punishment
Mother uses tangible rewards (pacifiers) for good behaviour
Crying in baby or clinging and whining in toddler a problem
Partner does not help mother with child as she would like

The child (Smith and Hanson, 1974)

Has a general developmental quotient of 90 or under on the Griffiths Scales of
    Mental Development
Physically neglected on admission to hospital
Has a history of failure to thrive
Mother says he is not wakeful (½hr +) at night
Mother says he is not excitable or lively by day
Mother says he is not tired during the day
There is delay in bringing the child to hospital for attention to the injury
Had low birth weight

Analysis of characteristics

62 of these key characteristics were subjected to a multivariate analysis which is described in this paper. Five were excluded. Low birth weight had been compared with the national figures readily available and the controls had not been checked for

incidence of this. Delay in attending hospital had been covered in the course of a 'Circumstances of Accident Schedule' not given to the controls (who were asked more appropriate questions concerning the circumstances of their child's admission to hospital). Mother's allowance, her own mother's means of punishment and her General Health Questionnaire score were thought to be represented by other, similar variables. However, for the time being, perhaps all five should be retained by the practitioner who wishes to obtain a picture of characteristics relevant to a young child hospitalised or dead as a result of non-accidental injury.

There was a score of further characteristics which were excluded from the multivariate analysis for a variety of technical reasons. Broadly, those that were included were applicable to the whole Index sample and could be dichotomised so that the feature was either present or absent in the case. A variable not meeting this criterion is not very useful to the practitioner meeting individual cases.

Details about the wording of questions, criteria for ratings and psychological tests used are either published or available, so that the 67 key characteristics may be applied and explored further.

There were many other features which significantly characterised Index rather then Control parents, but which occur predominantly in the 'lower' social classes. Thus, when more weight is given to the occurrence of such features in the middle classes and less to that in the lower classes in the Index sample, thereby matching the situation in the Control sample's class distribution, their occurrence is insignificantly greater than among the Controls. It would be useful to list these features as well, since they do, in fact, exist in a higher proportion of abuse cases through their social class link; it could help the practitioner to know which problems are related to the client's or patient's social *milieu* and which more directly to child abuse. However, the information can be found in papers published.

Another sizeable list consisted of features to be met quite often in child abuse cases, but also in the Control sample, so that the difference between them was insignificant. It would be illuminating to list these for reference purposes, and to prevent some time wastage among other researchers and practitioners, but space does not permit. Most hypotheses in the literature which could be obtained retrospectively from or concurrently with recent injury were obtained in the Birmingham study. If they do not appear among the 67 listed above it is likely that they were insignificant either before or after class control, but the reader can check in the papers to which reference is made.

Given our sample size, it was feasible to obtain correlations between the variables and to apply multivariate techniques of analysis so that more than two at a time could be studied in association. McQuitty's (1957) elementary linkage analysis was the method chosen to bring to light clusters of variables within the Index sample. Elementary linkage analysis is one way of bringing out major groupings among variables. A variable can belong to only one cluster and will be excluded from it if it is more closely associated with a variable in another. But, as a corollary, the inclusion of a variable in one cluster does not prevent its being almost as closely associated with a variable outside that cluster. There is not the space here to consider all the intersting findings which emerge when a number of important variables are inter-related. The correlation matrix for 62 variables contains 1,891 correlations, of which about 600 are significant (at or well above the .05 level of probability). It is impossible to publish the whole correlation matrix but the information is available from the writers.

Quite a few little groups of just two or three variables emerged which made sense but did not seem to have far-reaching implications. For example, mothers who said they had an unhappy childhood were invariably those who re-called two or more neurotic symptoms in childhood. In fact, in the psychiatric interview the question about unhappiness in childhood followed directly upon the one about thumb-sucking, bed-wetting, nail-biting etc., and answers could have been prompted by reflection on symptoms.

Mothers who said they got on badly with their parents were invariably those who recalled getting on badly with them in childhood, and they tended to be those who seldom saw their parents at the time of the study. It may suffice for the practitioner to ask only one of these questions in an interview aiming to cover all the relevant areas. However, further research is needed to show whether any of the questions found to be significant in distinguishing between abuse and control cases remains so in a shorter interview in a different context.

In a separate cluster, we found that mothers who said they got on badly with their siblings were usually those who had done so as children. Perhaps the problem really began early, or perhaps their memories were coloured by recent experience. If one question is to be selected for this area, it would be better to choose the one about recent experience as probably being the more reliable, but the finding that the problem may be of long standing is of practical importance, and predictive studies set up should allow themselves the luxury of exploring early family relationships.

Mothers who could not discuss child-rearing with their partners tended to be those who made the decisions for the family in general. The absence of the child's natural father actually tied in more closely with a different cluster, but it has a correlation of .37 with mother having to make the decisions which was significant at the .001 level.

Another small 'group' on its own, in the sense that other variables linked with it are linked more closely with other groups, is the association between physical neglect and failure to thrive. In other words, a baby who is physically neglected on admission to hospital may well prove to have a history of failure to thrive, suggesting perhaps some underlying attitude to the child on the part of the mother, rather than, say, a medical condition on the one hand and a social on the other.

Mothers who said the child prevented them from getting on with their work, by crying or clinging, were often those who said they withheld love as a means of punishment. A link such as this does not tell us which, if either behaviour, produces the other, and protagonists could be found for both viewpoints. Most children in the Birmingham study seemed to settle down well in the hospital setting and did not spend a lot of time demanding attention, when their mothers were not there. It has been noted above that mothers of abused children tended to describe their reactions to crying as extreme in one way or another, and it is widely held that either extreme of responsiveness can produce some form of behaviour problem in the older child.

The larger clusters are of greater interest, since features which impinge on numerous others may be thought more worth tackling in treatment.

The largest cluster of variables (which may be seen in Fig. 5.1) hinged on the link between mother's unmarried status and the absence of the child's natural father. Associated with the former were the illegitimacy of the battered child, the first child having been conceived pre-maritally and the lack of basic amenities in the home. Linked with the absence of the biological father was mother not getting on well with her current partner. The abandoned mothers were also more likely to use physical punishment on the child. Here we probably have a rather crucial link. Feelings of inadequacy, depression and wretchedness in child care may well stem from the mother's situation *vis-a-vis* the father of the child. Although it is to be hoped that the mother can be trained to look positively at her relationship with the child and be taught, with the aid of techniques borrowed from behaviour therapy, to manage the child effectively (Reavley & Gilbert, 1976), and to appreciate that her responsibility is also a privilege, it will perhaps be found, more valuable to help the parents in their marriage (or lack of marriage) at the same time. If we continue to describe this large cluster of variables with which we are concerned, the point will become more obvious. Linked with mothers' incompatibility with their partners was their general dissatisfaction with their situation, complaints that fathers did not help with the children as much as they might, and opinions that fathers rejected the children. Linked with their partners' unhelpfulness was the mothers' abnormality of responsiveness to the children's crying and their emotional involvement in feeding the children. Via abnormal responding there was a further link with children *not* being wakeful at night, which has been discussed elsewhere as lethargy and quite plausible as a symptom of brain damage.

A rather smaller cluster (Fig. 5.2) had to do with the mother's psychological state, but drew in her relationship to the child and to outsiders. Mothers' extreme general sense of guilt tended to be associated with their projection of hostility in a paranoid fasion onto other people. More ordinary criticism of others was linked with the latter. In other words, here we have a generally high level of hostility directed both inwards and outwards. Mothers who felt guilty tended to be more often diagnosed as neurotic by the psychiatrist than did others! The prominence of anxiety and depression in the diagnosis fits in with test results and in the general population could indicate suicidal tendencies. Neurotic mothers in this sample were also very likely to be considered personality-disordered, and they were often the ones who had no friends. They were often the ones who wanted ready obedience from their babies or toddlers, which again suggests that the mother is less provoked by the child than by her unhappiness in relation to adults. This is another cluster which has considerable potential for further exploration for treatment purposes and its bearing upon prognosis.

Two clusters hinged on the EEG abnormalities of fathers and mothers respectively, but since the numbers therefore included in these clusters were very small, and since, in the practice, EEGs will rarely be obtained, we shall not describe these.

A cluster of four variables (Fig. 5.3) was based on the link between mothers having few social activities and their having few opportunities to be free of their responsibility for the child. Those who lacked these opportunities also said they did

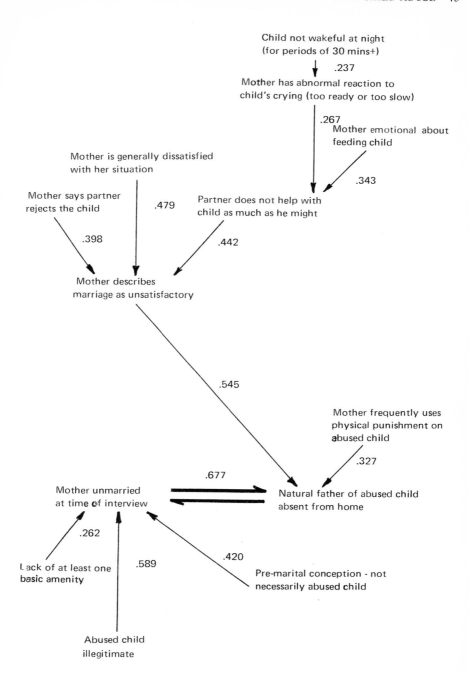

Fig. 5.1. Mothers unmarried status and absence of the natural father.

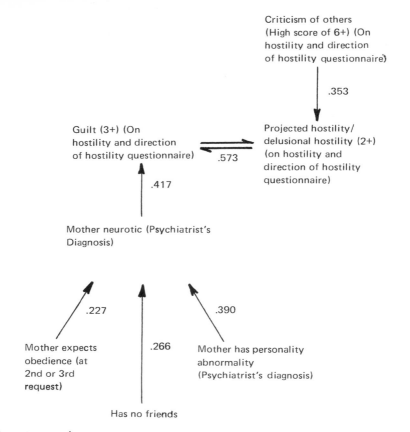

Fig. 5.2. Mother's psychological state.

not keep close track of the child's whereabouts or well-being! And those not keeping careful track also tended somewhat to have inactive (?lethargic) children. This cluster indicates a very inconsistent situation, which may nevertheless give a fair picture of what goes on in the home and what state of affairs can lead to child abuse.

Finally, a second cluster of four was found (Fig. 5.4). This time fathers were more directly involved. If fathers got on badly with their own fathers it was highly likely that they got on badly with their own mothers as well, and they were fairly likely to be diagnosed as personality-disordered. This does not tell us much about child abuse, but if we add a link, between bad relations between father and *his* mother and the fact that his child's mother was a teenager when the child was born, we are reminded of the 'cycle of deprivation', in this case facilitated by an unhappy child escaping from home in circumstances which are likely to produce another unhappy home.

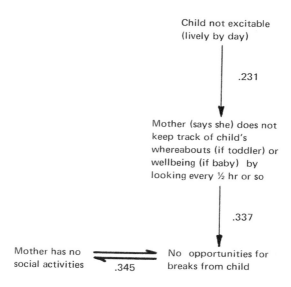

Fig. 5.3. Mothers' social activites.

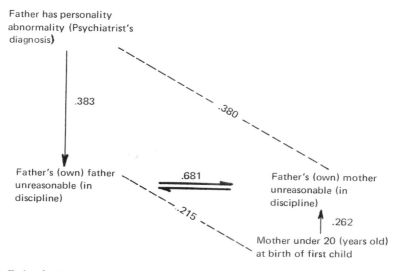

Fig. 5.4. Fathers' relationship with his parents.

These, then, are the major clusters of variables. Many other associations exist which are secondary to them but which may be useful and are available for perusal.

Validity

There will be questions about the generality of the clusters we have found, and some comment is called for. The Birmingham study was deliberately designed to exclude as far as possible cases where abuse had not occurred. For this reason, most children were selected because they had been brought to hospital casualty departments and two doctors were in agreement that, on medical grounds, the injury was unlikely to have been accidental. Hence nothing is being said about cases where suspicion is low or where the child is 'at risk' only. Some similarities will, however, be noticed between the findings of studies of such cases and parts of our data, but if the whole range of key characteristics is to be applied to children 'at risk', a fresh investigation is needed.

For cases of child abuse, of a wide range of severity, the findings described in this paper may be considered applicable, and the basic data relatively reliable in view of of the care taken in the selection of a control group and the formulation and timing of questions. It has to be remembered that some kinds of variables are less reliable than others. Those consisting of a single, *ad hoc* question in a social or psychiatric interview are of course less reliable than those based on a scale consisting of dozens of questions and whose validity is well established. But the phrasing and context of the single question are as important as validity studies, and the months of consideration given to the contruction of interview schedules at Birmingham at least took care of this aspect of reliability. Sighs have been heard for uniformity among researchers in instruments used. It is unlikely that slight variations will distort the major findings if they are of real significance, while of course, such things as the professional role of the inquirer and the intervention processes between the injury and the inquiry will make a great deal of difference. At Birmingham, each parent saw a psychiatrist for an hour, and a psychologist for an hour, both in hsopital, and then saw a social worker for an hour at home; all interviews were held within a few days of the injury. These circumstances were felt to be very helpful. Where there was overlap between the interviews, findings were in good agreement. Reliability of the clusters as such is a slightly different matter, since any method of multivariate analysis is sensitive to the number of variables included. But if the data fed in are sound, we must not shirk the complications which should then reflect the real situation. Confidence in puzzling or complex results is increased by the small clusters consisting of predictable links.

It would be very useful now to see a second large-scale, controlled study carried out with a comparably broad basis. In fact the basis could be narrower in some respects since many questions currently in use could be discarded; it should be broader in others to include findings from predictive studies, such as those on prenatal and neonatal observations, provided these relate to cases of established abuse, and not merely 'risk' where reasoning soon becomes circular. It would be better still, if a predictive study could be mounted which would incorporate all variables significantly associated with abuse. It is not difficult to envisage a study, in which all teenage pregnancies were assessed on these variables and followed up. In fact, a section of such a sample could receive preventive attention based on present knowledge, so reinforcing (or negating) the predictive value of research on the remainder of the sample.

Recognition in the individual case

Helpful as surveys and overall statistics may be in enabling us to come to grips with the nature of the problem, we have at some point to move from large-scale analyses to a description of the individual case. There are many cases where the diagnosis is difficult; cases where the parents deny injuring the child; and it has often been asked, which or how many characteristics must the family possess for the child to be regarded with confidence as physically abused?

This is a more difficult task and it may be helpful if we pinpoint a few problems which arise. First of all we have asked whether one can differentiate an abuse from a control case in terms of the number of adversities by which it may be described.

Of the 62 possible adversities considered in the exercise, Index sample cases had an average of 21 while the controls had an average of eight. The two distributions of numbers of adversities show (Fig. 5.5) that only three of the 53 Control cases had more than 14. So that possessing a score of 15 or more adversities, here, is a fairly good indication that we are dealing with a case of child abuse, although the occasional mistake may still be made.

But 28 of the 134 Index cases were just like the Controls in having fairly few adversities, so how do we deal with these? There are some characteristics which never occur in the Control sample, so that we might be able to say that if there are under 15 adversities, *and* if such and such a characteristic is found, we can be fairly sure we are dealing with child abuse. Now those characteristics are: acquaintance of less than six months before marriage, marriage unsatisfactory, partner rejects the child, mother says she was a poor scholar, her own mother was unreasonable in discipline, as was father's own mother, and mother has a criminal record. But the occurrence of these characteristics is not that much more frequent in the Index sample, although in each case, it is significantly more so. The frequencies range from 15 to 45 per cent of the sample being affected. How often do these characteristics occur among Index cases with fewer than 15 adversities? We can identify only a further 10 among the 28 by the criterion of possession of just one such characteristic.

One lesson brought home by the distributions is that non-abusing families can also present with quite a few of the key characteristics in child abuse, so that far from thinking in terms of any one factor which is typical of child abuse, we should withhold judgement on the individual case until we have a more wide-ranging and balanced view of the situation.

The Control families were very young and for that reason probably incomplete. It is possible that those which had many similarities with abusing families, became such, later on, and these families with difficulties could probably do with help in any case.

In this kind of analysis where individual profiles of features are being drawn up, one discovers the quantity of factors on which, for an individual case, we know nothing. Taken as a whole, the results were very acceptable, the average number of known characteristics among the 62 being 50.4 (81 per cent) for the Index and 52.5 (85 per cent) for the Controls.

However, this still means that a great many individual profiles have gaps where adversities may or may not exist. If we exclude all cases which have more than six

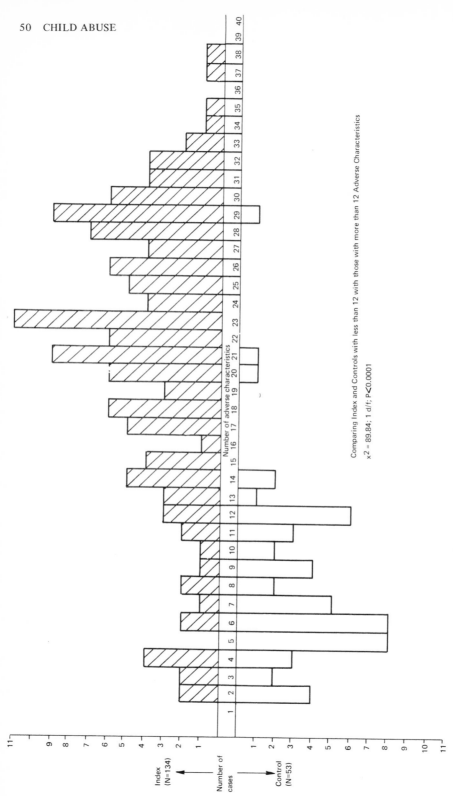

Comparing Index and Controls with less than 12 with those with more than 12 Adverse Characteristics

$x^2 = 89.84$; 1 d/f; $P < 0.0001$

Fig. 5.5 Frequency Distribution of Number of Adverse Characteristics

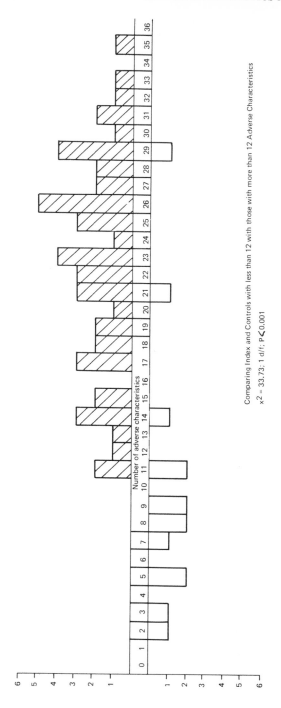

Comparing Index and Controls with less than 12 with those with more than 12 Adverse Characteristics

$x^2 = 33.73$; 1 d/f; $P < 0.001$

Fig. 5.6 Frequency Distribution of a Number of Adverse Characteristics for Cases in which the number of 'unknowns' is less than 7.

'not knowns', (the figure is half way to the average number of unknowns) we are left with only 50 Index and 14 Control cases to compare. This time the two distributions of number of adversities shows (Fig. 5.6) that no Index parent had fewer than 11 adversities. This suggests that many of those marked as having few adversities in the total Index sample in Figure 5.5 are also those who have many 'not knowns' in their profiles. Perhaps therefore, it would be fruitful in practice to make a special effort, in cases of suspected child abuse where the sum of known adversities is low enough to hinder differential diagnosis, to obtain as much information as possible on all key characteristics. But it has to be admitted that a similar effort with a non-abusing sample will produce cases where there is a higher sum of adversities too.

We probably have to conclude that the matter of identification must be left to the now-familiar methods of vigilance and medical opinion, but that a large number of variables have been found, which occur considerably more often in abuse cases. One might go so far as to say that cases with more than about 15 adversities among 62 key characteristics are highly likely to be abuse cases. This figure is not, of course, to be taken as absolute, but for the time being may be a fair guide in the matter of prediction or identification. Furthermore, links have been found between certain key characteristics which are meaningful and may be of use in treatment and prevention of re-battering.

References

McQuitty, L.L. (1957) Elementary linkage analysis for isolating both orthogonal types and typal relevancies. *Educational and Psychological Measurement,* **17,** 207-229.

Reavley, W. & Gilbert, M.T. (1976) The behavioural treatment approach to potential child abuse - two illustrative case reports. *Social Work Today,* **7,** 166-168.

Smith, S.M. Hanson, R. & Noble, S. (1973) Parents of battered babies: a controlled study. *British Medical Journal,* **4,** 388-391.

Smith, S.M., Honigsberger, L. & Smith, C.A. (1973) E.E.G. and personality factors in baby batterers. *British Medical Journal,* **2,** 20-22.

Smith, S.M., Hanson, R. & Noble, S. (1974) Social aspects of the battered baby syndrome. *British Journal of Psychiatry,* **125,** 568-582.

Smith, S.M. & Hanson, R. (1974) 135 Battered children: a medical and psychological study. *British Medical Journal,* **3,** 666-670.

Smith, S.M. & Hanson, R. (1975) Interpersonal relationships and child-rearing practices in 214 parents of battered children. *British Journal of Psychiatry,* **127,** 513-525.

Discussion

Case work is an affair of the heart, epidemiological study of the head. Can epidemiological study identify abusing parents through the recognition of clusters and if so, with what degree of certainty? In order to direct social work to the client with the greatest need, the prediction of the potential abuser and the concealed abuser was a priority for child abuse work but left the much larger problem of families in danger of breaking down, where the need for help might be as great and where the chances of rehabilitation might be greater. The study reported by Ruth Hanson provides satisfying evidence that certain clusters of data have a predictive value. The question was raised whether data on abusing parents could be compared with data from a 'normal' population. Some tendency towards violent and abusive behaviour could be present in controls. What would be of great value would be to know what concentration of risk factors are shared between those who abuse and those who do not. Common observation suggests that within the same harmful socio-economic *milieu,* child abuse is not a constant and many violent people spare their children. Such a study, hard as it would be to mount, might shed light on causative factors.

6. The questionnaire as a research tool

ROGER D. FREEMAN

*'There is no virtue in the mere attachment
of numerical values unless the numbers
have a point and a purpose'.*
Rutter, 1977

Introduction

Questionnaires are in common use for research purposes; we probably all receive them, from time to time, in either our professional capacity or as citizens. Potentially, they represent an economical way to answer certain kinds of questions without more extensive interview techniques. However, their design and interpretation involve problems which are often poorly appreciated by those designing them. Results may therefore be vitiated before one starts. This contribution is an effort to assist those choosing the questionnaire as a method to design it more effectively and to realise some of its limitations.

General principles

1 Establish goals. This is an essential step upon which everything else depends. If there is a specific hypothesis to be tested, this should be spelled out.

2 Define the sample. Defining the goal and the available population from which the sample will be drawn will help determine the target group. The methods by which this sample will be selected must be very precisely set out, both initially and for analysis and reporting of results. Otherwise readers will be unable to convince themselves that the findings are suitable for generalisation.

3 Review similar projects. Who has done something similar, or with a similar group? What problems did they have in obtaining and inerpreting the information? A questionnaire that has already been used and found to be relevant, reliable and valid, may possibly, be adapted with little, if any, change.

4 Obtain necessary sanction. It is not uncommon for questionnaires to be sent out by students or professionals to people who find them unwelcome or who fear that they may get into trouble by revealing information. If, for example, parents are being surveyed, the sanction of parents' organisation is helpful. If professionals or facilities are receiving questionnaires, it is very important to obtain the approval of the relevant professional or organisational body. Often a covering letter from that organisation provides the necessary reassurance to respondents.

5 Brevity. The longer the questionnaire, the lower the rate of return. With a low rate of return, questions will invariably be raised about the differences between responders and non-responders. To avoid this criticism or the necessity for a separate study of non-responders, which if often very difficult, a reasonably high rate of return, in fact greater than 60 per cent is important.

6 Other ways of maximising response. It often helps to state the goal of the research succinctly. The questionnaire should be designed in such a way that little work is required, especially at the beginning of the questionnaire. For example, sometimes specific statistics are asked for which are not readily available in the form requested. This may take special effort. Similarly, questions of a highly personal nature should probably be placed further on in the questionnaire after the ones which are less difficult, or else be omitted entirely, if they are not highly relevant. Enclosing a return envelope with a stamp on it is another standard technique for increasing rate of response.

7 Pretest the questionnaire. One of the most common errors is to omit pre-testing. No matter how good the questionnaire may seem to be, no matter how clear the questions, it must be tested in advance on a small group of persons smilar to those who will be receiving it. Actually, two phases of pretesting are necessary to ensure that the first revision is effective. A tremendous amount of later effort can be saved by this method. Otherwise, unrealised ambiguity of questions or terms leads to strained interpretation of replies or the necessity to omit that part of the analysis altogether.

Problems

1 Relationship between reply and behaviour. It is well known that responses to questionnaires or in interviews may not represent actual behaviour under the given circumstances (Costello, 1966). For example, the theoretical question of whether or not a facility will accept a certain type of case may be unrelated (or weakly related) to the acceptance of an actual applicant. People often reply on the basis of their judgement of appropriateness. Thus, *validity* must be demonstrated through some other technique.

2 Semantics. People working in a special field become accustomed to certain terms and expressions, and may wrongly assume they are generally understood. The pretesting procedure will help identify these ambiguities. But some attention also needs to be given to the phrasing of questions. For example, questions which are semantically opposite may not be replied to in identical, but opposite, fashion. This is a question of design which is beyond the present discussion, but covered in Costello (1966) and Anastasi (1968).

3 Temptation toward over-inflation. It is not uncommon for colleagues who discover that a questionnaire survey is planned to attempt to 'piggy-back' questions or interests of their own on top of it. Generally, it is wise to resist this because of the relationship between brevity and rate of response.

4 Class intervals of numerical data. One very common problem is to inquire about numerical data such as income, or frequency of a behaviour, have the respondent check a box representing an interval, and then code this later. The difficulty lies in dividing up the continuum. For example, there may be no responses in a particular class interval, and too many responses in another. Or the class interval may be so large that the within-group differences are larger in many cases than between-group differences. As an example, suppose we are asking how long a particular type of behaviour has been present. If the respondent has the possibility of choosing 0 - 5 months; 6 - 11 months; 12 - 17 months; and 18 months or greater, one can easily see that replies of 5 months and 6 months, differing by only one month, will be placed in two different classes, and the coding for research purposes will be the same as for answers of 1 month and 11 months, a 10 month difference. In such a case, one would have to consider either using the actual number or dividing the class into a larger number of intervals (Guildford & Fruchter, 1973).

5 Who answers the questionnaire and who is supposed to answer it? One must consider whether questionnaires should be answered by a particular person in a particular role, or whether this does not make any difference. For example, if it is going to parents, does it matter whether the parents collaborate on the answer? If it does, then one has to have some method of ensuring that it is done either together or separately. One must also consider parent-substitutes, whether their responses are to be included, and whether in fact, there is an opportunity for such a person to indicate his or her relationship to the child. If the questionnaire is going to a facility of some sort, there may be a tendency to have the director delegate it to a subordinate within the facility to answer it, so that one may have to consider directing the questionnaire to a person in a specific position, if this is important. It is always a good idea to request the name and position of a person answering the questionnaire in a facility response.

6 Sample size. Depending upon the nature of the hypothesis, and how the results will be used, it may be necessary to obtain statistical consultation on the required number of responses. Often this is not thought of, and then the conclusions obtained are of questionable value. This is a subject fully covered in Guildford and Fruchter (1973). It is best to think about a minimum 60 per cent return rate.

Format

1 Appearance and legibility. There is nothing worse than trying to fill out a questionnaire about which you are not enthusiastic when it is difficult to read or was typed on a defective typewriter. Sometimes the effort is made to cut down the number of sheets in a questionnaire by crowding everything onto one or two sides. This can be a mistake, for the person filling it out needs to have some sense of progress rather than going endlessly from one question to another.

2 Provision for coding. This will be covered to some extent in the following section on computerisation, but it is often helpful to leave a narrow column at one side of the page, clearly set off as 'for official use only', in which there are numbered boxes into which the coding numbers will be inserted. These have to be arranged in such a way that they correspond to the question and to the coding sheets used. Sometimes, if this is done properly, keypunch operators will work directly from such sheets without an intermediate step.

3 Additional categories of choice. Several things may happen to responses which you have not anticipated. First, they may be entirely omitted or the respondent may indicate that they are 'not applicable' for reasons specified or unknown. Sometimes an answer is given, but it is clear that the respondent has not understood the question and therefore it cannot be taken at face value. Sometimes the respondent wishes to indicate that he does not know the answer or is unsure. All of these possibilities must be considered, and categories provided for coding purposes. If, on the other hand, narrative descriptions by the respondents are to be used, rather than checking a box for a pre-established category, the categories into which this information will be coded should be established by pretesting. Even after some pretesting, a coding choice of 'other' will be necessary. This will cover unanticipated or unusual responses, and will be a signal to those working with the questionnaire that these answers may need to be looked at again.

4 Inclusion of rating scales, etc. Some questionnaires may include previously-validated rating scales, semantic differential designs, and other techniques. The problems in use of such measures are discussed in Costello (1966) and Anastasi (1968).

Computerisation or analysis

1 Coding. As previously mentioned, it is necessary to have clear criteria for the categories. Operational definitions must be established in advance. It is even necessary to establish a convention for dealing with double answers or when a person marks a space midway between two choices, such as on an ordinal or interval scale.

2 Use of Fortran sheets. In North America, we usually use these sheets which have 80 vertical columns and 28 horizontal rows. They are used by keypunch operators, but can also be employed, when the amount of data is not huge, for visual inspection. If it is not certain whether complex operations on the data will be necessary, it is best not to depend upon transfer of the coded material directly from the questionnaire sheets to the keypunch cards. The data should be transferred to Fortran sheets so that a certain amount of work (or all of it) can be done directly from them if computerisation is not necessary.

3 Case numbers and control numbers. Ordinarily a case number is assigned to each child, family or facility. If a control case is being used, it is often helpful to give it the same number as the index case, using a separate column to indicate whether the reference is to the index or the control. Thus, one might have two, three or four columns for the case number (depending upon the total sample size), then the next column to indicate index or control, going on to additional material in subsequent columns.

4 Treatment of large number of variables. If the 80 columns are exceeded, it is necessary to use two or more rows for each case. A few extra columns should be left at the end of the row, in case additional unanticipated material needs to be introduced later. (*Example:* In a recent questionnaire, I received a number of multiple responses from a few facilities. The questionnaire had been photocopied for each member of the staff to answer. It was necessary to use a separate column to indicate whether or not this had occurred. Some of the respondents sent important enclosures and an additional column was needed to indicate this, so that the information could be retrieved later. Beyond that, some people wrote comments on the questionnaire sheets which could not be coded, but which needed to be taken into consideration. This involved still a third unanticipated column).

5 Visual inspection methods. If visual inspection of Fortran sheets is used as the method of analysis, rather than computerisation, it is often helpful to use different colours when the data exceeds one row. For example, one may use blue ink for the index case and red ink for its control case. Then one can run one's eye down a column and pick out easily all of the indexes or controls. Alternatively, where one is not using controls but has two rows of data, the first and second rows may be done in different colours for similar reasons. Otherwise, one will have to keep checking the left-hand margin to find the appropriate row, and many errors will be made.

6 Correspondence between question number and Fortran sheet number. Although this may seem a very small and technical point, errors are frequently made in transferring data from questionnaires to Fortran sheets and then to keypunch cards because there is no correspondence between the item numbers on the questionnaire and the columns used on the Fortran sheet. For example, item no. 1 in the questionnaire may turn out to be in column 7 or 8 on the Fortran sheet because of the necessity to enter case numbers, as well as other demographic data, first. Some items will require two or more digits. One can attempt to solve this problem, which can be a very frustrating one, either by using the Fortran sheet column numbers on the questionnaire items (which may confuse some respondents) or by spacing the items on the questionnaire in such a way that the coding boxes on the right hand side of each page (which will be set off from the body of the questionnaire) are arranged in a pattern which is unambiguous; then the number next to the coding box corresponds to the Fortran column and not to the questionnaire number. Of course, one can also deal with this by having no numbers at all attached to the questionnaire items themselves.

In any event, it will probably be necessary to obtain consultation not only from a statistician, but from people who know the computer facilities to be employed. The layout of the questionnaire will then match the subsequent steps and avoid problems and unnecessary effort. I cannot emphasise enough the importance of this procedure which is omitted by many investigators. They are so concerned with the questionnaire itself that they forget how much drudgery is going to be involved for themselves (or others on their behalf) at a later point. When using the computer, 'debugging' of errors can take many hours and cost sums of money because of errors made in transferring numbers from questionnaires to Fortran sheets and then to the keypunch cards.

Summary and comment

By now it may seem that the task of preparing an adequate questionnaire must be quite overwhelming. This is not necessarily so, and once one has done it, subsequent ones are infinitely easier.

These remarks are applicable to many questionnaires, but probably not to all, and I have not attempted to address myself to the specific area of child abuse. I would imagine that questionnaires in this field might involve such possibilities as:
1.   Those addressed to facilities or agencies to determine current practices or numbers of cases being seen;
2.   Questionnaires to individual practitioners, such as physicians, attempting assess either their numbers of cases of this type or their opinions about management and referral;
3.   Questionnaires to the general public;

4.   Questionnaires to be used with child-abusing parents and perhaps a control group in an attempt to determine differences in personality, or to predict future abuse. Each of these approaches will require different methodology and format. Prediction may be particularly difficult. One reason for this is that child abuse is more likely to occur in unstable families who may be more difficult to locate for follow-up. The establishment of area-wide or country-wide case registers so that families can be located even if they move far away may be one way to deal with this.

For a more adequate investigation of attitudes and certain areas of personal functioning which may influence child abuse, questionnaires may be insufficient and interview data may be necessary.

I have not attempted to review here questions of research design, a complex subject in itself (Campbell & Stanley, 1966; Rutter, 1977). However, it is hoped that this presentation of some of the difficulties in the use of questionnaires will be of value.

References

Anastasi, A. (1968) *Psychological Testing,* 3rd Edition. London: Collier-Macmillan.
Campbell, D.T. & Stanley, J.C. (1966) *Experimental and Quasi-Experimental Designs for Research.* Chicago: Rand McNally.
Costello, C.G. (1966) *Psychology for Psychiatrists.* Oxford: Pergamon.
Guildford, J.P. & Fruchter, B. (1973) *Fundamental Statistics in Psychology and Education,* 5th Edition. Tokyo & London: McGraw-Hill.
Rutter, M. (1977) Surveys to answer questions: Some methodological considerations. In Graham, P. (Ed) *Epidemiological Approaches in Child Psychiatry.* London: Academic Press (in press).

Discussion

The importance of questionnaires was generally accepted not only for the gathering of information but also as a tool both for research and to assist practice by listing and defining data of importance. Most professionals assumed that it was within their competence to design and to interpret questionnaires, although this was not, by any means, certain. Even advice and criticism from the statistician was not enough. The sociologist and the psychologist besides commercial advisers could give essential help in the design of the actual questions and their order. The problems of confidentiality also arose; an especial difficulty could be the ethical one of whether information could properly be extracted from a client who had not been warned of the purpose for which the questions were being asked. In North America there were legal implications since from the point of view of the law the information might be used 'against' the client in criminal proceedings. The questioner was truly seeking information in order to help the child and the family, yet the client who was afterwards prosecuted for cruelty or neglect could hardly be expected to see it in this way.

On the other hand, the value of the questionnaire would be greatly reduced unless the client gave spontaneous replies, hence the inadivisability except for matters of fact, of posting questionnaires for filling in at leisure. The public knowledge that questionnaire studies were being made might cause some clients to seek their advice and help elsewhere.

7. Development of children from abusive families

CAROLYN OKELL JONES

The Battered Child Research Department of the NSPCC operated as a community based social work project which accepted referrals from hospitals, general practitioners, maternal and child welfare clinics and other social agencies in three Inner London Boroughs between January 1970 and September 1973. The main thrust of therapeutic intervention was directed towards meeting the parents' needs and fostering their emotional development through long-term, intensive, home-based case-work, including the provision of practical help. It was hoped that they in turn would become more sensitive to their children's needs and the skewed dynamics of parent-child interaction would be altered. Relief from the children was regarded as a vital part of treatment. Part way through the project, the Department opened its own therapeutic day nursery in premises close by the office, for some of the battered children and their siblings.

A detailed account (Baher, *et al.*, 1976) of the Department's work with twenty five families in treatment over a period ranging from eighteen months to four years has recently been published. Additional papers by the writer (Jones, 1975, 1977a, 1977b) have included a summary of the main findings and a critical evaluation of the progress made by the parents and children. This report is confined to findings relating to the children at the time of final evaluation. It highlights the shortcomings of the service in meeting their psychotherapeutic needs and makes some recommendations about future intervention.

All the children accepted by the Department were under four years. Fourteen had severe injuries, two moderate and four minor. The remaining five had no current injury on referral, but were considered to be at high risk of abuse. Two children died and four suffered permanent physical or mental handicap as a result of their *referral* injuries.

At the time of final evaluation, twenty of the surviving battered children were living at home with their parents. All but three of the children were placed in some kind of care, day or residential, at some point in treatment, as casework alone was regarded as an insufficient safeguard.

Subsequent injury to the battered child and siblings

The supportive, intensive care provided for the families was, in the main, effective in reducing the incidence of repeated, severe non-accidental injury to the children.

However repeated, minor undefined injury in these children in our care represented a major problem for the social workers and the parents alike. The problem is compounded by the fact that children already defined as battered or at high risk of abuse are under closer surveillance and the likelihood of observed injuries is greater. In recording subsequent injuries, all those for which there was no definite proof of accidental cause were included. On reflection this criterion may have been too rigorous in that any external marks, be they scratches, bumps, or bruises, were listed if no adequate explanation was forthcoming.

During the three year period after referral, twenty two children were available for possible injury in the home. Of these, twelve received injuries for which there was no adequate explanation. These figures might appear to be high, but, in fact, only two children suffered a serious injury and three moderate injuries during this period. The rest suffered minor injuries which did not warrant medical treatment and none sustained permanent physical or mental disability as a result of post-referral injuries. The highest rate of injury occurred during the first year of treatment.

Subsequent injuries to siblings of the battered child were also recorded. Out of a possible total of thirty two, seven siblings were thought to have been injured by their parents during the three year period following referral. One child received moderate injuries and the remainder minor injuries, with two children suffering recurrent minor injuries. The fact that siblings were also injured lends support to the view that there is often very little difference in parental treatment of the siblings and the battered child.

An important point to emphasise, when considering criteria for successful intervention, is that even if the risk of physical injury has diminished, there still remains the question of whether the home environment is conducive to the child's emotional development. This remained a matter of great concern in a number of our cases and raises issues far beyond those related to non-accidental injury.

Parent-child interaction

Only slight positive changes were noted in most aspects of parent-child relationships, leaving many doubts about the effectiveness of our treatment service in improving the quality of parenting. Lack of acknowledgement of parenthood and failure to enjoy children persisted.

The majority of children still had homes where empathy and sensitivity to their needs were lacking, where inconsistent, often harsh discipline remained the mode, where parental expectations remained inappropriately high and where little positive reinforcement took place.

As we have sensed that most of our parents were demonstrating an emotional rather than an intellectual block to understanding their childrens' needs and development, we tended to underplay direct educational work with them. We now feel, that more attention should have been focused on helping the parents to learn and try out alternative child rearing techniques and different approaches to daily child care routines, once a relationship of trust had been established. In recent years other practitioners, (Alexander *et al.*, 1976, Jeffery, 1976) have developed practical ways of changing parent-child interaction in families of children at risk of abuse, which we would fully endorse as part of a comprehensive treatment programme.

The development of the children

Psychological assessment of the children showed marked improvements in language and cognitive skills which is encouraging. It seems that the Department's system of care helped to restore the child's overall developmental status in most cases, those placed in the therapeutic day nursery showing the greatest improvement of all. However, psychological assessment also indicated that these children's family relationships remained distorted, especially their relationships with their mothers, and differed from those of non-abused but deprived controls.

At the time of the final evaluation, the social workers in the team observed that the children tended to fall into two groups, the introverts and the extroverts, displaying clusters of symptoms similar to those described by other practitioners (Galdston, 1975; Bishop, 1975; Martin and Beezley, 1976a).

The introverts were children who, at the time of referral, had seemed withdrawn, controlled, wary and generally lacking in energy and interest. Now they appeared healthy but delicate, fairly sprightly and spontaneous, aware of themselves and sensitive to their surroundings and other people. Some of these children showed traits of obsessive neatness in their behaviour, wariness of their parents and perhaps an over-eager compliance and willingness to please others. They seemed to be holding in their feelings but the appearance of recurrent problems such as enuresis, food refusal and sleeplessness, suggested that these were highly sensitive and anxious children.

The extrovert group consisted of robust, hyperactive and clumsy children, careless of personal danger in the environment and often prone to accidents. Some were aggressive or destrictive, uncontrollable and liable to temper tantrums. They were easily frustrated and distracted and unable to involve themselves with others Interaction with groups of children or their parents tended to trigger this reckless, violent behaviour, which seemed imitative of their parents or siblings. Though many of these children had shown similar characteristics at the time of referral, a few developed them at a later stage.

In our estimation only eight of the twenty three surviving children seemed to be making reasonably satisfactory and *sustained* emotional development. Of the remainder a few had serious emotional problems which caused grave anxiety about their future development. A few were like weathervanes, reflecting the moods of their parents be regressing or displaying disturbances when the home situation was particularly stressful. Some of the battered children and their siblings were already presenting problems at school.

Shortcomings of the service in meeting the psychotherapeutic needs of the children and recommendations for the future

Our findings suggest that insufficient attention was paid to the psychotherapeutic needs of the battered children and their siblings both in the treatment programme as a whole and in the therapeutic day nursery. In the day nursery setting, we now think that we tended to overemphasise the therapeutic claims of the parents over the children leading to some degree of confusion and conflict for the satff. Whilst some formed special relationships with individual children they were not able to provide the specialised help which many needed. Consistent paediatric care and development monitoring, speech therapy, physical and/or occupational therapy, special educational help and various forms of psychiatric therapy, such as play therapy, group therapy, or individual psychotherapy should all form an integral part of future treatment programmes. It is vital in our attempts to meet these children's needs that at least one adult has the concern, skill and time to earn their trust and to enter the world of their thoughts and feelings. Clearly training programmes for all workers, who are likely to come into close contact with abused children, should pay more attention to developing their communication and therapeutic skills with children. Another pre-requisite for such workers is a solid grounding in normal child development in order that they may quickly recognise the abnormal, including the more subtle signs of disturbance. For example, some abused children, especially those who are quiet, overly friendly (forming indiscriminate attachments to adults) and who exhibit 'good', compliant behaviour, may be regarded as normal, but in fact have significant deepseated psychological problems.

Ideally we think that the workers treating the parents and those involved in providing therapeutic day care for the children should be based under the same roof. Galdston (1975), Ten Broek (1974), Lynch and Ounsted (1976), Bentovim (1977) and Alexander et al., (1976) have discussed the great value of special day or residential family centres in which a multi-faceted treatment programme can be offered. This kind of setting also helps to avoid polarisation of parents' and children's needs and facilitates close communication and mutual support between all staff involved in the treatment process.

Another questionable aspect of our intervention in relation to the children arises from our choice of placements when separation was deemed necessary. In twelve out of thirteen cases where we placed children in care for varying periods of time, we opted for small residential nursery or family group home care rather than foster care. This view depended on a favourable prognosis for the child's rehabilitation with his family. We hoped that the children would not need to be in care for long periods and we were making their emotional needs a less important criterion for choice of placement than the extent to which the parent-child relationship could be encouraged and enhanced during the separation. In a group care setting the child-caretaker relationship is more diffuse and seems less threatening to the parents.

With hindsight we now feel that in some cases a consistent, warm foster home would probably have proved a more emotionally fruitful placement for the young child than a children's home. Unfortunately it is difficult to predict the length of this stay when making initial plans or to guarantee the consistency and therapeutic value of foster care. A matter of increasing concern amongst practitioners is that it is not uncommon for battered children to evoke an abusive response from hitherto satisfactory foster parents. Undoubtedly, foster parents take on a very difficult task when accepting an abused child into their home. They require a great deal more support, education and consultation in dealing with abused children and their parents than they receive at present. We would endorse Martin and Beezley's (1976b) plea that such foster parents should be regarded as part of a multi-disciplinary thera-peutic team which provides consultative services and shares information to the full. It is increasingly apparent, that simple manipulation of the social environment (e.g. foster home placement) is not enough to correct the psychological trauma of child abuse. Removing a child from an abusive situation must not be regarded as the end of treatment, but merely the beginning. There is an urgent need for systematic research into the relative merits of various kinds of protective placements for abused children in comparison with the home environment.

Undoubtedly, permanent separation of the child from his family is another *therapeutic* option which should be considered more frequently than it is at present in child abuse cases. Again with the benefit of hindsight we now feel that in several of our cases the child's interest might have been better served if the focus of our intervention had been on helping the parents to relinquish their child rather than on working towards rehabilitation. However, in the recent move in child care thinking towards a greater emphasis on the rights of the child as an individual, (Goldstein, Freud and Solnit, 1973), there has been a tendency to assume that it is relatively easy to decide that a child has no long term future with his family. In our experience, such a prog-nosis may be difficult to make until one has known the family for some time, and yet, only if decisions about separation are made early on in the casework process, can frequent disruptions of caretaking for the children be avoided. Of help here, would be the setting up of more residential assessment and treatment centres similar to the one at the Park Hospital Oxford, England or Circle House, Denver, U.S.A., where the whole family could be intensively observed in a safe place over a period of weeks or months. The family's response to efforts to augment their caretaking abilities and capacity for change could then be evaluated, as well as the quality of parent-child interaction. At the same time the child is protected and assured optimum growth and development by means of a stimulating environment. Another goal would be to establish more scientific and legally acceptable criteria for court determination and disposition than are now available. This seems vital, in view of many of the provisions of the Children Act 1975, for example, the provision which has been brought in, as additional ground for dispensing with parental agreement to adoption, that the parent or guardian has seriously ill-treated the child and, because of the ill-treatment or for other reasons, the rehabilitation of the child within the household of the parent or guardian is unlikely.

It is evident from our study and the few follow-up studies conducted by re-searchers in other countries that abused children and frequently their siblings experi-ence considerable physical and emotional suffering and that their development is impaired in a variety of ways for a variety of reasons. However, it is important to emphasise that the information available so far is mainly derived from relatively short term follow up studies. There is an urgent need for resources to be allocated to longi-tudinal studies of these children. In future, child abuse treatment programmes should include comprehensive developmental assessment of all non-accidentally injured children (and wherever possible of their siblings) and should ensure that they are kept under periodic review by medical, psychological and social work personnel so that their development can be closely monitored. Longitudinal studies of an inter-disciplinary nature, which such a review would provide, would enable assessment to be made of the long-term effects of various types of therapeutic intervention, and would alert professionals to any ongoing special treatment needs of abused children. Such an approach would enable us to learn more about what happens to abused children when they start school, during latency and adolescence and during the period when they find marital partners and embark on parenthood themselves. It is only by obtaining more insight into the mechanisms underlying abnormal inter-generational patterns of parenting, that we can hope to break the cycle of violence so often detectable in these families.

In the last decade concern about early identification and protection of abused children has increased dramatically. This concern is reflected in the Department of Health and Social Security memoranda (1974, 1976,) on non-accidental injury which consistently emphasise that the safety of the child must, in all circumstancnes, be of paramount importance and offer a blue-print for a national rescue service. However, it is now time for professionals to be encouraged to extend their therapeutic goals and concern themselves with the needs and rights of abused children in a broader context than that of physical safety. A future DHSS memorandum should draw attention to the research findings on abused children to date (cf LASSL(75)29) and provide guidelines for long term treatment planning aimed at improving the quality of life for these children, to supplement those on 'saving'. Martin's (1976) Child Protection Team format would serve as a useful model.

References

Alexander, H., McQuiston, M. & Rodeheffer, M. (1976) Residential family therapy In Martin, H.P. (Ed) (1976), *The Abused Child: A Multidisciplinary Approach to Developmental Issues and Treatment,* Ch. 19. Cambridge, Mass: Ballinger.

Baher, E., Hyman, C., Jones, C., Jones, R., Kerr, A. & Mitchell, R. (1976) *At Risk: An account of the work of the Battered Child Research Dept.,* NSPCC, London: Routledge & Kegan Paul.

Bentovim, A. (1977) Therapeutic systems and settings in the treatment of child abuse. In Fránklin, A.W. (Ed), *The Challenge of Child Abuse,* Ch.20, London: Academic Press.

Bishop, F. (1975) Predictive & preventive studies. In *Proceedings of First Australian National Conference on the Battered Child,* Western Australia: Dept. of Community Welfare, pp. 16-19.

DHSS (1974), LASSL (74) **13** Memorandum on Non-Accidental Injury to Children.

DHSS (1975), LASSL (75) **29** Memorandum on Non-Accidental Injury to Children.

DHSS (1976), LASSL (76) **2** Memorandum on Non-Accidental Injury to Children.

Galdston, R, (1975) Preventing the abuse of little children. *American Journal of Orthopsychiatry,* **45,** 372-381.

Goldstein, J., Freud, A. & Solnit, A.J. (1973) *Beyond the Best Interests of the Child.* London: Collier-MacMillan.

Jeffrey, M. (1976) Practical Ways to Change Parent-Child Interaction in Families of Children at Risk. In Helfer, R.E. & Kempe, C.H. (Eds), *Child Abuse & Neglect: The Family and the Community,* Ch. 12. Cambridge, Mass: Ballinger.

Jones, C.O. (1975) Predictive and preventive studies. In *Proceedings of First Australian National Conference on the Battered Child,* Western Australia: Dept. of Community Welfare, pp. 19-25.

Jones, C.O. (1977a) A critical evaluation of the work of the NSPCC's Battered Child Research Department. *International Journal of Child Abuse & Neglect,* Vol. 1, No. 1. In press.

Jones, C.O. (1977b) The fate of abused children. In Franklin, A.W. (Ed), *The Challenge of Child Abuse,* Ch. 7. London: Academic Press.

Lynch, M. & Ounsted, C. (1976) Residential therapy - a place of safety. In Helfer, R.E. & Kempe, C.H. (Eds), *Child Abuse & Neglect: the Family and the Community,* Ch. 11. Cambridge, Mass: Ballinger.

Martin, H.P. (1976) Child protection team format. Appendix A. In Martin, H.P. (Ed), *The Abused Child - A Multidisciplinary Approach to Developmental Issues and Treatment.* Appendix A, pp. 283-285. Cambridge, Mass: Ballinger.

Martin, H.P. & Beezley, P. (1976a) The emotional development of abused children. *Developmental Medicine & Child Neurology.*

Martin, H.P. & Beezley, P. (1976b) Foster placement: therapy or trauma. In Martin, H.P. (Ed) *The Abused Child - A Multidisciplinary Approach to Developmental Issues and Treatment,* Ch. 15. Cambridge, Mass: Ballinger.

Ten Broeck, E. (1974) The extended faily centre - a home away from home for abused children and their parents. *Children Today,* 3, 2-6.

Discussion

A common complaint about the attitude of the law is that it seems to concentrate attention on the criminal, while displaying little interest in the victim and his sufferings. In child abuse, to some extent the reverse holds true. The moral of Harold Martin's talk, that our concern is with abused children rather than with child abuse, seemed to bias our thoughts in the direction of the victim, the child, a natural view for both child psychiatrist and paediatrician. Yet neither group thinks of children alone and out of the context of some kind of 'family' care. It can be argued that the parents, who act criminally are themselves also victims. The discussion therefore, while starting with the child, his reactions to abuse and neglect and even his contribution to his own abuse, after considering his needs moved to the needs of families and how these could be supplied. The importance of studying the impact of this intervention provided Carolyn Okell Jones with one of her main themes.

The study of abused children shows a diversity of reactions or adaptations in which personality and character play a large part. The style can be 'withdrawn' or 'obstreperous', 'aggressive, noisy, hyperactive', or 'compulsive, neat, orderly and worried by mess'. The children seem locked into a narrow range of behaviour. Valued for what they do and not for what they are, they have a low self-esteem. They do not known how to have fun and many of them 'tease' their caretakers by fighting, temper tantrums or bed-wetting. How far are these reactions innate and how far the results of neglect and deprivation? The effects of maternal depression on a child and his own reactions to depression need study. Poor nutrition diminishes brain growth, lack of verbal stimulation and lack of opportunity to explore may limit abstract thinking, conceptualisation and the growth of language skills. The child who already has a mild neurological defect may invite abuse and neglect, which in its turn removes all chance of his improvement. The child's food refusal, vomiting or soiling or screaming at an inopportune moment may trigger the crisis. The severity of the injury that results is a matter of chance. The effect of dashing a baby on its cot depends in the event on where and how it lands.

The child's needs vary with age, but a thread runs through, the need for 'object constancy', for the certainty of having 'someone else who is important to you whatever happens', without which the future will always remain uncertain and unpredictable so that the child, especially the 'separated child', is insecure and feels deprived. The child is deprived of what is now called nurturance and later of that balanced mixture of discipline and stimulation which is essential to the build-up of independence and eventual maturity. The follow-up studies of Carolyn Okell Jones and of Harold Martin allow us to define and draw a picture of some of the long-term effects in childhood of abuse and neglect. Many more follow-up studies are needed and for much longer periods. Does the outlook vary with the age of the child at the time of the battering or of the consequent separation? How far is the future influenced by the quality and the character of the professional intervention? The first two or three years of life were thought to be the most sensitive.

The discussion moved to the problem of providing the child with 'good' parents, a necessary safeguard for the child's right to health. If left with his own biological parents after abuse, the absence of evidence of further abuse or injury was an insufficient guide. In many abusing families the abused was also the neglected child. The biological parents need instruction from workers visiting the house, and family surveillance by regular visits to a health centre or a hospital clinic. For children over 5 years old, retired teachers might form a valuable pool of helpers from which to draw. For younger children, nursery schools can provide a good environment in which mothers can learn, but at present the places are occupied by children whose mothers think that their children need them and often the educational element is lacking. Day fostering can relieve mothers of the strain of continuous responsibility, but in all these environments the staff must be aware of the family's problems and needs. Child-minding should be more than a convenience and should make a positive contribution to the child or the baby's development as well as helping to show the mother how to cope with her problems. Toy libraries and play visitors can contribute.

With regard to foster-homes, the group, while aware of the personality problems that can arise, felt that much more could be done to include fostering in the treatment of the whole family. The foster-parents should be prepared so as to act as and be recognised as part of the caring team.

Besides providing the child with 'good parenting', they also help the biological parents to come to terms with their problems. This is seen as a triangular relationship between child, biological and foster parents. The psychiatrist and the psychologist have important parts to play not only with parents and with children but also with those giving care. What is needed is to improve the relationship between child, parent and care-givers and this cannot be done through work with any one of them in isolation

Types of combined family activity could be explored and discussed with parents.

When short-term fostering is used, the question arises of how long a time should be given to the biological parents to re-establish themselves. The criteria suggested for deciding when the time has come, which must vary with the age of the child, are these. Do the parents now enjoy the child - and each other? Are parents really co-operating and managing the child? Are there ready life-lines which the parents are prepared to use? Have they achieved better control of their impulses so that in a crisis they can think out rather than act out? What has been their reaction to recent events? A time limit should be set for rehabilitation of the family, perhaps of one or two years, and failure then should in the child's interests lead to the severing of the parents' rights. If the child does return home, the family will certainly need continuing help and guidance.

The group felt that many more substitute family homes with professional back-up services are needed in which can be given the kind of therapeutic care outlined above. Without the biological parents, the child loses contact with family lore and has no sharing of family history and family jokes, important contributions to the child's feeling of identity. On the other hand parental access to children in foster homes is a fruitful source of conflict. Some consider that these meetings might be better arranged in social welfare offices, but others suggested that the emotional problems natural in the circumstances should be talked over openly and that such discussions would not only improve relationships but also provide important insights into the meaning of good parenting.

Of paramount importance is the recognition of vulnerable families and the establishment of a bridgehead before damage is done. A good relationship then can in time allow the worker to exercise an acceptable influence on family interactions. Pregnant high risk women should have regular ante-natal meetings, and extra support in and for a time after the peri-natal period. Ante-natal care can only develop into this new pattern after obstetricians have a greater awareness of the nature of the problem. Both medical social worker and paediatrician should be involved and psychiatric help should be available.

Older children, who have lived all their lives in violent families, may be excluded from school because of their own violence and lack of discipline. If, as seems likely, these children are inviting abuse as a form of testing out, then these children are candidates for self-mutilation, over-doses and delinquency, and psychiatric units for their treatment are required. Such deviant behaviour as truancy, delinquency and drug over-dose, is common in the history of abusing parents. Deficient nurturance or outright rejection are features of the child murderer's background.

The needs of two other groups of people, the sibling and the helpers, were also discussed. In all follow-up plans as well as studies, the progress of siblings should be assessed. The stress on helpers who work with abusing families should be recognised by their employing authority and the necessity for support and for good conditions of work given practical expression.

This wide spectrum of needs which follows our concern with child abuse and neglect should be examined in each area. This may be one of the functions of the Area Review Committees.

The needs of social workers and of other care-givers were discussed in greater detail after Carolyn Okell Jones' paper. In practice, getting on terms with the family presented difficulties, which were not lightened by the knowledge that the family had been entered on the 'register'. Different views were expressed about the wisdom of informing parents about their registration. Provided the worker can get close enough to the parents and share their worries first, a degree of direction can be accepted once they can recognise their need for help. Team work lessens the intensity of the personal involvement of the worker. Difficulties remain about the withdrawal of help in the interests of diminishing dependence.

The damage that might follow inexpert and insensitive handling of children during clinical examination in hospital, is a matter for discussion with the British Paediatric Association. Unfortunately, insistence that only senior hospital staff members should undertake these examinations gave no guarantee of better handling. The adoption by the doctor of an accusatory attitude towards the parents was deprecated. These misfortunes in hospital, besides the harm done to the children, only increased the difficulty experienced by the social worker in maintaining a good relationship.

The difficulties of communication with children, especially the under three year olds was also discussed. Here a psychologist might help. Practical suggestions about training made by Ms. Jones were approved by the group and are printed in full in Chapter 28.

8. The monitoring scheme in Bath

ANTHONY C. FAIRBURN

Bath (population 86,000) was one of the first cities in the U.K. to set up, in October 1970, a local interdisciplinary surveillance panel for child abuse, and has now accumulated six years' experience.

Last year we reported (*New Society,* 31 July 1975) after 4½ years:
1.   The number, based on knowing the actual prevalence, of families at risk of child abuse to expect to have to monitor at any one time in 'a city like Bath'
2.   How the participation of the local panel worked, in giving through two of its members, regular fieldwork guidance aimed at *very early intervention*
3.   How defining the size of the problem helped the planning of better facilities
4.   The way the panel 'gelled' and the time needed to accumulate local lore.

We suggested also that such a local interdisciplinary linkage system has potential as a model for extending 'into the wider field of child deprivation and neglect'. It could provide an early-warning system for all pre-school children, who might need enrichment or possibly more drastic measures at the earliest stage.

This last has not yet been done, but a considerable extension 18 months ago almost doubled the catchment (156,000) by taking on two small country town and commuter town areas in what was part of Somerset, spilling over the halfway mark to Bristol.

We also became embedded in the Avon County central register, and reported thereafter in DHSS Memorandum terms. Because we retained our practical way of working, with automatic monthly review for our high-concern families and quarterly review for the lower-concern ones, we can still give comparable figures. The system is assumed to be over-inclusive, simply because, as each year passes, we are not picking up late referrals in trouble.

'Level of concern'

We have always regarded the level of concern as the key concept to which to work, reflecting as it does 'what we *know* to be going on in this family at the moment'.

High - For practical working we split the families into 'B's, who could not be left for longer than a monthly update. This did not preclude every other type of acute intervention, and we were usually aware of a 'core' group of 6 to 12 families of major concern at any one time.

Low - The larger numbers of a low concern (twice as many again) included some 'B's' whose family circumstances had changed towards stability. Most were, in fact,

71

just routine checks of all significant bruising and all fractures in under-three-year olds. Most of these came off the register after two or three reviews, as we became satisfied about them.

With such a clearly over-inclusive system the temptation was to forget this bigger task. The system, through which were picked up a few, mostly mild but undoubted, child abuse cases, had to be kept up.

DHSS categories

The titles recommended by the DHSS, 'Known', 'Suspected' and 'Potential', have less practical usefulness than the statistics collector might think. Of our 'Known' cases (of past child abuse), three are of low concern to us, because of what we know of the family and their relationship with the field-worker. While they are reviewed quarterly, on the look-out for their individual danger signals, it would be wrong to equate their 'Known' category with 'Most serious'. Conversely, the least strong DHSS term, 'Potential', often all that the lack of observed facts allows one to say, include 7 (half) of our present high-concern families. It would be a great mistake, we think, to treat these three DHSS categories as though they indicate 'risk' categories.

Prevalence in Bath

Figure 8.1 illustrates rough numbers of cases in Bath. The cumulative totals probably have the highest validity. Below them (hatched) are represented out fluctuating population of families, entering and leaving our categories of high concern ('β') and low concern.

Many variables affect the panel's judgement, the members' experience, the accumulation of 'local lore', the need (or not) to override a field-worker's assessment. Too much should not yet be read into the apparent small drop in high-concern cases.

The addition of 70,000 rural, country town, ex-coal mining and commuter town people has not thrown up many extra high-concern cases. How much the drop in births is sequentially altering the picture remains to be seen.

In quiet times, one must guard against being lulled into a false sense of security, and we are only too aware of the differences between our area and the large city-centre populations in the U.K. whom Selwyn Smith and his colleagues and the NSPCC teams have studied. Nevertheless we keep in mind our neighbour Jack Oliver's notable emphasis in winkling out evidence of serious pathology, by intensive cross-checking with all agencies in largely rural Wiltshire.

Case conferencing and the local panel system

The value of a tight, local-linkage monitoring panel system is not least because of its usefulness and stiffening effect in case conferences. These usually come together broadly in these ways:
1. Initial/bedside type
2. Urgent crisis blows up
3. A major policy issue is the be decided (Section 2 care: graduated return to parents)

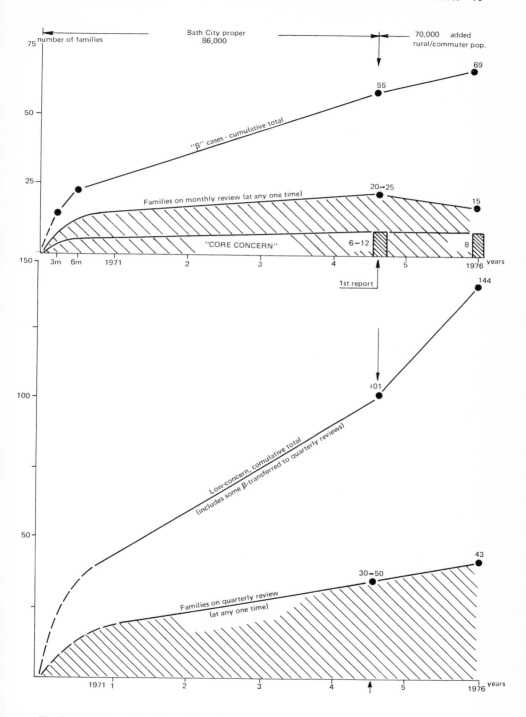

Fig. 8.1. Numbers of families under review.

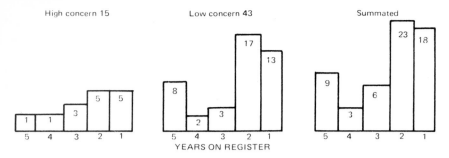

Fig. 8.2 showing the length of time the present group of families has been kept on the register in the two categories

4.   To over-ride the local system
      a)   panel not 'gelled' yet
            i)   still inefficient
            ii)   to help educate and train
      b)   departmental disagreement
      c)   police, for instance, advise prosecution where surveillance and casework are felt adequate
      d)   headlines, or just a feeling that responsibility is getting too heavy and must be shared

We would like to suggest that the large case conferencing system, once the initial crisis is past, is necessarily ponderous and inefficient in monitoring week-to-week, month-to-month alterations in a family. It is no substitute for the quickly reacting, locally sensitive panel, once that is fully established. The strain of devolving responsibility from the centre is probably unimaginable to those of us on the periphery, yet it must also be remembered that a good local panel will be just as sensitive in calling conferences over crises and policy matters.

We would like to hear views on the degree of overlap with the work of 'co-ordinating committees' for problem families. The partly overlapping areas of emotional neglect and child cruelty need to be defined and the amount of extra work this would entail, estimated. Would work with emotional neglect and child cruelty be seen only as a dead-end job because of the lack of facilities for enrichment of the young children?

Discussion

The group accepted Fairburn's point that level of concern about the family was in general of more importance in determining management plans than seriousness or apparent triviality of the injury. Some cases where abuse was known to have occurred were in the low concern group, while half of the cases of high concern were among potential, not known, abusing families. This approach could be used to control the overloading of any monitoring system. There were some problems related to the concept of consensus about management decisions. Did this mean a majority reached by a show of hands, a practice deplored by the group, or was it something more subtle? A case conference which fails to reach a consensus view can appeal in

Bath to the monitoring panel, at which the field worker is not present. The appropriate member of the panel then discusses the panel's view with the worker of the same profession. That not every profession is represented on the panel seemed to the group to present a difficulty. In some areas and districts, the review committee has appointed a sub-committee to resolve such problems. It would be helpful to hear from Area Review Committees how they tackle the question of consensus.

PART 2

The educational element

9. Mother's introduction to her newborn baby—the Denver film

HENRY KEMPE

The parent-child interaction is an accidental by-product of a controlled predictive study on the prevention of child abuse based on observations made in the delivery room and in the first day of the baby's life. The labour room nurses were asked, as part of the study, to give an answer to each of three questions:

1.   How does the mother (father) look?
2.   What does the mother (father) say?
3.   What does the mother (father) do?

Video taping, with both parents' permission, obtained both before and after taping of several hundred consecutive deliveries was for the purpose of validating by independent observers the nurses' observations on parent-child interaction. The tape showed that nurses were highly accurate in this study.

Some of the vignettes were thought to be of use in teaching nurses and doctors good and bad practices in their conduct of a confinement, and films specifically directed towards nurses and doctors are being made. The vignettes for the parent-baby interaction film on the other hand were made specifically to sensitise students of nursing and medicine as well as practitioners in some very obvious observations which can now be routinely expected as part of good health care. The omission of these observations should be considered as serious as failure to obtain a blood pressure or to ask about a history of toxaemia of pregnancy. In sum, without invasion of privacy, these standard observations of early parent-child interaction can be expected to become as much a routine as the standard history and examination.

The base line of a happy and healthy bonding is shown in the first experienced couple having a fourth child who turned out to be a much desired boy. It is followed by a rather depressed couple with a third and definitely undesired child. The next vignette is of an unmarried but happy bonding mother with her first baby and shows that a supporting husband is not essential for a good bonding. The final four vignettes are typical either of non-bonding or of mothers slow to bond.

The first of these was a woman who had been on heroin and who had unfulfilled expectations of her first baby beginning with its being of the wrong sex. The second mother was by nature cold and instead of greeting her baby with pleasure complained of its ugliness. She did later achieve bonding with her baby.

The third had battered her first baby and described this second baby as looking like an ape. The last, unsupported by the father and producing a girl instead of a preferred boy, became depressed, failed to mother her daughter and gave her up. The baby's reaction was to cry excessively.

10. Can good parenting be taught?

CYNTHIA REYNOLDS

The nineteenth century policy of social reform to improve the standards of health, hygiene and nutrition amongst the working classes led to the introduction of Mothercraft classes for girls in some elementary shcools. These remained in existence, perhaps more generally under the name of Child Care, in various schools - which later in the 1920's became secondary modern - up and down the country. Frequently Health Visitors made a substantial contribution to the teaching of such courses and until the 1960's they remained primarily concerned with the physical care of babies and young children.

The 1960's saw the publication of much research on under-achieving children and considerable evidence was offered to support the view that many children were arriving in school at 5 years old, deprived of the breadth of linguistic and play experience - and family security - which would enable them to benefit to the full from their education. A perpetuation of poor child rearing practices was observed - very often, but not always, in areas of poor housing and low income. Consequently a view began to be expressed that there should be some education or preparation for parenthood whilst young people were still at school (Stanton, 1969). This gained some momentum and was supported further in the early 1970's (Pringle, 1974; DHSS Consultation 1973).

At the same time the advent of comprehensive education and the raising of the school leaving age, ensured a new interest in courses which were described as 'meaningful' and 'relevant' in secondary education. Considerable expansion in the curriculum led to the introduction of studies in the Humanities, Health Education, Community Education and Social Education, to name but a few, all of which were integrated courses with components on the family and most probably Sex Education as well. The role of parents was considered and some courses offered further components on the development and the care of young children.

Some schools went further than this and offered a complete one year or two year course in Parentcraft or Child Development. The content and style of these courses varied according to the interests and backgrounds of the teachers who initiated them, and their growth tended to be in regional pockets although some sprang up in relative isolation. In some cases, where a Child Care course had already existed, this was overhauled to fit in with the new knowledge on the needs of children. The National Association for Maternal and Child Welfare had for many years offered schemes and examinations in Child Care and Parentcraft and they, too, engaged in up-dating and revising their schemes. Many of the schemes adopted by schools or innovated entirely from within them were associated with the relatively new Certificate for Secondary Education, a teacher controlled examination offered under the auspices of various regional boards. This was because the general ethos of the secondary school is directed towards examinations and even if head teachers were willing to allocate time for such a subject as non-examination Parentcraft or Child Development the pupils themselves demanded an examination. Generally, these courses covered the average or low ability range and only a few schools offered courses for academic pupils. Most of them were options and only occasionally did a school offer a comprehensive, albeit a shorter, course to all its boys and girls in the fifth year.

It can be seen that the picture over the country at the present time is very variable and it is virtually impossible to draw any hard and fast conclusions. However, since 1971, the Inner London Education Authority has initiated courses in 'Child Development and the Family' and supported them with two advisory teachers working full time, helping teachers and organising in-service training, under the direction of the Authority's Inspectorate.

The London courses have always been based on the following central core of work regarded as crucial:
the young child's need
1.   For loving and secure relationship;
2.   For communication through talk and being listened to - books, stories, nursery rhymes, etc.;
3.   For play as a means of learning and relating his own inner world to the world outside;
4.   For acceptance as a person from birth

Practical experience with under fives in playgroups, nursery classes and day nurseries has also been regarded as integral to the course. Every attempt has been made to try to ensure that pupils have been carefully prepared to maximise this experience. Sessions with junk and paint, clay and dough beforehand, to enable them to work through their own play needs and to learn how much a child gains from such simple materials have been consistently successful. Learning how to read and tell stories and acquiring a repertoire of nursery rhymes and singing games have also proved to be invaluable. Armed with adequate guidance from the teacher and going out to playgroup leaders and others involved with under-fives, who have been informed before hand on the course, and the expectations for the pupils, has ensured that the young people's involvement has been of benefit to the little children and to themselves. Repeatedly, reports have come back of youngsters transformed and of 'school refusers' not only attending their playgroup or day nursery with consistent regularity, but also performing with outstanding success. Failures in this area of the course have nearly always been related to a failure on the part of the adults concerned. For example, teachers fail to contact and visit playgroup leaders beforehand, or to visit the pupils whilst they are out on their practical experience. Or the playgroup leader or nursery class teacher did not really want the youngsters and failed to give them purposeful jobs or to treat them as adult helpers.

Teachers in London are encouraged to make as many links as possible with those people in the community who can contribute to the courses several sessions or even just one. Health visitors, Pre-school Play group Association advisers, social workers, nursery school staff, day nursery matrons, children's librarians, health educators, even sometimes a hard-pressed general practitioner or educational psychologist, have been involved. There is also growing involvement of young parents and this kind of link is proving to be of mutual benefit. A number of schools use the skills of several members of staff and run the course on an inter-disciplinary basis. Sociology, Human Biology and Home Economics are the three subject areas most likely to produce teachers who are interested in Child Development.

Because the subject area is a new one it means that teachers have to be continually engaged in learning themselves, and this is one of the strengths of the courses at the present time. The danger of the examination course is that it will become too 'fixed' and after a time lose the freshness and spontaneity that comes with teachers handling new material and new learning experiences. There is no doubt that teachers form different relationships with their pupils in this work, provided the groups are fairly small, and if they have a sensitive and sympathetic approach. In fact, it often seems as if the adults involved in the teaching are being 'good enough' parents to their pupils.

Over the past five years we have learned that Child Development courses need lengthy and careful preparation and that only adults who are enthusiastic about the work should do it. We believe that the courses should be optional and do not agree with all pupils taking a compulsory course. Apart from the sheer magnitude of the organisational difficulties this would create, we think that to force young people into this delicate and sensitive area of work to do with human beings and human relationships would militate against all we hope to achieve.

Inevitably, when studying the needs and care of young children, many issues arise relating to the parental role. There should be recognition of factors which affect the way in which parents handle children including those which impose stress and make difficulties for any parent. The importance of parents as the child's first mediators between himself and the outside world - as well as his first teachers - must be emphasised. Nevertheless the fact remains that no person really knows about experiences until he or she is actually a participant. Abstract theorising on how to handle children is divorced from reality and some of our pupils have not reached the cognitive levels to enable them to deal with hypothetical considerations and abstractions that bear no relationship to their own experience. This is why interaction with young children is, in our opinion, an essential component of any course because here is a real learning situation.

Because of the diverse nature of the courses and the fact that they only cover a relatively small number of pupils, no attempt has been made as yet to discover if they really do have any effect on the way pupils handle children when they become parents. It would be interesting to know if the self-selection process inherent in an option system means that potentially poor parents who may engage in child abuse never participate in courses of this nature.

Our highly subjective observations suggest to us that a number of pupils do show a marked increase of maturity and acceptance of personal responsibility through taking part in a Child Development course. This may be because they find a sense of self-worth and acceptance in their adult role as helpers with under-fives. It is perhaps a truism to say that this could happen equally well in other areas of the curriculum which spark off interest and motivation in learning.

A school course can offer an opportunity for pupils to learn some skills which will help them as future parents. Many parents need help with their task of rearing children in a highly complex and changing society where urbanisation and job mobility have done much to break up the old established patterns of family living. Our society and the education system ought to be producing persons whose person- alities are growing towards maturity and who have a correct perception of them- selves and the world around them. The whole school should be offering a framework for the development of persons who will be able to cope with their future lives as adults and parents and handle their children accordingly.

References

DHSS (1974) The Family in Society: Preparation for Parenthood, *Consultations 1972-1973,* London: HMSO .
Pringle, M.K. (1974) *The Needs of Children,* London: Hutchinson.
Stanton, M. (1969) Education for Motherhood. In *Trends in Education,* DES, London: HMSO.

Discussion

To open the discussion Mrs Carol Dukes, a health visitor, described her recent experi- ence in teaching parentcraft for two one year courses to girls in a class of fifteen in a comprehensive school. The syllabus, resembling that of ILEA, was covered in twenty meetings each lasting from one to two hours and held in a converted house, an annexe to the school, which had been decorated by students. She felt that cultural and class differences between teacher and pupils provided a real obstacle. She herself began by sharing with the girls her own experiences of family life and of relationships with siblings. The pupils tended to be those unable to cope with academic subjects. She remains uncertain about the best age to start but she would have liked to include boys. She blamed commercial advertising for giving too rosy an expectation of parenthood so that disappointment and failure were likely to result from experiencing the inevitable strains and difficulties. In general the objectives of these courses needed to be more clearly defined. On evaluation of success, she could only claim that the girls got more from the course than they had expected. The group listening to Mrs Dukes, felt that she was a born teacher, capable of imparting her own enthusiasm to any class or age. The question remained, how typical is she of parentcraft teachers?

The general discussion revolved round the questions of whom to teach, when to begin and what to teach. The co-operation of the teaching staff was essential and professionals such as health visitors and doctors (general practitioners, child psychiatrists, even community physicians with a special child health interest?) should be drawn in. The course should not be limited to the non-academic pupils and boys should be included, although generally teachers preferred to take the non-academic boys gardening. In some parts of the course, girls might be less frank in the presence of boys and most agreed that for some of the talks the sexes should be taken separately.

The question of when to begin was variously answered: perhaps all through primary school, perhaps at the top, perhaps not until 13 or 14 years old, although then girls tended to be at a giggly stage. In any case some further opportunity, if not for talks at least for discussion, should be made when a girl became engaged. The fact that more younger girls were now becoming pregnant must influence the decision about when to begin and this raised the question of what to teach.

The bias of the course had to be towards successful family life, home-making, home economics and all that contributes to parenthood. The most controversial element concerned sex education. The cool contemplation of human biology and of the reproductive organs had to be linked with concepts of health and the more emotive ones of religion and moral standards. The fact that girls of 13 and 14 years were now becoming pregnant in increasing numbers, suggested that girls at least needed early instruction not only in a theoretical knowledge about sex but also in its practicalities.

Here we approached the question of the objectives of the course and also its relevance to child abuse. If too early and too frequent pregnancies increased the liability to abuse, the understanding of contraception was certainly relevant. Did such knowledge encourage sexual experiment? If so, did that matter? Should the general practitioner prescribe contraceptives to girls under the age of 16 years? If so, should he do so without the knowledge of the parents? These far from rhetorical questions found no agreed answers.

Everyone did agree that awareness of these problems did not solve them. A well run course could, however, give the children a greater insight into themselves as individuals and this must be an advantage.

Only a slight reference was made in the discussion to the important part, which a knowledgable teacher could play in identifying children who were being neglected or abused. A closer co-operation and sharing of information between the Head teacher, the class teacher, the education welfare officer, the school doctor and the social service department was desirable. A better balance must be drawn between the safety and protection of the children and the feeling that a family's social problems or descent into delinquency or doubtful ability to care adequately for their children are private matters. Key observations besides obvious evidences of bruises or injuries include frequent school absences or truancy, inattention and decline in educational progress. The possibility of emotional as well as physical deprivation must be borne in mind in any assessment of the child's condition. The sibling, not the object of abuse, may also suffer.

11. Prediction and prevention— an obstetrician's view

MARY ANDERSON

In spite of great technological advances over the past few years in methods of monitoring the clinical well-being of mother and fetus, there has also been developing a greater realisation of the psychological needs of the pregnant woman. This has meant a considerable alteration in traditional attitudes of both doctor and midwife, but a great deal has still to be achieved in this respect in many maternity units. There seems no doubt, however, that the end result of attending to the psychological (and social) needs of the pregnant woman should be a closer bond between mother and baby and a lesser likelihood of later child abuse.

It seems appropriate to outline some of the efforts that obstetricians make to achieve a 'psycho-social rapport' with their patients, using the routine employed in my own hospital which is typical of most busy service units. I will then pick out areas where we may be deficient in this respect and suggest where we might improve our arrangements and our attitudes.

The Antenatal period

The booking clinic

In the booking clinic the history of the patient, both medical and social, is traditionally taken by the midwives. The examining doctor will often enlarge on the medical aspects of the history and we are now very much geared to picking out the woman 'at risk' in her pregnancy, medically or obstetrically speaking, and as pregnancy progresses, the fetus 'at risk'. A battery of monitoring investigations has been developed over the past few years for use during pregnancy to predict difficulties and, so far as is possible, to prevent major problems from arising. Obvious social 'at risk' women, picked out whenever possible at the first booking visit to the antenatal clinic, include the single girl, especially the young teenager, the parous woman with housing and financial difficulties and the woman with the unwanted pregnancy, too far advanced for termination. These are clearly in need of support and are referred at an early stage to the Medical Social Workers' Department.

Here I raise the first query. We are not as skilled at detecting the psychologically 'at risk' mother as we are the medically 'at risk'. Should we not be paying much more attention to the social and personal history of our patients and not just leaving the midwife to record a few, often un-noted, facts? We ask, for instance, in the past obstetric history if existing children are 'alive and well', but should we not be enquiring into the health and well-being of these children in greater detail? Have they had hospital admission and, if so, why? What about the patient who has lost her baby at a few months following a 'cot death' or from 'unknown causes'? We are not, I fear, as scrupulous as we might be in obtaining from other hospitals, family practitioners or social workers, records which may prove highly pertinent to the management and future supervision of the mother and her baby. The study by Frommer and O'Shea (1973) has already suggested that simple questions about the mother's own childhood should be incorporated into the antenatal history. They showed, for instance, that where childhood separation has occurred in the mother, then that mother is more at risk of running into problems in managing her infant later.

Home versus hospital confinement

From the obstetrician's point of view there is no substitute for the safety of a hospital confinement. Many women feel, however, that to bond a mother more closely to her baby there is no substitute for delivery in the familiar surroundings of her home, supported by other members of her family. I cannot accept that this supersedes the profound potential tragedy of a dead baby or an ill mother who may, in any case, have to be transferred urgently to hospital. The happy medium must lie in earlier discharge from hospital and the management of the puerperium at home.

Shared antenatal care

In most hospitals, an extensive system of 'shared care' with family practitioners has been developed. Here the mother attends her family doctor for intermediate antenatal care and is seen in the hospital at two or three salient times in her pregnancy. If the practitioner is well known to the mother and has looked after her and her other children for some time, this system must surely help towards developing the feeling in her that the new baby is indeed to be part of the family unit and an extension of the existing family circle. It is to her own familiar family doctor far more than to the unfamiliar hospital doctor that a mother will express her fears and worries.

Motherhood classes

These are provided in most maternity units and are usually well attended. They include a series of talks given by midwives, doctors, health visitors and physiotherapists as well as practical demonstrations on the care of the newborn and visits to the labour ward. Those attending these classes are the more interested, caring and intelligent women, and probably not the women who are liable to abuse their babies later. Efforts should be made to urge many more women to attend these classes, although restrictions on numbers are inevitable in most units through lack of space and staff.

One of the most important points in the prevention of child abuse is surely to develop as early as possible in pregnancy the feeling of a family unit to which the infant is to belong. Including husbands in at least one of the motherhood class sessions is important and still happens too rarely.

The routine antenatal visits

Many antenatal clinics are greatly understaffed and are too large. This means very brief examinations with far too little time for communication between mother, doctor and midwife. Failure of communication with the mother and her feeling that she is just a body containing a fetus to be palpated, must produce much distress and in some cases may even lead to a growing lack of interest in the developing baby, since no one takes the time or trouble to explain or discuss anything with her. One apparently insurmountable difficulty is that the patient may have to see different doctors at each visit to the clinic. In so many units, a number of these will be overseas doctors often with restricted command of English and a much too rigid adherence to textbook scientific obstetrics. Regrettably, too, conflicting advice or comments are given by members of the same staff, something which must alarm many mothers and produce, in some, fear of and indeed distaste for, the unborn child.

To avoid these problems in my own clinic, the senior sister interviews each patient at the end of her clinic visit to give her a final opportunity to talk and to ask questions. As the consultant in charge, I endeavour to see each patient at least once in her pregnancy to act as final arbiter where confusion or doubt has arisen in the patient's mind.

Technology

I have already commented on the explosion of technological advances which has taken place in recent years. Many methods now exist to monitor the fetus in pregnancy and all can and should be explained in simple terms to every mother, even to the least intelligent. This will help to avoid the dangerous possibility of a mother feeling quite remote from her developing baby because the sheer mechanics of the management of a pregnancy have overtaken and obliterated the human aspects of the care of the mother.

Fortunately - or perhaps unfortunately, in the present context - these monitoring methods may finally rescue small babies who are dysmature and require intensive care for a considerable time after delivery. This is a group, which we know is especially liable to abuse later, when returned to their mothers after a long separation. It could well be that greater explanation of what may happen after delivery, given at as early a stage in pregnancy as possible would avoid some of these problems later.

Labour

Preparation for labour must be as complete as possible. Nowadays this should include not just an explanation of physiological events but an introduction to the battery of equipment which the mother may face on entering the labour ward. The syntocinon drip, the technique of, and reason for, induction of labour, the cardiotocogram, are all amenable to simple description and explanation. There seems to me to be a considerable danger that, in our absorption with technicalities, we, as obstetricians, as well as the midwives are at risk of converting the process of birth into a fine piece of scientific achievement. We must never forget the mother at the centre of it all and the new human being who is first and foremost part of that mother and her family unit and not just the end result of our technical skills. Creating this dangerous attitude must surely engender in the mother a feeling of remoteness and alienation from her baby.

Three aspects of the labour ward are particularly important in the present context.

1. The husband should be encouraged to remain with his wife throughout labour if this is the couple's wish. Most maternity units accept this now, but he must be made to feel welcome and an important part of the proceedings. In this way the feeling of a family unit is enhanced.

2. Pain relief in labour is of the essence. A painful labour for a mother who does not really want this baby anyway must surely be the last straw. Epidural anaesthesia is now in widespread use and has a great deal to commend it, provided it has been thoroughly explained to the patient and not administered without discussion.

3. When the baby is born, the most distressing sight to be seen in a labour ward is the removal of the baby to its cot without the mother catching even a glimpse of it. Fortunately this is rare, but it may be inevitable in some deliveries for the baby to be handed to the paediatrician for immediate resuscitation. Even then, however, the mother should be talked to by the obstetricians and mid-wives and wherever possible an explanation of what is going on given to her. It goes without saying that as soon as possible the mother should be given her baby to hold for as long as she wishes.

The puerperium

Breast feeding

In most hospitals now the baby is with the mother all the time, and this should be universal practice. Removal of the baby to the nursery to give the fraught mother a restful night should, however, be equally common practice. Breast feeding, which should have been encouraged during the antenatal period, must be given every support and supervision. No greater bond can be established than by this mode of contact. On the other hand the mother who does not wish to breast feed, and this can be for a variety of valid reasons, should not be made to feel guilty or inadequate.

Depression

The well known phenomenon of puerperal depression must be remembered in those at risk. But the lesser 'fifth day blues' must not be dismissed as of no consequence, especially if they take the form of ignoring or neglecting the infant.

Separation of mother and baby

This we know is of great importance with regard to later child abuse. Ill babies have to be transferred to special units so that intensive care can be given to them. Although a more appropriate subject for the paediatricians, may I as an obstetrician make a special plea? There is a sad tendency for failure of communication between paediatrician and obstetrician so far as these ill babies are concerned so that the obstetrician is not always kept entirely in the picture and is, therefore, ill-equipped to act as mediator between mother and baby. The obstetrician is often at fault and perhaps all lying-in ward rounds should be preceded by a visit to the Special Care Baby Unit.

Regular visiting by the parents to the Special Care Baby Unit, preferably together, to see their baby, to handle it and to feed it, if possible, and to talk to the medical and nursing staff is essential. The difficulty arises when the mother is ready to return home long before the infant is fit enough and this may constitute a considerable problem. Mothers should be encouraged to visit their babies as often and for as long as they can and a special mothers' room should be available in all special care units.

What seems an unforgiveable separation of mother and baby is when ill babies have to be transferred to distant specialist units where the mother cannot also be accommodated. In many hsopitals there are cubicles in the postnatal wards to house the mothers of babies transferred from outlying hospitals, and these should be much more commonly available.

Conclusion

At present the obstetrician is largely unaware of the full extent of the problems of child abuse and has not as yet set about developing monitoring and prediction skills such as he has developed in the clinical field. It is perhaps no exaggeration to say that the obstetrician, supported by the midwife, could in many instances have the earliest opportunity of anyone for detection and therefore protection of those women or families at risk.

References

Carter, J. (1974) Ed. *The Maltreated Child,* London: Prior Press.
Franklin, A.W. (1973) *Report and Resolution of The Tunbridge Wells Study Group on Non-Accidental Injury to Children,* London, DHSS.
Frommer, E.A. & O'Shea, G. (1973) *British Journal of Psychiatry,* **123**, 149-56.
Harrison, L. (1976) *Nursing Times,* July 22.
Jones, W.L. (1975) *Nursing Mirror,* 23 October, p. 49.
Renvoize, J. (1974) *Children in Danger,* London: Routledge & Kegan Paul.
Smith, S.M. (1974) *British Medical Journal,***1**, 443.
Smith, S.M. (1975) *Nursing Mirror,* 12 June, p. 48.

12. The gentle art of neonatology

ALFRED WHITE FRANKLIN

Man and wife make the marriage, the birth of the first child makes the family. Every single circumstance of this initiation into family life is important.

The recognition of the newborn baby as a person with considerable awareness and positive feelings and reactions is a recent development in our culture, in which the baby has been seen as a passive recipient rather than an active partner in human relations. It is true that for many mothers, although never for all mothers, the happy event was greeted with joy and delight. The names, like the bassinet and its contents, were ready waiting, as perhaps also were the inheritance, career and even, in exalted circles, the future spouse. But babies in general, especially those belonging to exhausted multipara living in squalor, were not treated with consideration for their feelings, nor were they highly regarded. When death rates were high, the feeble, the deformed, the unwanted and those whose bonding mechanism had gone awry, could be submerged without trace beneath the flood of those dying naturally from such perinatal happenings as intra-cranial haemorrhage and serious infection.

Obstetric improvement and paediatric advances

The high mortality rate, and the high perinatal mortality rate, meant that birth and death were inextricably linked in childbirth in the minds of everyone. Concern for the safety of the mother nearly always outweighed concern for the baby. Puerperal sepsis, puerperal toxaemia and obstructed labour were rightly the pre-occupations of doctors and midwives. A wastage of new life was 'natural' for babies. In the nineteen twenties men like Eardley Holland unravelled the mechanics of labour and devised methods both of avoiding foreseeable disaster and of managing the complications of delivery, especially preventing intra-cranial haemorrhage in the baby. With the spread of this knowledge, birth-deaths declined and obstetrics became safer for the mother. In the nineteen thirties Leonard Colebrook's meticulous studies on sulphonamide therapy at Queen Charlotte's Maternity Hospital led to the defeat of puerperal sepsis. Ten years later, neonatal spesis succumbed to penicillin and the newer antibiotics. In the fifties light began to dawn on the hitherto mysterious pathology of the newborn. In the nineteen forties exchange transfusions largely solved the problem of death from haemolytic disease of the newborn; elucidation of kernicterus had to wait until the fifties for studies of bilirubin metabolism by chromatography and electrophoresis.

Modern medicine has its roots in morbid anatomy, but only in the last twenty five years have fetal and neonatal organ and tissue changes been interpreted in ways different from those of adults. Failure of the lungs to expand at birth was equated with lung collapse from obstruction of the bronchus and death from asphyxia with death from drowning or other forms of suffocation. The idea of developmental progress, of something happening or failing to happen for the first time, was introduced only with the adoption of the paediatric developmental point of view.

The recognition of the unique nature of the histological changes in the newborn allowed clinical syndromes to be regrouped. A truly remarkable series of enlightenments have followed at an accelerating pace during this last period: lung histology, chromosome analyses, the identification of hitherto unrecognised enzymes. A mass of metabolic and biochemical studies including fetal blood sampling have revealed the important, sometimes the vital differences, between mature and neonatal physiology and between the responses to stress and to infection which are specific to the immature baby and the early hours and days of life. Accurate prediction, the envy of those who work with child deprivation and abuse, is possible. Preventive action can be taken against genetic faults in the first trimester of pregnancy and against impending disaster in the last. With new knowledge techniques changed. Passage through the Valley of the Shadow of Birth has become a safer journey.

Hospital delivery

Hospital confinement was originally for the abnormal, the homeless and especially for the unmarried. It was not meant for the normal married poor even when home conditions were bad, with hot water from kettles, newspapers for bedclothes, absent window panes and a gang of assorted gaping children watching. But even when hearths were cold, hearts were warm and grateful father was ready with a cup of tea for actors and spectators. The contraction of middle-class households, the disappearance of retainers, servants and extended families, led to a demand for maternity homes. Every town soon had its quota in which new recruits to the professional classes were joined by upper working class wives who feared death in hospital, which they were a little ashamed to enter, and yet not happy to risk at home the failure of the midwife or doctor to arrive in time. This intermediate stage, ended only by the opening of new hospital maternity wards in the National Health Service, had among many disadvantages, too small a margin of safety. A converted house, despite inadequate plumbing, contrived labour ward and an unsafe nursery, reminded patients and relatives of the bedrooms at home, producing an atmosphere of comfort and usually of false security.

The staffing was poor, one certified trained midwife satisfying the legal requirements. The other staff members, who in practice often had to shoulder responsibilities both for the conduct of labour and for the care of the babies, were inadequately trained and not always of high quality. The small annual turnover gave an appearance of safety, belied by the number of avoidable deaths from infection and from treatable congenital defect, when the results were gathered together from a number of small homes. It was against the background of the rising popularity of these poor quality maternity homes that the newly formed College of Obstetricians and Gynaecologists ordained that hospital confinement was to be the pattern for the future.

Changing professional relationships

New knowledge and improved techniques have changed the relationships of all the members of the cast, obstetricians, anaesthetists, paediatricians, laboratory consultants and technicians, nursing staff and midwives.

The obstetrician

Fifty years ago the obstetrician had his two hands, his five senses and a few obstetrical instruments. He was a skilful clinician but he was no statistician and no epidemiologist, nor in his hospital practice was he, with a few outstanding exceptions, especially sensitive to the environment and the social circumstances from which his pregnant patients came and to which they, with their babies, would return. Age and clinical experience set him in his ways, supremely confident in his techniques. He became an increasingly authoritarian 'chief'.

His scientific interest was absorbed by maternal mortality. When prontosil brought puerperal sepsis to an end, the other problems that replaced maternal mortality were not entirely within his power to solve. Meanwhile he began to lose his status. Once the cynosure of the governing committee which had appointed him, with a matron anxious to please, midwives anxious to learn from him and do his bidding, laboratories at his command and a continuous supply of captive mothers and babies, he found that the needs of his patients for other experts and for other skills were growing.

The anaesthetist

The administrator of anaesthetics, starting from Simpson's chloroform and passing en route the Minnitt gas and air apparatus, has made a long journey on the way to becoming an anaesthesiologist, an expert on such diverse matters as homeostasis and neonatal laryngoscopy. In his efforts to spare the mother and to assist the obstetrician he may adversely have affected the fetus, a happening revealed only after a series of tragedies. Fortunately the influence of drugs and anaesthetics on the fetus and particularly on neonatal behaviour and function is now recognised and studied. Experience suggests that this new knowledge will penetrate the system slowly because of the conservatism inevitable with strictly supervised routines.

The paediatrician

The paediatrician arrived late in the maternity department of the hospital bringing little knowledge and less experience. Queen Charlotte's had in the twenties invited a specialist in diseases of children on to its staff. A fount of wisdom on the care and feeding of normal infants, he could predict when a baby was going to die but found it difficult to distinguish intra-cranial haemorrhage from lung pathology. He had little treatment to offer. His first success came when exchange transfusion saved babies from dying of haemolytic disease. Later, penicillin enabled him to help babies to overcome some of the previously fatal infections. Sharpened by radiology and better pathology, his clinical accuracy improved and now he knew what was actually happening, though still lacking the means by which to control events.

The diffusion of paediatricians into the community by the National Health Service first gave most paediatricians access to the newborn baby and the baby the benefit of his help. That the obstetrician had some grounds for resisting this change cannot be denied. The paediatrician twenty-five years ago knew little about the newborn. The knowledge did not exist. On arrival in the maternity department, flexing his muscles and feeling his new power, he turned topsy-turvy many traditional treatments. He removed from the premature baby the gamtgee jacket and woollen bonnet, the dropper used for feeding, the binder and the cord powder. Now the baby lay nude without fluid for a few days while the cut end of his umbilical cord dangled unprotected in the air. The sudden availability of incubators in which temperature and humidity could be efficiently controlled and the oxygen percentage raised to undreamed of heights, together with a sudden increased use of oxygen for no clear reason, set the stage for a series of disasters. The resulting dehydration could be corrected by intravenous fluid, but hypoglycaemia usually remained unrecognised. Most serious of all was the epidemic, in all the departments that were dazzled by novelties, of retro-lental fibroplasia and permanent blindness from the effects of too much oxygen.

Despite these initial tragedies, the transfer of a very special kind of patient to a specialist doctor has been followed by many valuable advances in treatment. Now instead of being a disposable object, the baby has become a subject for scientific study. Technology has invaded the nursery. The compulsion for more accurate and earlier diagnosis and the need for instrumental control of potent and potentially dangerous forms of treatment has transformed the nursery into a laboratory of great sophistication. The neonatologist has arrived. The baby shall not be allowed to die.

Laboratory staff

None of this work can be accomplished without the wholehearted support of the laboratory staff. What has been happening to laboratory consultants and their technicians? In early days the clinician could turn his hand to the job helped perhaps by an assistant whom he was training. Now the laboratory has its own independent life and much of its work has no direct connection with the patients in the hospital. For one thing the hungry appetite for employment of all the vastly expensive equipment could not be satisfied by only the routine work of the hospital. Nor could the salaries of the men and women who dutifully tend and serve the equipment be justified. Research, sometimes clinical, but preferably basic and the need for material for Ph.D. theses keep these complex concerns going. Loyalties are therefore divided. The obstetrician no longer stands in an employer/staff relationship with the laboratories. The names of the technicians appear quite properly in the list of authors in many scientific papers. The needs of the patients are of course fulfilled and patients are called upon to provide material for the researches on the success of which the financial health of the laboratory may depend. That ethical problems arise is not surprising. Priorities may become confused and perhaps investigations are carried out that are not strictly necessary for the clinical management of the patients. To

serve the clinical staff and the patients is only one part of the function of the
laboratory.

The nursing staff

The laboratory is not the only place where loyalties are divided. Right in the very
heart of the hospital, in the labour ward itself, tensions and divisions are felt which if
directly affect attitudes to the patient. Most maternity units are performing a number
of functions, among them education. The patients are essential for education in
clinical practice, both of doctors and nurses. Nurses in training need to have attended
at a specified number of deliveries. It is not unknown for the patient to be told
'stop pushing' because the baby must not be born until the pupil has arrived. Of
course the nursing staff perform invaluable service to the mothers and the babies,
but the needs of duty rotas, lectures, rest periods cannot be gainsaid.
    Loyalties to the nursing hierarachy also influence attitudes. There is a colonel
in command with staff officers and the foot-soldiers engaged in short term service
as part of their training. Among their other duties, they are fighting the unending
battle against human error. This is a defensive war routine procedures minutely
observed providing the main safeguard. Routines are designed to protect foolish
mothers and careless midwives. They exist to spare the need for thought and therein
lies their danger. Their advantage is that in the day of disaster, if routines were found
to have been correctly followed, no-one can be held responsible and no-one can be
blamed. It is routine, taught and practised by command, that prevents flexibility
and this is what delays changes from yesterday's routines religiously learned. They
are the hierarchy's Queen's Regulations.
    Tension arises when the needs of education run counter to the needs of treat-
ment. All rhesus sensitised mothers should be delivered only in hospitals with a
twenty-four hour pathological service and a staff experienced in exchange transfusions. The safety of the baby demands it. When the plan cannot be operated
because a hospital, lacking facilities but which is also a training school, must admit
every kind of case, here is indeed a disarray or priorities.

Routine practices

Routine practices are necessary safety measures, but they need review. They may
be out of date; and when a new one is added, a determined effort should be made
to remove an old one from the list. No-one has the task of watching with the expectant mother's eye every detail of her handling through the antenatal department,
through the labour ward with its strange faces and disturbing apparatus, into the
ward where she will make her first attempts to care for her baby. No-one in the
hospital is actively fighting for the happiness of mothers and babies during their
initiation into family life.
    A new orientation in maternity work in hospital is beginning to stem from
examining all the techniques of management from the expectant mother's visit to
the booking clinic until she reaches the labour ward. What happens in the delivery
room and thereafter until she goes home should be influenced by recognising the

need to keep mother and baby together. The way in which the mother is greeted and handled at her first visit is important. So is the person who takes the history and the way in which the questions are framed, which ought to include matters relevant to the mother's ability to care for a baby and, with multiparae, to the condition of the siblings. Emotional and social elements will influence the mother and her success in mothering. The preoccupation with illness and with physical states cannot and should not be changed, because obstetric safety for mother and baby hold their priority. Nevertheless, the price may be too big if this interferes with the mother's ability to nurture her baby successfully.

The baby should be given to the mother to hold immediately and the policy should not be to send the baby to special care for observation lest it might need some special treatment but rather the reverse. The baby should go with the mother unless some reason actually exists for separation.

When I first visited Queen Charlotte's Maternity Hospital forty years ago, all babies delivered by forceps or Caesarian section, however, good their conditions, were cot-nursed for 48 hours and not once picked up, certainly not by the mother but not even by a nurse. After much argument over many months the rule was relaxed when the paediatrician had examined the baby and pronounced picking up safe. Feeding was inflexible at 3 hourly intervals by day, and night feeding was discouraged. Discipline and authority were vested in the Matron and only after her retirement was it possible to institute 4 hourly feeding, when this seemed what baby and mother (and not Matron) wanted, and eventually, although reluctantly, on demand feeding and night feeds as of right rather than of favour. The importance of at least visual contact between a sick mother and her baby in the special nursery was difficult for the staff to recognise. To take the small baby in its incubator to see the mother on another floor or to allow the mother in a wheeled chair to visit the baby in the special nursery seemed to the authorities ventures far too dangerous. At last, such things began to happen and finally the mother was given permission to hold her own baby's hand through the port-hole of the incubator.

The hardest battle - and these were all hard battles, although it is difficult for the modern generation to realise it - was fought over allowing children to visit mother to see her and the new baby during the puerperium. But finally, even this was permitted. Later the stimulus of Professor Nixon at University College Hospital gave fathers some status in the initiation into family life. All of these changes happened many years ago. On a series of recent visits to obstetric departments, my pleasure at finding all these techniques in action was slightly diminished by the impression that in some the changes were relatively recent. My experience was limited to half a dozen centres of excellence in university hospitals. Would, I wonder, the conditions be so good at District level?

These changes were prompted by intuitively held feelings of the needs of mothers and their babies, helped by a strong dislike of routines for routines' sake. So often a routine method begun for sound reasons continues long after those reasons have vanished. Now these humane practices are being given a scientific basis by ethological studies of animal and human behaviour. Is it a measure of our hardness of heart even in the compassionate professions of nursing and medicine that such studies are necessary? Must humane practice always bow before scientific proof?

Should mothers be given more responsibility over decisions about anaesthetics and drugs? Or indeed about other elements in their care? The pendulum can swing too far in going 'back to nature', but treating a mother as though she has no responsibility for what happens to her in this critical period cannot be a good preparation for confident care of a first born new baby with whom she is shortly to be left alone. To recognise the importance of the interaction between the mother and her professional caretakers is nothing new but is now beginning to be understood. In the Denver film a newly delivered mother was urged by the nurse to look at her baby and not to look down the other end at the doctor who was 'sewing her up'. Her alarmed expression was striking to observe. Puerperal depression is a common experience for midwives to see, but entirely new to the mother. The suffering mother is not helped by and indeed cannot penetrate the nurse's artificial cheerfulness.

By the time the baby is born, the maternity staff should realise which mothers and babies need special support and cannot be treated according to the normal routine. Such understanding and flexibility are expected to contribute to the prevention of child abuse and deprivation.

The future

The hospital maternity service grew up for the care of the abnormal, the homeless and the single woman. Once, many mothers and babies were expected to die and even in childbirth the over-riding need was to overcome death. Now death is a rare visitor. How much this is due to the improved health of our community, how much to improved obstetrics cannot be accurately measured. Certainly labour is not now obstructed by a rhachitic pelvis. We must ask how necessary are the safeguards and precautions that originated in those dark ages and how far they contribute to a new set of emotional problems. We must also ask whether the socio-economic element in health and disease should influence decision making.

The original occupants form the minority. If every normal healthy woman is to produce her expectedly normal healthy baby in hospital, we need a new philosophy Let critics of the routines continue to press for changes in what seems unnecessary, harmful or even ridiculous. But let them realise that present methods were developed to secure the greatest safety for the patients. If modern medicine has its roots in morbid anatomy, death and disease are its progenitors. It is the psychosoematic branch that now needs tending. Obstetrics should look in this new direction and ask the question 'what interferes with the initiation of family life?'. To find the answer requires that all our techniques and routines are re-examined from this point of view.

One possiblity is for the 'maternity area' to consist of two related but separate parts, a maternity home for the normal and a specialised hospital for the abnormal. Mothercare, fathercare and baby care could be practised and taught in the former, and problem obstetrics and neonatology practised and taught in the latter. Selection of cases, always difficult, will never be perfect. Nevertheless many at risk groups can already be recognised and further study could surely refine selection. What would be the worst that could happen when an unexpected problem arose in a supposed normal? An emergency transfer? This is never a good thing. The loss of a baby who might otherwise have lived? But we shall always lose some babies. Should we not balance these against the mass discomforts and less than good handling of the initiation of family life for the normal and healthy?

The science of neonatology is flourishing. Professional competence depends on knowledge and technical skill. Where there was once scarcity there is now abundance. Professional excellence demands something more, a full understanding of human relationships within the hospital. And more than anything else, knowledge of how positively to promote the health and happiness of the family that is beginning there. This is the gentle art of neonatology.

Discussion

The Tunbridge Wells Study Group drew attention in Resolution N (see p.186) to the importance of obstetric practice in relation to bonding between mother and her new baby.

In Chapters, 3, 4 and 5 of this book, the observations reported by Pamela Howat, Margaret Lynch and Jacqueline Roberts, and Ruth Hanson and her co-workers, all add importance to the stress associated with an abnormal perinatal period. The group does not confine its interest to the abnormal, the small for dates, the premature or the sick baby, but believes that successful family life demands a fresh look at maternity practice even for the normal. The presence of an obstetrician, Dr. Mary Anderson, was especially welcome.

Although there is, she said, no official obstetric view, she believes that obstetricians are realising, as she herself does, that they have a responsible part to play not only for the mother and the baby, but also for the whole family, and so they become involved in child abuse in ways which must of necessity be preventive. She is planning a prospective study of the outcome of pregnancy in a population in which observations relating to prediction of child abuse will be included.

The group did not enter deeply into the question of hospital versus domiciliary midwifery, but rather sought a compromise, 'There should be more home atmosphere in hospital and more hospital atmosphere at home'. The district midwife in conjunction with the health visitor and the general practitioner could, more often than they now do, supervise the antenatal period once the mother has had her first examination and has booked in, just as the postnatal examination of mother and baby at eight weeks can be made in the Health Centre. Close co-operation between the primary health care team and the hospital maternity service is vital and the general practitioner should be in the best position to discover the mother's wishes about her confinement.

The involvement of the father has long been recognised and in all maternity departments he should be welcomed, if he so wishes, in the labour ward, preferably with something to do besides holding his wife's hand. He should have been allowed to attend some preparation classes and he should be willing and helped to give up two weeks of his annual leave to prevent his children from going into care while his wife is in hospital with the new baby.

The persistence of bad habits and thoughtless routines is discussed in detail in

Chapter 12 with particular reference to the special care baby unit.

'Pain relief in labour is of the essence', claimed Dr. Anderson. Yet some mothers complain that they are 'not present' at their own delivery. The time may have come for the mother to have a greater share in the making of decisions about the timing and place of her delivery, the use of sedatives and anaesthetics and the feeding of her baby.

Miss Howat's moral in Chapter 4 is that the labour ward staff can easily be taught to observe and record how the mother looks at her new baby, what she says and what she does. Before she realises the meaning of these simple observations, even the experienced observer is likely to state categorically that she has never seen a mother who rejected her baby at the first contact. Since, according to Miss Learmont the midwife is the most senior person present at 76 per cent of deliveries, the need is great to systematise what the midwife should look for and what she should do. Her observations will never foretell which mothers will abuse their babies, but only who is vulnerable and who needs support because she may break down under stress. Observation of the mother alone will not reveal much about the father, although their reaction to each other may be informative.

The prediction of vulnerable families and especially of vulnerable mothers should substitute extra care and sympathy for the natural annoyance with and antipathy to a mother who seems ham-handed in managing and cold in her attitude towards her baby. The midwife and the health visitor who should be aware of the situation need to form the best possible relationship with such a mother so that she can accept their help and their advice and not regard it as being critical of her, very sensitive, self. No harm would be done if time so spent deprived some of the obviously successful mothers of some attention.

In all this discussion the mother or the family is assumed to be prepared to book in, to attend parentcraft or other preparation courses such as those run the National Childbirth Trust, and to co-operate cheerfully with all the plans. The vulnerable family cannot be relied upon to behave in this way. A difficulty discussed in Chapter 16 has been introduced by the attachment to general practices of health visitors who thus lose their geographical responsibilities. The suggestion has been made that health visitors should be notified of a pregnancy as well as of a birth in all areas, and not only in a few as at present. The abusing family with its predilection for isolation, its fear and dislike of authority and its general attitude of non-cooperation which result in 'non-attendance', could in this way be reached.

The highly controversial question of statutory removal of a newborn baby from a mother known to be violent and considered not to be amenable to treatment is the subject of Chapter 26.

PART 3

Current views from the professions

13. Prediction and prevention in general practice

KEITH BESWICK

Introduction

The aim of this paper is to describe how a primary health care team became aware of the problems of non-accidental injury. The events leading to the acceptance of the problem are discussed, and the changes which occurred in the team that led to the development of a management programme. Further changes in the team occurred after the institution of the programme.

Didcot is a small town of 16,000 people with a further 16,000 in the surrounding villages. Employment is varied but includes research establishments, a power station, light industry and the automotive complex in Oxford. A very small proportion commute more than 25 miles. Housing is good but there are mobile caravan parks and a small army camp.

The patients (9,250) in this study are all registered with one practice which is housed in a modern Health Centre. The primary health care team consists of four male doctors, three health visitors, three nurses, a midwife and an auxiliary. Also in the building are the local Social Services, offices for the health visitors and the Home Help service.

As to the size of the problem, we recognised 12 cases of abuse which occurred between January 1973 and February 1976. There was a further case of a child of 6 months who died of a subdural haematoma and had a sibling dying as a cot death. Recent information has indicated that there is a strong possibility that there was abuse. We also had another 22 families on our at risk register in February 1972.

Coming to terms with abuse

The general practitioner working alone when presented with a child who has been injured is in serious danger of making the interview both collusive and ritualistic. The general lack of management programmes for dealing with the problem in the community means that early warning signs are ignored. Most of us find the idea of abuse repellant and too horrible to be thought out in isolation, especially those of us who have recent personal experience with our own children.

The need to discuss topics of mutual interest and a desire for both the Primary Health Care Team and Social Services teams to work more closely, resulted in the sharing of the common room at coffee time each day and the setting up of seminars in the Health Centre each Friday lunch time to discuss topics of interest. These joint team meetings enabled us to obtain realistic expectations as to each other's ability and method of working. The feeling of strength and back-up generated from one's colleagues is of great help. The resulting improved relations with Social Services coincided with the realisation that child abuse problems needed to be discussed together and in depth.

At first the members of the team were only aware of the gross cases of abuse, in which asphyxiation had been attempted or a femur fractured. Sharing clients with the Park Hospital for Children, Oxford, educated the team and made us more aware of early warning signs. This in itself created a bigger problem, the earlier we saw that families were in trouble, the harder it became to help. At first we were frightened to approach them for fear of putting the idea into their heads that they might injure their children. Experience has since shown that the more honest the approach the better for both sides.

The development of management programmes

With the Park Hospital we have developed the following programmes of management. First comes prediction. The primary health care team is well placed to predict the families at especial risk. This should ideally be from the time the woman reports that she might be pregnant. Though most patients are delivered in hospital, the discharge letter may divulge various clues, such as prolonged labour, operative intervention or the child's admission to the Special Care Baby Unit. The health visitors and midwife have become expert at recognising those mothers who are not enjoying their babies. The receptionists, too, have developed a sixth sense when children are at risk and arrange for the children to be seen by the doctor, even if they present at most inconvenient times.

A register of children at risk is kept by the health visitors. It is important that all members of the teams be aware of which families are on the register. By trusting each other, fear of loss of confidentiality is avoided. Those registered should preferably be reviewed at frequent intervals and the inclusion of a family on the list should not be taken as a failure by the worker concerned. The start of a therapy group is a good time for review.

Identification can be made by any member of the primary health care team. What is important to recognise and accept is that the patient has a problem. Often it is impossible and undesirable to deal with it in a busy surgery. Time must be made within a few days to go into the problem at a greater depth. Physically abused children are referred for hospital consultation immediately.

Both the general practitioner and the health visitor, and, ideally, a social worker, should be present at the diagnostic interview. The full history should be taken in the first part of the interview and then the problem outlined. Only then can a simple management plan tailored to the patient's problem be drawn up to make use of the existing services.

Help may be given in the following ways:
1.   By providing nursery or playgroup places to enable the mother to have the few hours of peace which she desperately needs.

2. By increasing socialisation, especially when new families arrive in the area completely without friends. This applies especially to Service families. Here the health visitor may well be able to help.
3. By attention to housing. Bad housing can be a contributory factor and help is often needed in getting the patients to accept the situation rather than in waving a magic wand with the Council.
4. By seeing the child at regular intervals.
5. By referral to other agencies. This can only be effective if there is a full understanding of what the agency can provide. These agencies will include hospital services from paediatricians and child psychiatrists as well as from adult psychiatrists. A home help or family aide may be life saving.
6. By specialist group activities.

Group therapy for mother and child as a community project

The simple management plan, outlined above, gave us some insight into the problem, but left us wanting to explore the problem in greater depth and from the community angle. For this reason, staff from the Park Hospital and a family doctor (KB) decided to set up groups for mothers and children in a Community Health Centre. Initially, this caused considerable anxiety in the primary health care team and the social services. These fears were talked out and the back-up facilities of the Park Hospital explained. Careful plans were made, drawing on former Park Hospital experiences. The aim was to help parents with those child-rearing difficulties which could lead to child abuse. Most parents had asked for help for themselves because they feared harming their child. An effort was made to exclude any mother who could disrupt a group or be rejected by others (e.g. the psychotic). Seven mothers with nine children under school age were selected. Six mothers attended regularly.

Groups were run simultaneously for mothers and children. The co-therapists in the mothers' group were a male family doctor and a female social worker from the Park Hospital. A play therapist organised the children's group with two voluntary helpers and a boy and girl from the local secondary school. The groups ran for six months.

The participating mothers, who showed many of the characteristics typical of child abusers, were helped in the following ways:
1. They developed greater self-esteem by learning that they were not the only mothers with problems and by discovering their own area of competence. They also lost their sense of uselessness by learning how to help others.
2. Their regular contact with other group members relieved their previous social isolation. They also began to set up social gatherings outside the group and, at a later stage, they took over the visiting of any member who did not attend.
3. They learnt to trust all the therapists and began to form real friendships with each other.
4. They acquired social skills and a knowledge of child-rearing.

Observation of the children revealed a disturbed group, needing considerable help in their own right. Their progress was monitored throughout the six months and the following changes occured:

1. Clinging, over-attachment was replaced by increased independence through careful handling of both mother and child on separation.
2. Watchfulness disappeared as the child established regular relationships with adults.
3. They learnt constructive play and the enjoyment of play.
4. They developed social skills through greater contact with other children and adults.
5. They made rapid physical and emotional developmental progress. For example one child gained 2 kgs. in weight in two months and a whining baby developed into a chattering extrovert toddler. Children with specific areas of developmental delay received special attention and teaching.

Time was available at the end of each session for a mother to talk to the play-therapist and to join in her child's play. The project therefore provided an opportunity to evaluate and treat both mother and child as individuals and to help them together with their relationship problems.

As planned, at the end of six months, the Park Hospital therapists withdrew. A new group has now been started by the community workers.

Discussion

The traditional procedures for dealing with the problems of child abuse and non-accidental injury left the practitioners with a feeling of frustration. At the case conference all available information is pooled so that a decision can be taken whether or not to instigate court proceedings. When a court case was considered inappropriate, the conference did not look towards the future or take into account the skills or willingness of those involved with the family to help plan further management. Hospitals can discharge patients, and general practitioners can remove patients from their lists, but these problems remain within the community.

The actual incident of abuse for which a child is admitted as an emergency is only an episode in a series of events. The work done on prediction had enabled us to recognise small injuries as warning abuse, or cries for help. This made the problem even harder as without a management programme we were powerless to help these families. Though it was often possible to get other professionals to recognise that these warnings were indeed important, we often had to make the decision to do nothing.

The main reasons for failure to act were lack of confidence; the absence of a local management programme; fear to act except in obvious cases; poor communication between professionals, especially in the presence of depressing legal advice; a feeling of failure by those already involved and a general feeling of hopelessness about the situation. There were usually too many reasons for not doing anything

At the introduction of the groups many doubts and fears were expressed. These mainly concerned the lack of specific training for the therapists; the fear of making things worse; an inability to deal with crises and doubts about back-up services for the therapists.

By involving both the primary health care team and the social services in the planning stages and allowing doubts and fears to be expressed, we were able to get initial widespread support. As the group progressed new cases were referred with greater optimism because of the realisation that we could help with these families in a positive way. The simplicity of the group in a Health Centre setting is attractive and often within the realms of existing facilities. The non-medical staff of the Health Centre have taken to the playgroup, which has become an established feature of the building.

Discussion of the group's progress at the Park Hospital enabled us to realise our limitations and also to withstand pressure to accept unsuitable mothers. We were also grateful for constant availability of the Park staff for advice in times of crisis.

The groups have given us a lot in greater understanding of problems in child handling and insight into families in times of crisis. They have also taught us to work more as a team, especially with social services. At times we almost felt that we were learning more than the group members, but the group had a great facility for bringing us down to earth with a bump.

14. General practitioners and child abuse

RICHARD STONE

At the end of the John George Auckland Report there is a table showing the lengths of contact with the family of various workers. Social and other workers came and went: one general practitioner was in contact from well before the first child's death until after the second (Fig. 14.1). This contrast is stunning and is common to many cases. Yet deaths occurred, and criticism of general practitioners is only thinly veiled.

The general practitioner is a notorious butt for despairing neglect by other workers. My plea is to look for every opportunity to create in him an interest in awareness of the early signs of abuse, and what to do if faced with potential or actual abuse, and working with others. 'We'll just have to wait for the old boy to retire' is not good enough. Anyway, retirement for a general practitioner is not at 65 as it is for hospital doctors. He is an independent contractor with the DHSS and can go on past 90 if he wishes.

Very many general practitioners know well what to do, and are fully alive to the need for multi-disciplinary co-operation. Among the others, there are three targets:
1.   New general practitioners,
2.   Receptive general practitioners who need to know more,
3.   Non-receptive general practitioners.

New general practitioners

Child abuse figures prominently now as a topic in medical student eduction. Changes in training are taking place. Yet we still produce young doctors who think little of medical activity outside the technological teaching centres and even less of non-medical workers. At present 40-60 per cent of new doctors go to general practice. A number will start out as the 'non-receptive' general practitioners.

However, this trend is dying in the medical schools and, more importantly, most young doctors are now subjected to a broadening post-graduate education before arriving as principals in general practice.

Receptive general practitioners

Before long every Area Review Committee will have sent out to every general practitioner in its area its booklet on what to do in child abuse. Even if read and kept

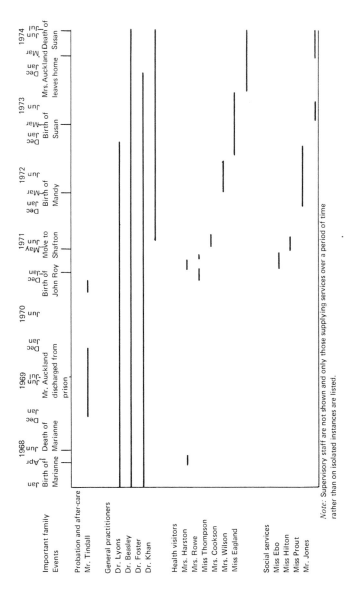

Fig. 14.1. Individuals providing services to the Auckland family 1968–1974.

somewhere accessible, it will be necessary to circularise booklets, say, every two years to keep the subject fresh in doctors' minds.

There are financial incentives for general practitioners to attend for postgraduate education under S.63 of the Health Services and Public Health Act, 1968. Many paediatricians have a stock lecture on child abuse, complete with gory slides and lists of early signs. The receptive general practitioner is likely to be exposed to this every year or two provided that clinical tutors and paediatricians remember to include the lecture in curricula. Full recognition under S.63 is readily applied to courses 'for doctors by doctors'. Difficulties arise when a course is run by, say, the NSPCC or social work departments: all those likely to be in primary contact with an abused child are invited. It is just such a multi-disciplinary meeting which is most likely to break down the barriers of communication so criticised in the Maria Colwell report.

Now, local clinical tutors have only a limited budget and are very unlikely to approve such courses, although it may help if the venue can be arranged to be in their lecture rooms. It is not widely known that Regional Post-graduate Deans exist (addresses from the British Post-graduate Medical Federation, 33 Milman Street, W.C.1) who have authority to approve courses outside medical centres, but only at 'zero rating'. This recognition contributes only towards seniority awards and incidental expenses. It does not cover costs of running the meeting so that approval for attending a study group like this one at Farnham does not provide for reimbursement of the course organisers for food and lodging of the doctor, nor for payment of the course fee by the doctor.

A good result from the recent integration of Health with Social Services could be that social workers might make a brief summary for the general practitioner after each major assessment of a family, including case conferences on child abuse. This should be sent only with the consent of the client. It could be a fuller version of the brief discharge note sent by housemen from hospital. A senior social worker tells me she feels it would be a good discipline for workers in the field to have to summarise problems in this way and could be useful for the social services themselves when a family transfers to another area. It would also ensure that families are encouraged to register with a doctor.

Non-receptive general practitioners

The Area Review Committee's booklet joined the medical journals in the waste-paper basket. Contempt for health visitors is only exceeded by that for social workers. Child Abuse did not figure in the syllabuses of the medical schools before 1969/70. 'Don't tell me what's wrong with that family: I brought the mother into the world/ They're the salt of the earth/for Heaven's sake, the father is a barrister'.

Many general practitioners protect themselves with an attitude of superiority. Sadly this is reinforced by their 'inferiors' who are frightened off by the rejection they receive. The inability to share responsibility is enhanced by years spent in a small surgery, cut off from other workers, even other general practitioners. It will sometimes take a great effort to overcome this isolation.

I urge all workers never to reject back, no matter what the provocation. If a polite telephone call does not work, try waiting at the door before surgery starts. Write a letter offering to hold a case conference at a time which suits the general practitioner's convenience, however awkward that may be. If necessary, hold it in his surgery. If all else fails, appeal to the elitist urge and ask a consultant paediatrician to make the contact. If approached often enough, the general practitioner may agree to a meeting, just to stop the pestering. It may well take only one successful meeting, or one brief and effective case conference to convert him to years of multi-disciplinary co-operation. It is worthwhile to try to make this miraculous conversion not just in cases of child abuse, but in any situation when it is felt the general practitioner has something to contribute. It is all too easy to fall into the trap of mutual rejection, to the detriment of patients and clients.

Community midwives

Some ante-natal examinations can be carried out in the home by community midwives. This has become possible with the reorganisation of the Health Service. Community midwives are now based in hospitals in close contact with consultant units. A number of advantages would follow, including the saving of money by transferring medical time from cost-intensive hospitals to the cheaper primary care team. The size of ante-natal clinics would be reduced. After booking, ante-natal checks in the early and middle months of pregnancy are medically dull, and can be looked on as a waste of skilled time for highly trained obstetricians. Removal of about half of these examinations would free them for the complicated situations where they are really needed. At the same time, the role, interest and responsibility of community midwives would be increased.

Lastly, and most important, in the concept of this meeting, greater opportunities would be provided for the prediction of child abuse. A midwife, perhaps with a health visitor brought in to help, would be able in the home to identify the known factors in an informal way.

My recommendations are printed in Chapter 29 (see p. 190, 191).

Discussion

Dr Beswick claimed to have been educated about child abuse largely through the staff of the Park Hospital for Children, Oxford, a privilege not available to general practitioners in other localities. The group agreed that the development of similar general practitioner services based on the same principles would be of great importance. In his turn, Dr Stone made valuable proposals as to how the interest of general practitioners could be enlisted and their skills increased, while, at the same time, conceding that some practitioners would not respond.

In discussions about the management of families, expectations of what each person in the team can achieve are often unrealistic; but a collection of professionals forming a team to tackle problems, which they all can see, could advance beyond recognition of the problem and referral elsewhere. Such good team work might be more effective in some cases than the large formal case conference, which tends to get caught up in discussions about court action. Team members play an invaluable part in supporting each other. Their participation in establishing play groups helps to extricate families from isolation and encourages their socialisation. Fathers need to be actively involved as well as mothers.

As regards numbers, Dr Beswick reported that eighteen families had asked for help in 8 months and only one child had been admitted to hospital on account of bruises. Patients who were used to attending doctors' surgeries might find it easier to discuss their problems and seek help there than in social welfare offices. Questions of confidentiality do arise, but with the caring approach to families, such difficulties can usually be overcome.

On practical matters, from the general practitioner point of view, any training meetings should have academic approval, which is more easily obtained for meetings held in medical centres. Should finance be a problem, the help of drug companies could well be sought.

15. The role of the health visitor in the prediction and prevention of non-accidental injury

JEAN DAVIES

Much publicity has been given in reports of recent cases of non-accidental injury to the actions of the health visitors concerned. There has been at least one common factor, namely the very high population covered by one health visitor. In the Inquiry into the family of John Auckland, it was reported as over 10,000 and, in the Steven Meurs case, 11,000. These are by no means isolated instances and in the present economic situation there is a danger that case loads will become even heavier. In such situations regular visiting to all families with young children becomes an impossibility and 'selective' visiting becomes the norm rather than the exception.

The health visitor's tasks

As long ago as 1956, the Jameson Report recommended a ratio of one health visitor to 4,300 population. The Department of Health and Social Security Circular 13/72 states:-

'While subsequent experience confirms this estimate as reasonable for some areas, a ratio of one Health Visitor to 3,000 population may be desirable in others; e.g., those with a highly developed system of attachments to general practice, or with a high immigrant population. Such provision would be exclusive of supporting ancillary staff'.

It is encouraging that the document on *Priorities in the Health and Personal Social Services* places such emphasis on the need to expand the preventive services; but what, in practice, can the health visitor do to help reduce the incidence of non-accidental injury?

Regular visiting

Over the last few years, there has been a gradual increase in the number of health visitors attached to group practices, although there are still some areas where geographical districts are worked. There are advantages and disadvantages of attachment schemes, and I propose only to examine their effect on the subject under discussion. One result has been to hasten the expansion of the health visitor's role. Because many more problems of the handicapped, bereaved, elderly, etc., are referred to her by the general practitioner, less of her time is spent with the pre-school child.

Why is this to be deplored?

1. Health Visitors have no right of entry to any person's home. Consequently, they have to establish good relationships with the families under their care. This cannot be achieved at one visit, but only over a period by regular contact.
2. Home visiting is essential for the detection of early signs of stress, which could lead to child abuse, e.g. depression or mental illness in either parent, marital disharmony, or financial difficulties. A change of behaviour or deterioration in the standard of home care may be the first tangible sign of trouble. Much misery and even tragedies might be averted if help could be given before a crisis develops.
3. Developmental assessment of young children, either at home or at a clinic, will give valuable information regarding both the physical and emotional health of the child.
4. It is now an accepted fact that some of the parents who abuse their children come from families where violence has ruled down the generations. Many of the parents were themselves unloved children. It is only by gaining the confidence and trust of the family that health visitors will realise just how much help and support is needed. This is unlikely to emerge in the clinical atmosphere of a surgery. Equally important, the attitudes of the parent to the child, and child to parent, can be seen in the home and when it is possible to see both parents, their reaction to each other.

Primary health care teams

Since reorganisation of the National Health Service, much has been said about the formation of these teams. Their effectiveness is obviously facilitated by good attachment schemes, particularly when social workers are included, but these schemes are not an essential pre-requisite to good liaison and cooperation at field level. The need for this cannot be over-emphasised. For example:
1. The health visitor and the general practitioner should work together in investigating the reasons for frequent visits to the surgery with apparently trivial complaints.
2. The midwife (hospital or domiciliary) and health visitor need to exchange information regarding families at risk. One of the London Boroughs has instituted a system of alerting health visitors to the birth of babies born in the District General Hospital likely to be at risk.
3. When social case work is required there needs to be cooperation between the health visitor and the social worker, with a two-way exchange of information. All too frequently, when a case is referred by one department, there is no feed-back from the other.
4. Informal discussions with all concerned will often result in the appointment of one person as the key worker to undertake the main support for the family, calling in the other agencies as necessary.

Change of Address

The health visitor, working in a geographical area, will quickly see or hear of a new family on her 'patch', often from neighbours or tradespeople. She then visits and lets the newcomers know of the services available. This is where we meet one of the disadvantages of attachment to group practices. The health visitor may have no record of the family and assume that they have registered with another practice. Information concerning new families with young children in an area needs to be carefully co-ordinated to minimise this risk.

Play groups and day nurseries

Responsibility for the registration and supervision of play groups now rests with the Social Service Departments. However, it is important that contact is maintained between the play group leaders and the health visitors
1. To discuss and give advice on any health problems of the children attending, and
2. To follow up children whose relationships with other children or adults reveal behaviour problems or difficulties
    Any suspicion of child abuse obviously needs to be investigated as a matter of urgency. It is unrealistic to expect the play group leaders to contact individual health visitors attached to each practice. In some groups in big conurbations there may be more than a dozen practices involved. One health visitor should be designated to act as liaison visitor for each play group.

School health

I do not propose to discuss here the procedure to be adopted when non-accidental injury is suspected. However, I feel that it is in the schools that more could be done to lower the incidence. What and where does the health visitor come in?

Health education
There appears to be a gradual increase in the amount of time devoted to 'education in personal relationships' in schools. Some of this is undertaken by specially qualified teachers, some by health visitors and some jointly. But, as I said in my original paper at Tunbridge Wells, *too many young people leave school and set up home without being able to adjust to each other, let alone have any children.

Child care and child development
Instruction on these topics is very patchy. In some schools quite comprehensive syllabuses are drawn up, often with the participation of the health visitor. In others such instruction is non-existent. Even where it is included in the timetable, the lesson is usually 'for girls only' and because of the pressure for examinations, often confined to those in the lower ability streams.

* See *Concerning Child Abuse, p.80.*

Perhaps I could quote my personal experience of one scheme. At a school where I was involved as health visitor/school nurse, the children (aged over 14 and all girls) were invited to bring their young brothers and sisters to the school one afternoon each week. There were usually ten to twelve children there, aged 1½ to 4 years. The class teacher soon realised that she needed professional help in dealing with some of the questions, so I was asked to give a few talks on child development. Out of this arose a series of discussions on the needs of children, as well as on human development. Whilst being delighted at this opportunity, I was left with at least two regrets, one, that boys were not invited and the other, that this type of education had not been given until the last year at school. It should start very simply in the primary school, to be dealt with in more depth throughout the senior school. It should not be left until children are adolescents.

Counselling in schools

What relevance has this to the subject under discussion? Experienced counsellors have been appointed to some large comprehensive and senior schools and are always available for consultation by the pupils. In other schools health visitors attend at specified times for this purpose. Children who find it difficult to communicate with their parents, but are in great need of help, are increasingly asking for it at school. Some of them come from homes where there is little love or attention given, so a sympathetic understanding could go some way towards preventing the perpetuation of the pattern.

Medical inspections and screening

Evidence of injury may be found at a school medical inspection when primary prevention has obviously failed. Warning evidence may be picked up at a routine screening session for hygiene or vision by the health visitor or school nurse. Deterioration in the standard of care, or a change in the attitudes or behaviour of the child, may be noticed or reported by the teaching staff. Not all children in these categories will be subjected to abuse but the presence of such changes does indicate stress and needs to be investigated. Where school nursing duties are delegated to less qualified staff, it is important that the health visitor maintains regular contact with the school.

Special problems

No access visits

One of their biggest problems is deciding what action to take after ineffectual visits to families at risk. This needs to be discussed with the nursing management and an agreed procedure drawn up. It is of prime importance that the date and time of such visits is recorded.

Need for adequate office accommodation

Many health visitors still work from home. Whilst this facilitates contact by their clients out of office hours, it does inhibit communications with other agencies, such as social workers and hospitals. There needs to be a central point where messages can be left. No office accommodation usually means no clerical support, so all reports have to be handwritten, and this is not conducive to good record-keeping.

Hospital liaison

Many schemes to improve liaison between the hospital and community services were in operation before reorganisation of the National Health Service in 1974, and it is to be hoped that these will grow and be extended. The recommendation by the Tunbridge Wells Study Group that the health visitor should be notified of all accidents to young children would, if carried out, produce a big administrative problem. In some areas nursing officers from the community are receiving lists of such casualties from their colleagues in the hospital, an idea that might well be taken up in other areas.

Recently the Department of Health and Social Security issued the consultative document, *Prevention and Health: Everybody's Business.* This phrase could so aptly be used to describe the feelings of this Conference.

The Court Report — 'Fit for the future'

This report, published since this paper was written, in no way alters the points made. In fact it serves to underline them, particularly in emphasising the importance of home visiting. If the recommendations of the Court Committee were adopted, child health visitors would be appointed undertaking both preventive and clinical duties in the home and clinics.

Reference has already been made to the dangers of large population to health visitor ratio. The Report suggests one child health visitor to 1,600 children (aged 0-15) with child health nurses to assist with the clinical nursing. This would certainly mean that all families with young children could be visited regularly.

Some of the recommendations are controversial and will be the subject of much criticism, but this will be debated elsewhere. Whatever one thinks of some of the suggestions, too many will be impracticable for years to come. It is encouraging that the needs of children should be highlighted in this way, and ways must be found to improve the situation now, even in these impoverished times.

Discussion

Some doubt was expressed about the general practice attachment of health visitors, although the advantages are seen to be considerable. One disadvantage is that whereas the health visitor used to get to know her geographical area and the families living in it, now she only has contact with families registered with the practice. Some ways must be found to achieve coverage for those families, possibly those most in need, who were not registered with a practice.

Perhaps even more serious is the new load of extra work laid on the health visitor, which often proves too heavy. In the worst areas she has not time to keep in touch with her mothers in the obstetric department. Her old commitment to advising on the rearing of children is also less honoured. Even if, as suggested, she should always be notified when a woman booked in at a maternity unit, she might not have the time to visit during the pregnancy.

On the question of visits to families when parents refuse entry, the group learned that health visitors oppose any compulsory powers on the grounds that such a change would harm her image. For families who move out of the area and risk becoming lost, the group learned that when a family in receipt of Social Security claims from a new area, the Social Security officer in the new area writes to the old area for the records. The Director in the old area may then be notified so that he can communicate with his opposite number in the new area.

The group stressed the importance of keeping a record of height and nude weight of all children whose progress is being supervised.

16. The current social work situation in relation to child abuse

SALLY BEER

Since the first meeting of the Tunbridge Wells Study Group in May 1973, the subject of child abuse has 'exploded' on the social work scene. The report on the death of Maria Colwell and the later enquiries about Richard Clarke, Stephen Meurs and the Auckland children have created an atmosphere in which many social workers themselves felt 'battered'. The comments made by, not only the popular press attempting to sell newspapers, but also fellow professional workers that have apportioned blame to young, named social workers, have saddened many of us who have felt that we have been forced into the position of defending actions or decisions that we hope we would not have taken ourselves.

The social service department has a duty to investigate any complaint that a child is being ill-treated (Children and Young Persons Act 1969 Section 2 (1)). Social workers in local authority social services departments are especially aware of the pressures of the community in the form of neighbours, doctors, the media, police and the social service department management itself. The present climate of feeling about child abuse produces high levels of anxiety amongst workers and the public. In some situations this may tempt the social worker to under-react in an effort to calm an already heated atmosphere. Although the response is aimed at a realistic assessment, the temptation to under-react to the pressures may be counter-productive in terms of protection of the victim, treatment and inter-disciplinary cooperation.

Techniques of management

During the past three years Local Authorities have set up Area/Borough Review Committees*, registers for children at risk of abuse, and many have involved and sometimes extremely complicated procedures for workers dealing with children 'at risk'. It has been noted by a recent BASW   Working Party on Violence in the Home†, that the management of several Local Authority Social Service Departments paid lip-service to their procedures, which they felt were being carried out when in fact poor professional practice or lack of resources inhibited effective work. Management is responsibile for ensuring that social workers are able to carry out the procedures that they lay down. Government circulars have concentrated so much on procedural aspects that there has been a tendency to think that this is all that need be done to ensure

* DHSS Circ. LASSL (72)2
† BASW evidence to the Select Committee on Violence in the Family

117

that the decisions made about child protection are effective. Much thought still needs to be given to the very complex question of the best way to enable a child to fulfil its potential.

The British Association of Social Workers has drawn up a Code of Practice for Social Workers and senior social workers supervising 'children at risk'. This document attempts to highlight responsibilities of the social worker in terms of good professional practice, but it must be clearly acknowledged that high standards of social work intervention depend also on effective structures for support and adequate resources.

The present cuts in Local Authority expenditure, with at best nil growth in most social service departments, has meant that the resources acknowledged by all to be necessary for efficient work with families who abuse their children, have developed very slowly, if at all. Research has shown that intensive help is required if re-injury of children in violent families is to be prevented. These cases are both anxiety provoking and time consuming, and management must, therefore, give appropriate weighting to them in the work load of the social worker. Despite the fact that most agencies acknowledge that priority should be given to a child at risk of physical injury, priority in terms of resources of man power, alternative care etc., it does not seem that the help given is enough.

Many departments now employ specialist workers but too many of these individuals are based at a central office. The specialist expertise and knowledge need to be area based. There should be a team with this specialist experience to cover each area, and, while in no way excluding other workers from taking cases, the team should ensure that back-up knowledge is adequate and that essential support is available. Social workers have a wide range of tasks to perform and one of the chief difficulties in large generic departments is how to get the specialised knowledge across to those young inexperienced workers in the front line. Following a study day in our own authority, I circulated the following check list for children at risk of abuse. The aim was to highlight some of the factors to bear in mind when visiting to investigate possible non-accidental injury.

CHECK LIST FOR CHILDREN AT RISK OF NON-ACCIDENTAL INJURY

A. Degree of social isolation - is there a life line? What is the quality of:
GP contact
Health Visitor contact
Family/Friends support
B. Family history - degree of mobility, previous history of family violence
C. Obtain a general picture of family health, especially that of the mother
It will be necessary to have the obstetric history at some stage in diagnosis
Do the parents have a poor self image and lack self value?
D. Assess growth and development of the child using developmental milestones.
Do you consider that the child's basic needs, such as warmth, food, play, physical contact, hygiene are being met
adequately,
intermittently,
not at all?
Is there evidence of neglect or failure to thrive?
E. *Signs of injury*
(1) Bruising - look for old brown bruises, blue bruises, fresh red marks. Facial bruising is important especially around the mouth - swollen lips.

(2)   Observe the way a child moves to assess if there is any injury.
Does he use all limbs? Is it painful for the child when picked up?
Are there any sore joints?
(3)   Note small round cigarette burns.
(4)   Note bite marks.
(5)   Note all unusual skin abrasions.
(All above can be seen by an observant worker without a special physical examination).

F.   Note if child has a high degree of awareness of adult movement.
G.   If child is injured or ill, is there any delay in seeking treatment, or refusal to do so? Are there any discrepant histories for the injury?
H.   Consider the fact that the abnormal/physically deformed child may be the abused child.
I.   What is the quality of the adult/child relationship?
(1)   How do the parents perceive the child e.g. ugly/attractive, bright/dull, loving/cold, clumsy/agile?
(2)   Are the parents' expectations realistic? Is parent's reaction to the child's behaviour appropriate to child's age?
(3)   Is the handling distant and mechanical especially in relation to feeding and nappy changing? Do the parents talk to the child, fondle him or smile at eye to eye contact?

The multi-disciplinary approach

Many of the problems noted by the Tunbridge Wells Group in relation to inter-disciplinary co-ordination have been resolved, but the difference in approach to the problem based on more fundamental factors would seem to have been highlighted in some areas. This is notably the difference between the police and social workers. Much of this difficulty has been well publicised and it is unfortunate that areas where liaison and cooperation are good do not attract the attention that some individual senior police officers achieve.

The liaison and cooperation between social workers and the Health Service has improved greatly, but it is noted that, as with the Social Service Department, there are some areas of the country in which it is difficult to find the necessary expertise in the form of medical advice.

The extent to which Local Authority Social Services Departments can play a significant part in preventing child abuse is limted by the demands for crisis inter-vention work. The Authority for which I work has set up specialist teams to work with under-fives. The aim of these teams is to work with young families with children at risk, to be a centre for expertise in child abuse for the area, and also to carry out some real preventive work, The team is responsible for all Day Care services for under-fives and attempts generally to raise the standards of child care for this age range.

Social workers are not involved nearly enough in prediction and prevention. Together with health visitors and other workers they should be able to understand and assist parent/child relationships, using the mounting supply of well researched information about situations likely to cause family breakdown. We need to develop and to provide preventive services such as good day care for under-fives and their parents, domiciliary help for families of children 'at risk', self-help groups of parents offering mutual support and effective 24 hour crisis centres.

However, the allocation of scarce resources in a time of economic cuts is largely a question of 'juggling' priorities. We must look much more closely at work carried out by small specialist units to see how their research findings can be applied in making the best use of precious resources.

A number of recommendations are printed in Chapter 28 *(see pp. 188 et seq.)*.

Discussion

The social worker is without doubt being given too many functions, too much work and, possibly considering that on average only 40 per cent are qualified too much responsibility. Voluntary bodies like the Family Welfare Association and the Family Service Units could make a bigger contribution and lay helpers could and should be mobilised selected and instructed. The supply of workers and resources is governed locally and not directly from central government. One serious drawback to training is the shortage of experienced training staff and, for field workers, lack of secretarial help, telephone and other time saving services. How much priority should be given to work for children and families? Helping them is an important exercise in prevention and seems therefore to be a high priority. Mobilising support for children and families and the need for the child's responses to be stimulated and enriched are discussed on page 64.

17. The present position as seen by a magistrate

W. E. CAVENAGH

The law is not a person. It cannot act, to put matters right or otherwise, on its own initiative. The legal system set up by society and the legal machinery which it makes available is simply one of the tools which may be useful in cases of child abuse. It can be used to enable whoever is managing the case to acquire legal powers so as to achieve some result, or take some action which they otherwise have no power to do. Examples might be the obtaining of a Care Order, enabling the social services compulsorily to remove a child from its parents, or the securing (by the police) of a conviction and sentence enabling them to have a cruel parent punished. It is the responsibility of whoever uses this tool to use it in a way which is appropriate to the end that it is intended to achieve. The party bringing the case must be prepared to take the initiative in starting proceedings and must bring the evidence and the witnesses necessary to a successful conclusion. In a court case, it is not the court's job to find out who did what. It is the job of the parties to bring the evidence and prove the case to the court. It is not the court's responsibility to seek out the evidence. The court has no interest in either party's case as such. Using the legal machinery does not always involve court proceedings, but the following outline of the position as seen by a magistrate may be helpful.

Court orders

A place-of-safety order
In crisis intervention this may well be the first step and it can for obvious reasons be of vital importance. Anyone at all may apply to a magistrate, and not necessarily in court, for power to remove and detain a child for a period not exceeding twenty-eight days pending care proceedings. These are judicial proceedings, but *the police* can remove a child *without making such an application,* and can detain him for up to eight days (though his parent or guardian on his behalf may apply for his release). In either event, there must be reasonable cause to believe that the child is endangered and that the need for care and control is shown both by the child's present situation and a reasonable assessment of his future.

The statutory criteria indicating a need for care and control are listed below. Firstly, as regards the present state of the juvenile, namely that
1. His proper development is being avoidably prevented or neglected, or his health is being avoidably impaired or neglected, or he is being ill-treated; or

2.   The above condition is probable following a finding in respect of another child who was, or is, in the household; or

3.   It is probable that the conditions set out in paragraph (1) will be satisfied in his case, having regard to the fact that a person who has been convicted of an offence mentioned in schedule 1 to the *Children and Young Persons Act 1933* (e.g. neglect, cruelty, etc) is, or may become, a member of the same household as the child; or

4.   He is exposed to moral danger; or

5.   He is beyond the control of his parent or guardian.

Secondly, as regards his future, that

1.   He is in need of care and control which he is unlikely to receive unless the court makes an order in respect of him.

Wardship proceedings

Any person having an interest in a child may by a simple procedure of issuing a summons make the child a ward of court. The court can then make orders to protect the welfare of that child if it is satisfied that it is in the child's interest to do so. In cases of extreme urgency, such orders may be made before the summons is issued (see Ch. 24), but the judge will not remove a child from home unless he is given reasonable grounds for supposing that such action is necessary.

Cases which are brought to court

These cases are heard in either criminal or civil proceedings, or both, according to what the party bringing the proceedings expects or hopes to achieve. Criminal proceedings are prosecutions brought by the police in the ordinary criminal court and if successful they render the convicted offender liable to punishment or probation. The criminal court has no power to make an order relating to the child. Civil proceedings are brought by the social services, the NSPCC or the police and are heard in the juvenile court with the child as the centre and subject of the hearing. The juvenile court has no power in such proceedings to order the punishment of an offending party. If the proceedings are successful the court has power to make an order for the child's welfare.

Interim care orders

The juvenile court can make an interim order, committing the child to the care of the local authority for not more than twenty-eight days at a time, at any time during the proceedings. Such orders may be necessary for any of a number of reasons, one of which may be that the child is at risk whilst an accused adult is on bail pending or during criminal proceedings.

Evidence

The weight of evidence required in a criminal case is such as to satisfy the court of the guilt of the accused beyond a reasonable doubt. In the juvenile court it is only necessary to satisfy the court that, on a balance of the probabilities, the situation appears to be such as the complainant alleges it to be. Those bringing proceedings must be prepared to prove the case. This involves producing the evidence to the court, and is a matter for careful consideration by social service departments expecting to appear as witnesses, complaints or social experts reporting to the court. Parents are allowed to help the juvenile and may question witnesses and must be allowed to make a statement or representation. In their absence, a relative may stand in for them if the juvenile is not represented. There is power in care proceedings for the court actually to exclude the juvenile during part of the evidence (except as to his character or conduct) if it thinks such a course desirable but parents or guardians must be allowed to remain in court. Conversely the court can exclude the parent or guardian whilst the juvenile gives evidence or makes a statement, if special circumstances make this desirable. But if it does so, then the parent or guardian must be told of any allegation which has been made against him whilst he was out of court, and must be given the opportunity of meeting it by calling evidence or otherwise. The child may be granted legal representation at public expense, but there is at present no arrangement by which the parent or guardian can apply on his own behalf, though this position is to be changed under the *Children Act 1975* when certain provisions are brought into operation. It is particularly important in a care case that lawyers on both sides should be familiar with court procedure and with the detailed provisions of the statutes under which the proceedings are brought. For example, some lawyers appear still to be unaware that proving the need for the court to make an order may enable the complainant to bring forward and the court to admit as evidence a great deal of family history insofar as it concerns factual evidence about relevant behaviour as observed by the witness, about the personalities involved and about the significance of these in relation to the likelihood of adequate care in the future.

Orders which can be make in successful care proceedings
The most important and the most frequently used of these are the Supervision and the Care Order.

The Supervision Order lasts three years or less if specified. The local authority social worker usually supervises unless a probation officer is already working with the family. The order can be discharged early on the application of the supervisor or the parent or the juvenile himself. There is a duty on the supervisee to receive visits but no right of entry for the supervisor and the supervision is of a general character.

The Care Order gives the local authority powers to override the parents or guardians in the exercise of most of their parental powers and duties. The court has no power to supervise the local authority's use of these powers. Whatever the court intended, the use made by the authority of the powers granted is a matter for them alone. The order runs until the juvenile is 18 if not discharged earlier, but the local authority must review each juvenile in care at least once in each six months. Discharge may be applied for by the local authority or the parents or guardian or the juvenile himself and a discharge may be granted completely or by the substitution of a supervision order.

Before deciding on the best order to make the juvenile court must consider a report made by a social worker on the child's social background, health and education. This may and usually does, include an opinion (with which the court is not bound to agree) as to what would be the best order for the court to make (since that is the object of the whole exercise from the point of view of the party bringing the proceedings).

This is not the same as evidence and cannot be produced before the finding in order to prove the case. Nevertheless the parent or guardian must be told of anything in it which is material to the question of how the child is to be dealt with, so that they have the opportunity to refute what is said if they do not think it is true. Similarly the child must be told (if he is of an age to understand) anything material about his own character or conduct.

Rights of appeal against sentences or orders
There is the usual right of appeal to the Crown Court in a criminal case. A right of appeal exists also against both finding and order in care proceedings. Notice must be given by, or on behalf of the juvenile within 21 days, and legal aid may be granted as for the original proceedings.

Summary of provision made in *Children Act 1975* for cases in which there is a conflict of interest between parent and child

The Act contains provisions dealing with this situation. They relate *only* to applications for *discharge* of Care or Supervision orders and appeals against the dismissal of such applications. They have at the time of writing, not yet been brought fully into operation. Under these provisions the court has power in certain circumstances to appoint a guardian *ad litem* and to order that the parent or guardian be given legal aid. These circumstances are as follows:

Parent or guardian not treated as representing the juvenile
The court *may* order that the parent or guardian is not to be treated as representing the juvenile or acting on his behalf in the proceedings if before or in the course of these proceedings it appears that there is, or may be, a conflict of interest.

The court *shall* make such an order where there is an unopposed application for discharge unless it is satisfied that to do so is not necessary for safeguarding the juvenile's interests.

These powers are also to be exercisable by a single justice before the hearing of the application (Section 64).

Appointing a guardian ad litem
Where the court makes an order as above it *shall* appoint a guardian *ad litem* for the purpose of the proceedings unless satisfied that it is not necessary to do so in order to safeguard the interests of the juvenile. For the purposes of the section 'court' is to be taken to include a single justice.

Rules of court are to be made relating to these appointments (Section 64).

Ordering legal aid to be given
Where an order is made that the parent or guardian is not to be treated as representing the juvenile, the court *may* order that the parent or guardian shall be given legal aid (Section 64).

Cautionary note
These provisions of the Children Act are *not* yet in operation at the time of writing.

Discussion

Most of the discussions about legal matters are gathered together on pages 194-5
but some special points were raised by Dr Cavenagh for discussion. She saw the
juvenile court as a gateway to social action and counselling. Doctors and social workers seem now to be overcoming some of their earlier unwillingness to come to court.
They must learn how to present evidence. A Doctor can always give his evidence on
affidavit. In the less clear cases magistrates can be difficult to convince. Juvenile
Courts do differ in their ways but witnesses should not be subjected to harassment.
The court is able to press for speed in hearing a case, something that should be
remembered when a speedy decision is important for the child. While the justices
should undoubtedly be instructed in a general knowledge of child and family development, experience and knowledge of social welfare should be in the court and not
on the bench. The recruitment of magistrates presents problems if the aim is as it
should be to gather from a cross section of the population with life experience. Young
people and black people prepared to serve were hard to find. Doubts were expressed
about the presence of school teachers as magistrates on juvenile benches before which
present and past pupils might appear.

18. A police view of the present position

MARY WEDLAKE

Introduction

Since 1829 the primary objects of the Police have been the prevention and detection of crime. Assault on a child is a crime, whoever is the perpetrator, and our duty is as clear today as it was in those formative years. Let no person think we will shrink from that duty; rather let them feel secure in the knowledge that we will fulfil it with vigour, determination and compassion.

Since the report of the Tunbridge Wells Study Group in 1973, there has been much discussion, rhetoric and protestation about police involvement with child abuse. Before I comment on the specific areas of police involvement as contained in the resolutions of 1973 let me say I am confident that the way to the end we are all seeking, the safety and comfort of our society's children, has been made much clearer.

Parliamentary select committee

Like other concerned parties the Metropolitan Police gave evidence to the Parliamentar Select Committee on Violence in Marriage. This was on 4 May 1976 and there is no need here to deal with that paper. Naturally we await with patience, yet some urgency, for the deliberations of that body. Any significant change in our methods or policy must wait for the consideration of their recommendations. It would not be too presumptuous to say that we believe that our current thinking and standpoint can stand the test of examination. Despite this constraint we have continued to seek ways of improving liaison with other disciplines and, despite notable exceptions, I believe we have done so.

Area review committees

With the establishment of Area review committees the Metropolitan Police took the view that police participation should be at the level of Detective Superintendent, an officer with considerable investigative experience of people and crime. It was hoped that representation at that level would lead to the formulation of sound and enlighten guidelines within which to work. A survey of Detective Superintendents in the Metropolitan Police Area has shown that there were differences of view and even total polarisations within certain committees. The Metropolitan Police would not seek to deny their share of the responsibility for this failure. One thing is clear, namely that Police were the only group who were positively discriminated against and whose role was severely questioned. This cannot be seen as a spirit of cooperation envisaged by the Department of Health and Social Security and the study group itself. If anyone doubts the discrimination, the point can be emphasised by particular reference to the important area of the case conference.

Case conferences

Police attendance at case conferences can depend on one or a number of considerations. The Chairman of one Area review committee stated that Police would not be represented at any case conference. His decision was final and had obviously been agreed privately, despite explanations of the legal and police position and the existence of the DHSS guidelines. Other considerations were that Police should be present only in very serious cases, or after the members of the conference had unanimously agreed that Police should attend, or provided the Police agreed to abide by the recommendation of the case conference, or provided the officer attending could give a decision there and then. There was even the proposal that separate case conferences would be held for those members with opposing views on police participation. Another committee felt that Police should be informed only where there was clear evidence of a criminal offence and the conference was unanimous in agreeing.

I became gravely concerned when I read the list of constraints, but, thankfully, I can confirm that there has also been real cooperation and progress. In one area where police particpation is excellent, the method employed is worthy of attention and recognition.

An officer has been appointed, and it happens to be a woman, with a special responsibility for liaison with the Social Services and other agencies in relation to 'care'. This officer becomes the natural choice for regularly attending case conferences and because of her continuous involvement with the members there is already a basis of mutual trust and understanding. Police policy at the case conference is the same. In practice, the officer reports the nature and views of the conference on a form which is seen by a senior officer and where an investigation is necessary it is made. Where abuse is reported to police by an agency, it is confirmed by a form provided by police. There can be no misunderstanding of what was reported to police. There is a general consensus that the whole system of case conferences operates efficiently and effectively.

Unilateral action on investigation and the decision to prosecute

As the law stands, and we would not seek to change it, the duty of the police is clear. Where a crime is suspected, it is to investigate the circumstances. It can never be overemphasised that the possibility of a police investigation is in itself a preventative measure, but, further, that such an investigation can be firm yet tactful; thorough yet considerate; and objective yet compassionate. Professional and experienced police investigators have the necessary qualities and skills.

Police have, and have exercised, discretion not to prosecute. Many examples exist and if they provide credence for others in our belief in the fairness and propriety of our right to take unilateral action, then one barrier of contention may have been breached.

A national register

The National Society for the Prevention of Cruelty to Children are considering the feasibility of establishing a national register of children at risk or abused and a resolution of this group suggested a working party be formed. For such a technique to be viable and of preventative value, it must have a proper foundation. The Commissioner has agreed to allow the expertise of National Criminal Record Office maintained at New Scotland Yard to be tapped by arranging for an experienced officer to address the NSPCC Advisory Committee on the problems related to the compiling and maintaining of such an index.

Education, interest and training

There is no doubt that the subject of child abuse has become and is a live issue, engendering interest and discussion at all levels within the Metropolitan Police. There is a real determination throughout the ranks to act in the best interests of the child at risk or abused. The quality and extent of our training has been under scrutiny and tangible efforts (such as the purchase of slides and tape cassettes for educational purposes) have been made. It is fully accepted that a basic preventative measure is the early recognition of child maltreatment by an officer who comes into contact with a family for whatever reason. The provision for additional training material and course is under review.

Conclusion

The Metropolitan Police is far from content with the position as a whole and is anxious to strive for real understanding of roles, meaningful dialogue and frank expression of opinions. We are always prepared to listen and consult but despite the misunderstandings or misconceptions we have to endure we shall not allow the rule of law, our duty or the interest of the child to take second place.

Discussion

Clearly the relationships between police and social workers and doctors still need to develop further towards collaboration. That there is a police viewpoint, his duty being both to prevent and to detect crime, is not disputed, any more than is the bias of social workers and doctors towards protecting their clients if there is sufficient doubt from the rigours of the law. Polarisation of those attitudes inevitably occurs and can only be reduced or prevented at the level of the workers by mutual understanding between them and by the establishment of a community of feeling for the families involved. The hard line with its pre-occupation with detection and prosecution can never meet the soft line aiming at rehabilitation yet an atmosphere can and in many areas is generated which allows the most productive and successful cooperation. A transfer of responsibility for child abuse from CID to juvenile bureau helps. So usually does working together on area and district review committees. The group hoped that as the result of closer working and better mutual understanding the preventive role of the police would be stressed while greater discretion would be permitted over investigation and prosecution. Simultaneously the other professionals must always keep in mind the duty of the police.

To what extent the top levels of hierarchies in the Home Office and the DHSS can document in simple language advice about the complexities of professional interchanges remains to be seen. More hopeful is the gathering experience of cooperation between those actually planning programmes and working in harmony over families. The professional workers should everywhere get together to sort out any differences and to try to reach an agreed code of practice.

The history of previous convictions which would certainly command attention in family flow charts, remains restricted information. If the police representative at a case conference expresses concern about the character of a particular individual, he should not be pressed for details and the delicacy of his position should be appreciated by the other members. All agreed that whenever a parent or caretaker is charged with assault on a minor, the social service department must be informed and a case conference should be called.

19. The present position in the probation and after-care service

R. W. SPIERS

I should at the outset state that as an inspector of the Probation and After-Care Department of the Home Office I am drawing upon experience arising largely from transactions between the Probation Service and the Home Office and between the Home Office and other Departments and services. Some of those transactions have involved fairly detailed consideration of particular cases which have been brought to notice and which have called for investigation. Others were concerned with the formulation of guidance to practitioners and some were in the course of surveys concerning the extent and nature of probation service involvement with children at risk of injury or other abuse. I need to make clear however that whilst I can speak about the service I do not purport to speak for it, and Mrs. Blooman, as Chief Probation Officer, may wish to extend in discussion some of the matters which I touch upon or omit, or to give a different impression of what may seem to her to be significant.

The suggestion originally put was that I might give a paper on the present status of the Tunbridge Wells resolutions. I see them, however, as a part of the historical background to more recent developments, and a base from which some of the guidance which has been given to services has evolved. The resolutions considered item by item do show some need for modification in the light of intervening experience. It is sufficient here to note that the matters, which have significance for the Probation and After-Care Service, have substantially been reflected in the subsequent guidance given by central government.

A general statement about the position of the Probation Service with regard to non-accidental injury to children might be along the following lines. The Service has in recent years become acutely aware of the seriousness of the problem of children at risk of non-accidental injury. It subscribes to the need to ensure effective co-ordination between services and supports the establishment of area review committees, whilst experiencing some frustration, arising sometimes but not exclusively out of boundary problems. It welcomes and is prepared to make full use of case conferences, whether as a participating service contributing information and knowledge or supporting agreed plans of actions, or as a service having primary responsibility to which others can contribute. Whilst accepting the need for safeguarding procedures such as registration and, in high risk cases, the special supervision of the worker by a senior officer, it bridles a bit at the establishment of such procedures which, for all their rationality in supporting good practice and service to clients, may be misinterpreted by some as more concerned with the protection of agency than of children at risk.

Some officers would therefore lay most stress upon professional competence and integrity, in which of course they would include not only individual skills but also sound inter-agency practice and liaison. In an ideal world, perhaps they would be right, but in the world as it is, we have necessarily to take steps to reinforce by agency practices and procedures, the adequacy of the service which is given, and we must accept that highly demanding high risk situations call for exceptional measures.

A general statement about the position of the Probation Service might go on to reflect the view that concern for non-accidental injury to children may be on too narrow a front. In the first place, there is the question as to whether registers should be confined to children in respect of whom there has already been an injury or whether they should extend to children reasonably believed to be seriously at risk. The relatively few such difficulties, as have come to notice, raise the question also as to whether a decision not to register should be within the absolute control of any one agency, or whether such a decision about registration should itself by a matter for case conference. Then it mayalso be suggested that in any case the emphasis in guidance upon non-accidental injury to children to the exclusion of other forms of child abuse, and indeed the proliferation of guidance, may be counter productive in the sense that staff coping with multiple tasks involving other high risk situations may become counter suggestible to undue focus upon one amongst so many of their priorities.

Tunbridge Wells Study Group Resolution I (p. 185)

One specific Tunbridge Wells resolution, (Resolution I) recommends the establishment of area review committees at area health authority and local authority level. This contains the elements of some confusion, especially for the Probation Service whose areas do not necessarily relate to either body. In the Probation Service the administration is related to the county, and in a Metropolitan county that may mean eight or more Metropolitan districts each having its own area review committee with perhaps no uniform agreement between them as to their practices concerning registration or on other matters.

With regard to case conferences I should like to pick up a difference in emphasis between the Tunbridge Wells resolution and the guidance given by DHSS in its principal memorandum of April 1974. The Tunbridge Wells resolution says that case conference should 'supervise the management of families involved', and in paragraph 14 the report of the group talks about case conference retaining an overall responsibility for each step that is taken. It concludes that the case conference should have the power to put its plan into operation or to modify it according to events etc. The DHSS memorandum (22 April 1974 paragraph 15) puts it differently and refers to case conference retaining 'overall concern for the management of the case', and it is this different emphasis which I think the Probation Service would uphold.

'Concern for management' implies that major decisions subsequent to the initial agreement about strategy, supervisory responsibility and action to be taken should normally be made through case conference so that all concerned are party to any consequential shifts of emphasis which may be necessary and can make the necessary adaptations. 'Concern for management' also means monitoring the action which is being taken, and this implies an obligation on individual agencies to keep the co-ordinator informed. It means a readiness to reconvene the conference to evaluate significant changes and to review developments. But case conference arrangements do not of themselves override or negate specific statutory responsibilities, which ultimately each agency has the right to fulfil. A possible outcome of case conference or inter-agency discussion may, for example, be a determination as to which agency or worker will have primary treatment responsibility. This may have implications for the acceptance by one service of a degree of delegated responsibility on behalf of another agency, or delegation to another agency of what might be a traditional duty of one's own service. In agreeing to act for others, or to allow some other body to act on our behalf, however, we do not shift the base of authority or statutory duty.

Case conference and other liaison arrangements may be used by an individual service to satisfy itself that duties which it has agreed to delegate are being adequately fulfilled. Likewise, an agency undertaking delegated responsibilities may use case conference to report upon its stewardship of those responsibilities which may not normally be those of that service, but which for the particular case have been accepted.

Guidance to this effect was given to the Probation Service by Home Office Circular No. 4/1975 when it was also and consequentially stressed that agreements or understandings between agencies should be recorded and confirmed between them in writing. This underlined the principle that agency responsibilities cannot lightly be assumed, delegated or dispensed with and that such inter-agency agreements, whether through case conference or otherwise, require to be endorsed at a senior level. So we emphasised that case conference should have a continuing concern for the management of a case, but distinguish this from authority or ability actually to manage across agency boundaries.

I should like to comment upon another aspect of practice about which too simplistic a view is sometimes expressed. Whilst acknowledging that case conference should be the medium through which significant decisions may be taken as to which agency or worker shall have primary responsibility, the arguments in favour of singling out a particular worker may be overstated, and the notion of the supremacy of the single worker may indeed in some respects be a myth. At one level we might recognise that there can be advantages in a vulnerable family having quick access to alternative sources of informed assistance. At another level there may also be some situations in which workers, in dealing with complex multiple relationships, would choose not to work alone. So far as workers from different agencies are concerned, although their basic skills and ethos may be much the same, they may nevertheless have different resources and supports which they can call into play. Whilst duplication of itself is not be be encouraged this need not be the inevitable consequence of service by more than one agency, if by agreement it is determined which is supporting and which is carrying primary responsibility for identified areas of interest, and if effective liaison is maintained.

The involvement of the Probation Service

The 1973 survey
I should like now to feed in some information arising from the surveys, which we have undertaken concerning the involvement of the Probation Service in matters

relating to non-accidental injury to children. In the first place, it was shortly after our interest was awakened following the availability of the Tunbridge Wells Study Group report in the autumn of 1973 that we set about obtaining information in order to make some assessment of the extent to which the service was in fact involved in supervision directly arising out of non-accidental injury to children. The results of that inquiry have been made available in detail to the group, and to other interested bodies. All I need to say is that relating to victims in the whole juvenile court age range, that is up to 16 years inclusive, as at a single date in October 1973, the Probation Service had responsibility for about 350 families in which a person was under its supervision as a result of an actual offence of non-accidental injury to a child. Of those families, about 200 had, at that time, been the subject of case conferences with other agencies. The inquiry also showed that, overwhelmingly, the most usual current contact was through a probation order in respect of the relevant offence. At least 67 per cent of the families thus had at least one parent on probation. The next most common occasion for contact was through release work with fathers who as a result of the relevant offence were in custody. This amounted to about 13 per cent of the cases. The substantial extent of involvement and the preponderance of probationers compared with after-care related to a custodial sentence were somewhat unexpected. The survey did not attempt to assess the extent to which the service was additionally involved in cases where non-accidental injury was otherwise known or suspected. That it did not do so was largely because of difficulty of defining criteria for inclusion compared with a known and proven offence. Yet it may be not least amongst this less well identified group, that there is the greater need for professional alertness, since potential risk will not have been pointed out by the offence giving rise to Probation Service involvement. Yet, it may be a probation officer, who because of a supervisory responsibility is in a position first to recognise, or at least to question, what is going on and then to do, or fail to do, something about it.

The 1976 survey
More recently, we have undertaken a survey of the number and types of cases registered by probation areas as at risk of child abuse, both under area review committee arrangements and for internal management purposes. This survey was not confined, as was that of October 1973, to cases where the responsibility arose directly out of an offence involving non-accidental injury to children, the later criterion being the fact of registration rather than the nature of offence or circumstances giving rise to probation service intervention. The more recent survey (see Appendix II) showed that 2,267 families were registered at 1 April 1976 for internal management purposes as being at risk of child abuse. Of these, over 1800 (81 per cent) were registered also under area review committee arrangements with the responsible central authority. The difference of just over 400 is accounted for principally by differences in criteria for registration, and in particular it highlights the fact that some authorities insist upon a known previous history of non-accidental injury before registration, whereas in the judgment of the Probation Service the risk of abuse was such as to justify registration with a view to the taking of special precautions.

A point I wish to stress is that of cases registered by the Probation Service, its particular responsibility arose mainly out of adult offences which were *unconnected* with child abuse (59 per cent), compared with about 17 per cent in which the adult offences did involve non-accidental injury to children and another 9 per cent involving some other form of child abuse. The balance of cases arose marginally from juvenile offences or care proceedings and, more substantially, from various civil matters such as matrimonial and wardship supervision. This latter group accounted for as many as 8 per cent of all cases registered.

I have earlier suggested that the demand for professional alertness on the part of the probation officer may be heightened where potential risk has not been pointed up by the circumstances or offence giving rise to Probation Service involvement. I wish now to reinforce this by reference to another factor derived from the earlier survey concerning cases in which the overt and intended purposes of supervision arose specifically out of relevant offences. From that survey, we learnt that as many as 76 per cent of the families were also in contact with other agencies, 66 per cent being with social service departments. Further, of child victims still living, that is between two thirds and three quarters of the sample, about 56 per cent were away from home in care, in hospital, with relatives etc. It follows therefore, that in a high proportion of those overt non-accidental injury to children cases at least one other agency would have a direct and recognised interest arising out of the same or similar circumstances, and therefore that the need for inter-agency understanding and clarification of responsibility should be readily apparent. By contrast, in the great majority of cases identified by probation officers as at risk and so registered, the involvement of other agencies, if it existed, might be understood or perceived to be unrelated to Probation Service purposes and would not necessarily or naturally give rise to co-ordinated effort. The professional responsibility upon the probation officer to recognise when to consult and to promote joint consideration or mobilisation of resources may in this less specific high risk group therefore be that much the greater.

Conclusion

Finally, might I observe that if it was not until after the publication of the original Tunbridge Wells Study Group report that the Probation and After-Care Service became aware of the significance of its involvement in this subject of non-accidental injury to children, there can be little doubt now of the extent and gravity of its involvement and of its commitment to making an effective contribution.

Discussion

The group was pleased to learn of the part played by the published report of the discussions at Tunbridge Wells in alerting the probation service to the problems of non-accidental injury to children. Concern had been expressed at that meeting that the social service department was not always alerted about the return from prison of a member of an abusing family. Attention was now drawn to a gap in supervision which might arise at the end of the period of probation in families in which abuse and even non-accidental injury commenced or recommenced later. Could the probation officer, before he left the family, introduce to them a member of the social service department from whom they could continue to receive support? This raised the problem of 'multiple agencies' and the probation service might prefer to make use of their own voluntary associates. Besides direct involvement with abusing families, the probation service is closely concerned with divorcing or divorced families where the children are at risk of neglect and emotional abuse as well as physical injury. Accusations of abuse by one or other party are by no means uncommon. The break-up of families and divorce are always extremely disturbing to the children and put them at risk of violence. The probation officer should always inform the social service department in professional confidence of any conditions needing investigation. Problems of custody and access can also be very damaging.

20. A coroner on ennumerating child abuse

D. R. CHAMBERS

Partaking in two of these interdisciplinary conferences on the problems of non-accidental injury to children, together with at least as great involvement in the investigation of sudden death in infancy, has given me a much greater insight into the difficulties of oth others directly concerned with both conditions. So far as the prevalence of child abuse is concerned, the particularly the number of deaths following such abuse, I can do no better than to quote from a recently published survey (Jobling, 1976) which states, '...estimates of children who die each year of their injuries range from 100 - 750. What the exact number might be has now become a controversial guessing game, some arguing that these figures are alsmost certainly an underestimate whereas others believe that the lower estimates are nearer the mark'. We all must have read in the newspapers headlines such as 'Parent attacks kill two children daily'*, but this article did contain the relevant criminal statistic that in 1973, the last year for which figures were available at the time of writing, there had been only 67 cases of murder, manslaughter or infanticide of children under the age of 16.

Estimates of the incidence of non-fatal child abuse are similarly not easy to reconcile. In April 1976 the then Minister of Health was quoted as saying that 97 English authorities, representing 90 per cent of the child population had reported a total of 5,700 known or suspected cases of non-accidental injury and 40 deaths in three-quarters of a year. If one assumes that the 90 per cent of authorities replying to the questionnaire are representative of all, then simple arithmetic would suggest a total of 8,400 cases with some 60 deaths; a figure clearly consistent with the criminal statistic quoted from 1973. The calculated number of abused children from this inquiry is, however, much below the numbers of neglected children known to the NSPCC for the same period†.

On the subject of incidence of non-fatal child abuse, the difficulty is, as others have pointed out, that there is great variation from area to area in classification of cases. The Annual Report of the Department of Health and Social Security 1975 (HMSO Cmnd 6565) notes the setting up of a country-wide system of area review committees and the compilation of registers. In my view, accurate statistics of incidence can be compiled only from the records available to these committees from the local registers. Demonstrably, there will be more cases of suspicion than of care proceedings being brought, but even a relatively unsophisticated breakdown of the figures, which must be known locally, would be very helpful in assessing the extent of the problem in the

* *The Daily Telegraph, 4 March 1975*
† *The Guardian, 1 April 1976*

living child. Until such national figures are compiled it appears unlikely that it will be possible to make much more than inspired guesses at the real totals of children involved.

As a full-time coroner my own interest is directed more particularly at death, at mortality rather than morbidity statistics, and two published sources are available relevant to the present problem. The Home Office annual Criminal Statistics give relevant figures of 'Offences currently regarded as homicide by sex and age of victim' (see Table 20.1). The other source is the Registrar General's Report DH4, referred to on page 139.

Table 20.1. Homicide figures from Home Office Criminal Statistics (1974 Cmnd 6168; 1975 Cmnd 6566)

Age of victim	Number of victims 1974			Number of victims 1975			Rate per million 1975		
	male	female	total	male	female	total	male	female	total
under 1 year	27	22	49	14	17	31	44.1	57.1	50.4
1 & under 5 yr.	19	14	33	17	10	27	11.7	7.3	9.6
5 & under 16 yr.	26	18	44	10	12	22	2.3	2.8	2.5

As the reports make plain, these figures relate not to convictions for proven offences but offences currently regarded as homicide. The other fact to observe is that there is no way of distinguishing those homicides by a parent from those committed by other persons nor of knowing whether the victim was killed following a period of abuse. Overall these figures seem to support the lower figure for deaths to be regarded as caused by 'non-accidental injury'.

This somewhat sanguine view has been the subject of challenge, usually on the basis that individual cases are known to those directly concerned with the management of an abused child where the death has not been the subject of criminal proceedings so that it may not be reported in these statistics. Indeed, in the area of my own jurisdiction, four inner North London boroughs, I am consulted, usually once a year, about the death of a child by the doctors, who have been concerned with it in life when I have chosen not to inquire publicly into its death. Such an inquest is mandatory, where the cause is violent or otherwise unnatural, but if, after a complete post-mortem examination by a pathologist well acquainted with the pattern of injury in children, nothing other than natural disease is disclosed, then no inquest is required (save in the rather uncommon circumstances that one is needed to dispel rumours about the death). The coroner, in these matters as in many others, is dependent upon skilled pathological advice.

Where the pathologist's report discloses that the cause of death is violent, the first question to be raised is clearly whether such violence was inflicted intentionally or with that degree of criminal recklessness which in law can constitute manslaughter. It is no exaggeration to state that in every child's death where violence is even suspected, the circumstances are enquired into immediately and with vigour by the local police and that the criminal investigation department is called in whenever the explanations given by witnesses do not exclude a criminal origin for the injuries. It is this very fact, which so often bedevils investigation of so-called 'cot death' as I have previously described (Chambers, 1974, 1976). The offence of 'child battering', as such, is unknown to the law; when death has been the consequence of injury inflicted unlawfully by another, the offence is homicide in one of its guises, murder, manslaughter or infanticide. Where there is enough evidence to justify such a charge, it will be brought. In a number of such cases the assailant admits the offence, but when the only witnesses are the parents who adhere to a story of a non-culpable 'accidental' origin for the injuries, the whole case will turn on the medical evidence. The English law of evidence would largely exclude much of the background information well known to those who might have been professionally concerned with the family. It is my view, that this fact is not fully appreciated by doctors and social workers accustomed to the standard of proof required to obtain a care order, and not used to the strict proof required at a criminal trial for homicide. Where it is clear that one of two parents must have committed the offence but neither admits to it, the prosecution is unlikely to succeed, as was illustrated by a trial in which the judge stated, 'It is quite clear that one of you was responsible for the death,* the accused couple were acquitted of manslaughter, but each was convicted of ill-treatment of their 4½ month son. Where no such prosecution for homicide is brought because the evidence is not strong enough, the matter is enquired into at an inquest. Here the coroner must first decide whether there be reason to suspect that the deceased came by his (or her) death by murder, manslaughter or infanticide. If he so decides, he must summon a jury.‡ At such in inquest, only relevant evidence is allowed, and this rule also serves to exclude much of the background which might prove damaging. As the law now stands, it is possible for a coroner's jury to commit for trial those it names as responsible for the death.† At the subsequent trial it is common for no evidence to be offered. There is, at the time of writing, a Bill before Parliament to remove not only the coroner's power of committal but any power to name a person 'guilty' of homicide.

A coroner who decides to proceed without a jury will hear all the relevant evidence and reach his conclusion. He may return a verdict of accidental death, misadventure, neglect, or he may leave the matter open. This open verdict might be interpreted as more or less the Scottish 'not proven' with its implications for those concerned in the death. The coroner, after inquest, returns a report to the registrar for the appropriate registration sub-district and from this information the tables of deaths from violence or injury published by the Office of Population Censuses and Surveys are compiled. The latest tables available are those for 1974, published in 1976. Table 20.2 gives an extract to illustrate what is available from this sourse.

It is always possible to argue that nestling within these cold tables of facts and figures there are undetected 'homicides', but each death recorded in these tables is so recorded as a result of inquest findings. There is a residual small category where it has not been possible to state whether the injuries were accidental or not (Table 20.3). A proportion of the deaths recorded, in which no definite finding was made at the inquest, might be unprosecuted crimes.

The present position cannot be described as at all satisfactory as on the one hand there is reported a discrepancy between the number of deaths categorised as homicide and the number of deaths known to observers as occurring in children known or strongly suspected of having been abused; and on the other hand there exists, in theory

* *The Daily Telegraph,* 23 October, 1976
† Coroners Amendment Act 1926, S. 13 (2) (a).
‡ Coroners Rules 1953, S.I. 205, rule 26.

Table 20.2 Showing deaths classified by nature of accident (Registrar General's Report DH4, 1974, Table, 4, No. 1)

E Code	Description	Age			
		0 - 4 yr.		5 - 14 yr.	
		M	F	M	F
E 880-887	Accidental falls	27	18	38	7
E 890-890	Fires	47	49	19	20
E 904	Hunger, thirst, exposure, neglect	11	7	-	-
E 910	Drowning, submersion	47	26	68	7
E 911	Ihalation and ingestion of food causing obstruction or suffocation	87	57	5	3
E 912	Inhalation and ingestion of food causing obstruction or suffocation	4	2	-	1
E 913	Accidental mechanical suffocation	39	30	16	5
E 916	Struck by falling object	8	4	14	6
E 917	Striking against object	3	2	17	3

Table 20.3 Showing deaths from injuries which may have been non-accidental

E 980-E988	Place of injury	0 - 4 yr.		5 - 14 yr.	
		M	F	M	F
	Home	5	2	2	6
	Farm	0	1	1	0
	Place of recreation or sport	0	1	1	1
	Other specified place	3	0	5	0
	Place unspecified	1	5	5	1
	TOTALS	9	9	14	8

at least, a means of resolving the problem. A figure or figures relating to the numbers of children at risk could be obtained from the local registers together with a record of how many of these have died and from what cause. An analysis of such figures would provide a more satisfactory answer than an attempt to extract from the tables quoted above the proportion of deaths which might be attributable to 'non-accidental' injury. If no such nationwide study of 'The pattern of death in children subject to abuse' is not under way, it appears to me that it is high time for one to be commenced.

References

Chambers, D.R. (1974) Legal aspects. In Robinson, R.R. (Ed) *Symposium on Sudden and Unexpected Deaths in Infancy, Canadian Foundation for the Study of Infant Deaths,* Toronto, p. 327.
Chambers, D.R. (1976 *The Listener,* May 6, p. 558.
Jobling, M. (1976) *The Abused Child.* London: National Children's Bureau.

Discussion

Many guesses have been made about the prevalence of non-accidental injury to children. The Tunbridge Wells Study Group provisionally accepted the estimates of Malcolm Hall (1974)*. These figures, which seemed to fit extrapolations from police records in Lancashire, did not fit with the violent deaths recorded in the Registrar General's Statistical Reports. The question was raised whether anything other than strict reporting of all cases in the country would reveal the true state of affairs. Did the number really matter? Apart from the help in planning that such information would contribute, the only other benefit of accurate knowledge would be to aid the management of later siblings in the family. For this reason, all apparently accidental deaths of children below the age of three years should be carefully studied, whether due to accidental falls, poisoning by drugs, cosmetics or domestic substances, drowning, burns and scalds or sudden infant death (cot-death). The problem would still remain of the starved or otherwise deprived child who died from 'natural causes', especially from respiratory infection or gastro-enteritis. The unavoidable conclusion reached after a spirited discussion was that everyone should be suspicious whenever a child died from an accident or suffered injury.

A confidential enquiry on the lines of the maternal death enquiry, by the DHSS was proposed into all deaths of children of three years old and under during one year. The newborn period should not be excluded and especial care should be taken to include data about ethnic group, social class, socio-economic stress, size of the place in family, psychiatric abnormalities, mental disease and disorder and personality disorder.

*See *Concerning Child Abuse*, p.11

21. Area review committees

G. C. M. LUPTON

It is, perhaps, a truism to note that the prevention, recognition and management of cases of non-accidental injury to children and rehabilitation of the children and their families involves many professions and agencies. It also goes without saying that those involved view non-accidental injuries in very different lights. At one end of the spectrum are those who see all cases as breaches of the criminal law, and at the other, those who see most as a manifestation of a malaise in the family and society as a whole and representing a call for help. Apart from the exercise by each of his professional skills, the standing of each of the professionals involved varies. The general practitioner and consultant have complete autonomy to pursue their professional practice as they think fit within available resources. The police officer acts as a member of a disciplined force. The officer of the social services or other local authority department, the health staff and the probation officer are each members of structured services acting as agents of their employers to carry out specific policies and programmes. Some voluntary agencies are nationally organised, some locally organised.

Non-accidental injury is a subject which lends itself to dramatic interpretation by the media; it attracts great interest in members of the public; it generates considerable political heat and gives rise to much emotional reaction which frequently serves to obscure the realities of complex and difficult circumstances and leads to misinterpretation of the actions and intentions of all those involved in cases. To reach agreement on policies and procedures represents for all the professionals a real challenge to their management skills, and to their dedication and willingness to compromise in the best interests of patients, clients and society as a whole. Guidance, issued by the departments of central governments, therefore, while emphasising the importance of action, has concentrated on the need to pool information and co-ordinate professional expertise, so that joint decisions on the best arrangements to provide care and treatment for the families concerned may be reached.

Co-ordination and co-operation

The need for co-ordination of services is not a new theme. It was advocated by a Government working party looking into the question of child neglect in 1950 when the Government advised the setting up of local committees with an officer to initiate liaison, regular meetings between services and a special officer to take referrals of abuse and neglect cases. The need for consultation between the professionals involved with individual cases was stressed in 'The Battered Baby' (1966) and circulated to Medical Officers of Health, Chairmen of Local Medical Committees and Local Authority Children's Departments by DHSS and the Home Office.

In the letter issued jointly by the Chief Medical Officer in the Department of Health and the Chief Inspector in the Children's Department of the Home Office in February 1970 (CMO 2/70) authorities with responsibilities in this field were asked 'to consult together on the situation in their areas to decide what further arrangements should be made to ensure that all necessary protection and assistance can be made available to the child, others at risk in the family and to the parents and other adults'. They were recommended to bring into their discussions such others as representatives of the Local Medical Committee, paediatricians and consultants responsible for accident and emergency departments, the police, the National Society for the Prevention of Cruelty to Children and other people and social agencies involved locally. The benefits of such co-operation were again referred to in the memorandum prepared by the Standing Medical Advisory Committee, circulated later that year, and were also emphasised in the Chief Medical Officer's letter of 31 May 1972 forwarding a copy of an analysis of the results of a survey made of action taken following the February 1970 letter. The report and resolutions of the Tunbridge Wells Study Group, commended to the attention of authorities in Circular 48/73, of 8 October 1973, also stressed the need for co-operation.

The functions of area review committees

When previous advice on the subject was brought together in the circular letter entitled 'Non Accidental Injury to Children' circulated to Health and Local Authorities in April 1974 (Circular LASSL (74)13 (CMO(74)8). Authorities were strongly recommended to set up what were now to be known as area review committees where they had not already been established, to provide a forum for consultation between all involved in treatment and the management of the problem.

The Area Review Committees were to be responsible for:
1.   The formulation of local practice and procedures and instructions for the detailed management of cases and the monitoring of their application
2.   The encouragement of education and training programmes to heighten awareness and understanding of the problem
3.   Advising on the need for enquiries into cases which appear to have gone wrong and from which lessons can be learned
4.   Advising authorities and agencies on the optimum use of the appropriate available resources both of finance and manpower.

A comprehensive list was made of those recommended to be members. Similar advice was issued in Scotland and Wales and these committees are now operating throughout the country.

The circular letter entitled 'Non Accidental Injury to Children: Area Review Committees' (LASSL(76)2 (CMO(76)2, CNO(76)3) issued in February 1976 summarised the main points made in reports forwarded by authorities on arrangements made in their areas on the lines recommended in LASSL(74)13 and advised, in particular, that membership of Area Review Committees should include representatives of legal and administrative departments of local authorities and other appropriate voluntary bodies. It also made certain recommendations regarding sub-committees, and suggested that meetings of the full Committees should be held quarterly.

Area Review Committees, therefore, take their place in the historic sequence of the development of services in this country aimed at the prevention, recognition and management of cases of non-accidental injury to children and rehabilitation work in their families. A committee on these lines is now generally recognised as the only forum in which the necessary meeting of minds and reconciliation of policies between authorities, agencies and professions can be sought. It is this recognition which has provided the impetus to the establishment of the committees throughout the country and to which can be attributed much of the progress already made. The extent to which consensus has been reached, even if it has been only an agreement to differ, but not to interfere, shows how much can be achieved, given the will, co-ordination of services, ironing out of overlaps and conflicts, and agreement on the best possible use of very limited resources.

Some fundamental difficulties

Consensus has not been achieved without difficulties. In the rest of this chapter, some of these difficulties are described.

1. T The committee cannot take executive decisions or decide on policy as members can only act *ad referendum* to their sponsoring authority.
2.   The committee cannot put matters to a vote and must seek consensus whenever an agreed view of the committee is necessary, as the membership, in covering all disciplines and agencies involved with non-accidental injury to children, is unbalanced in its representation of one profession or interest *vis-a-vis* others.
3.   Differences between the organisational structures of the authorities and agencies represented affect the contributions members can make. Some, such as representatives of voluntary agencies, will be able to speak for their agency, though others may not. Some, such as consultant specialists or general practitioners, though seen as representatives of their profession, may express personal views which would not necessarily be supported by their colleagues. Some, who are agents of elected authorities, may require to seek endorsement from their authority for accepting recommendations made by the committee. Others are members of a hierarchy who will require to seek endorsement from their seniors for decisions recommended.
4.   The members may represent attitudes which are irreconcilable.
5.   The members have different levels of responsibility in their organisations.
6.   Though the statutory position of the Director of Social Services under the children's legislation gives him an inbuilt interest in the good functioning of the committee, no one authority or profession is in a position to undertake a permanent lead role.
7.   Overlaps between professions and agencies call for particular sensitivity in developing procedures so as to ensure that they complement rather than duplicate each other.

8.   Co-ordination is further complicated by the different internal organisations of authorities. Some are related to client groups, others to the provision of particular professional skills and some to geographical areas.

9.   The committees have had to consider co-ordination of services and initiate new procedures without additional funds specifically provided for the purpose at a time when authorities and agencies have been experiencing extreme pressure on all their resources.

The health authorities and most local authorities were at the same time involved in a major reorganisation which meant that many officers, at any rate initially, were uncertain of their roles in their own organisations and *vis-a-vis* other authorities and agencies.

Inherent in the area review committee structure are, therefore, disparate elements which can create particular difficulties in management and which, to achieve real results, require much compromise between conflicting interests, attitudes and approaches. In another context it has been suggested that only by creating an autonomous structured service could such a wide range of interests be accommodated and reconciled. For the moment, however, this would not be practical in dealing with child abuse. Though we must not under-estimate these difficulties and the many differences still requiring to be resolved, it is particularly encouraging to note the degree of progress that has been made throughout the country in developing, through area review committees and elsewhere, the necessary policies and procedures for the management of cases, the inauguration of training facilities, monitoring past cases, etc. This speaks particularly well for the degree of dedication of all those working for abusing families and their children and augurs well for the possibility of a future general increase in co-operation between different professions, agencies and authorities.

References

Memorandum by the Special Standing Committee on Accidents in Childhood of the British Paediatric Association (March 1966) The Battered Baby. *British Medical Journal,* 1960, **1,** 601-603

22. Case conferences—cause for concern

RAYMOND CASTLE

'Although we realise how busy you are with re-organisation, recent events have left us in no doubt of the need to repeat the professional guidance about the diagnosis, care, prevention and local organisation necessary for the management of cases involving non-accidental injury to children'.
DHSS Circular (LASSL (74) 13 22 APL 74)

Introduction

The above quotation is taken from a DHSS Circular recommending the setting up of Area Review Committees following the tragic Maria Colwell case. Since that time, other cases have been brought to the attention of the general public via the media, all of which have highlighted a common problem - the breakdown of communication and co-ordination between the professionals involved.

Whilst Area Review Committees are doing much to ensure better management of cases involving non-accidental injury to children, and most have produced documents laying down guidelines, some doubts have been expressed about the general effectiveness of case conferences.

Indicative of the concern expressed are the following extracts from an editorial in the *Lancet* (1975).

'In this summer it is difficult to know who are the battered and who the most at risk. Is it the newspaper reader who is battered each morning by a succession of headlines - "Baby hit by mother went blind"? Is it the paediatrician, battered by too many case conferences and at risk of neglecting other needy families and ill children because this week he has cancelled his visit to the special care baby unit on Wednesday afternoon because of a case conference and has cancelled his Friday afternoon spina-bifida clinic in order to attend yet another case conference? The Friday conference, like the others, was attended by eight highly-paid, highly trained professionals, who sat solemnly around a table discussing a robust, healthy child, with a bruise on his bottom.

'Multi-disciplinary case conferences emerge as a vital part of the early management, but probably few people realise how much time they take from the lives of busy people with many other commitments.

Some of the teams concerned with non-accidental injury and some of the Case Committees are finding an increasing proportion of their time spent with trivial and doubtful cases'.

Another point of view suggests that much valuable time is wasted, not because of over-attendance at case conferences but rather by the lack of attendance on the part of key personnel who are actually working with the family. Certainly, recent events in which agencies and workers have been singled out for criticism have led to a high level of anxiety. Many workers now see the case conference as a primary source of support and protection and sometimes have unrealistic expectations of what might be achieved through its use. They feel disappointed and frustrated when these expectations cannot be met.

The DHSS Circular (1974) already quoted, states:

'A case conferences is recommended for every case involving suspected non-accidental injury to a child. In this way, unilateral action will be minimised and all those who can provide information about the child and his family, have statutory responsibility for the safety of the child, or are responsible for providing services, will be brought together to reach a collective decision which takes into account the age of the child, nature of injuries and a medico-social assessment of the family and its circumstances'.

'The case conference should retain overall concern for the management of the case and should be prepared to reconvene at each successive development in it or when any professional worker is particularly worried about the family'.

In examining the DHSS Scheme, Jan Carter (1976) points out two possible limitations with regard to co-ordination.

The first is that it tends to view co-ordination as the application of a set of static procedures, rather than as the negotiation of a dynamic process which is highly dependent for its definition on the accuracy of the perceptions of the professionals involved in the case.

The second is the assumption that its recommendations for co-ordination are applied in an ideal world. Professionals are assumed to be rational, harmonious people who demonstrate goodwill and commonsense and who reinforce each others' roles. Hospital and Social Services departments appear as efficient organisations with sufficient resources and adequate numbers of trained staff working to agreed objectives. In fact, such ideal conditions are rare.

Following on this theme, Tom Tomlinson (1976), writing on inter-agency collaboration, suggests that the reason various agencies do not collaborate more effectively lies in the fact that collaboration between agencies and workers is based on personal relationships and that the quality of those relationships is determined by the attitude of the participants. When it is positive and reassuring, good collaboration can result even though the participants may start with essentially different view points. Where the attitudes are destructively critical, the participants become defensive and are disinclined to expose their own work and ideas to possible ridicule.

Findings from the present study carried out by the NSPCC's National Advisory Centre on Battered Children highlight a number of interesting aspects.

The NSPCC's case conference project

The study had two aims:
1.   To examine areas of concern and identify significant trends and
2.   To establish whether any improvements in procedure are necessary.

Method
The National Society for the Prevention of Cruelty to Children has social workers in most regions covered by Area Review Committees, and therefore, by using the Agency' personnel, information was obtained on a national basis. The study was carried out during the 3 month period from 1 March to 31 May 1976. A detailed questionnaire was designed for completion by each case worker involved in case conferences on families with whom they had been working during the study period. It consisted of

nineteen main sections and included questions on the number of conferences attended, the number involving non-accidental injury, the conference venue, personnel attending, duration, ages and whereabouts of children at the time of conference and any legal proceedings taken. There was also a section inviting workers' comments on the effectiveness of case conference procedures in their own particular areas (see Appendix III p.205).

The study has limitations, being based on information provided by social workers, many of whom are covering large geographical areas and working under considerable pressure.

The sample

From the beginning of March to the end of May 1976, a total of 777 case conferences were attended. Of the total, 343 conferences (55.85 per cent) were the first on the families concerned, and of these initial case conferences, 248 (57.14 per cent) involved non-accidental injury to children. Thirty-six conferences (4.63 per cent), were called do discuss re-injury to a child previously the subject of a case conference. A further 13 (2.99 per cent) were convened in respect of first time non-accidental injury to the sibling of a child previously injured and the subject of an earlier conference.

Table 22.1 Initiation of Case Conferences

Case Conferences were initiated by:

N = 777		per cent
Social Services	419	53.92
NSPCC	202	26.00
Hospital staff	68	8.75
Area Health Authority	34	4.37
Probation Service	15	1.93
Other	39	5.03
Total:	777	100.00

It is interesting to note that on the 39 listed under 'other', four were concerned by the police, one by a general practitioner, one by a child guidance clinic and the remainder by education welfare departments.

Table 22.2 Chairmanship

Case Conferences were chaired by:

N = 777		per cent
Senior member Social Services	562	72.33
Hospital consultant	94	12.09
Senior member NSPCC	56	7.21
Senior member Area Health Authority	25	3.22
Senior member Probation Dept.	6	0.77
Other	34	4.38
Total:	777	100.00

Table 22.2 shows clearly that the largest number of case conferences, 72.33 per cent, have been chaired by senior members of Local Authority Social Services Departments. Although the next largest number, 12.09 per cent, are those involving hospital consultants, generally paediatricians, this is quite a low percentage of the total. Others involved have included senior members of Education Departments, NSPCC Inspectors, and so on, and on one occasion, a senior police officer.

Table 22.3 Case conference location

Conferences were held at:

N = 777		per cent
Social Service Department	434	55.85
Hospital	212	27.28
General practitioner's surgery	22	2.83
Probation Department	7	0.90
NSPCC Local Office	9	1.17
Other	93	11.97
Total:	777	100.00

A number have taken place in Education Departments and in a few instances, Area Health Departments.

Table 22.4 Duration of case conference

N = 777		per cent
Up to one hour	329	42.34
One to two hours	407	52.38
Over two hours	41	5.28
Total:	777	100.00

This table shows quite clearly that the largest number of cases are taking up to two hours or more.

Table 22.5 Medical and police attendance at Case Conferences

Personnel attending case conference

N = 777		per cent
Attendance of hospital consultant	262	33.72
Attendance of general practitioner	209	26.89
Attendance of medical personnel	471	60.61
Attendance of police	396	50.96

Out of the total number of case conferences held (777), hospital consultants attended 33.72 per cent whilst general practitioners only attended 26.89 per cent.

Table 22.6 Location of child or children

Where child or children concerned were at time of conference

Total number of children involved: 903

N = 903		per cent
At home	529	58.58
Hospital	180	19.93
Residential nursery	38	4.20
Foster home	94	10.42
Care of relatives	21	2.33
Other	41	4.54
Total	903	100.00

Of the 903 children available, 110 (12.18 per cent) were already the subjects of Care Orders or Supervision Orders.

Table 22.7 Age range of all children involved, including siblings

N = 1275

Age range in years	Number	per cent
0 - 5	696	54.59
6 - 11	454	35.53
12 - 16	126	9.88
Total:	1275	100.00

As with most other studies concerning child abuse, the largest number of children are in the youngest age category.

Table 22.8 Legal proceedings at initial case conference

N = 144

		per cent
Juvenile court proceed-ings	127	88.19
Adult court proceed-ings	17	11.81
Total:	144	100.00

Of the 434 initial case conferences, 144 resulted in Court proceedings (33 per cent).

Table 22.9 Agency initiating Juvenile Court Proceedings

N = 127

	Number	per cent
Social service depart-ment	70	55.12
NSPCC	48	37.80
Police	4	3.15
Other	5	3.93
Total:	127	100.00

The table indicates that Social Service departments are now initiating the largest number of Juvenile Court proceedings. Those under 'Other' were initiated by Education Departments.

Table 22.10 Agency initiating Adult Court Proceedings

N = 17		Per cent
Social Service Department	1	5.88
NSPCC	4	23.54
Police	12	70.58
Total:	17	100.00

Discussion

A number of factors are highlighted by the statistical information and comments contributed by the 220 NSPCC fieldwork staff who participated.

Duration
Since the initial hypothesis suggested that case conferences were too time-consuming, it is useful to discuss this aspect first. One cannot be dogmatic and it is recognised that some cases will take longer to discuss than others. However, it can be seen from Table 22.4 (p 149) that, in this sample, the majority of conferences have taken two hours or more. Most participants felt strongly that this is too long, and suggested that a reasonable period is about one hour.

In many instances, time has been wasted because those attending have not prepared a *resume* of their involvement and have had to delve into large files at the meeting to extract relevant information.

Personnel attending
Concern has been expressed that key personnel are frequently represented by another member of their department, who may have no personal knowledge of the family involved and consequently cannot be effective in the decision making. In particular, the absence of the general practitioner (see note to Table 22.5, p. 149) means that vital decisions must sometimes be delayed and occasionally a conference re-convened. It is suggested that any relevant and involved person who cannot attend should be required to submit a report.

The conference chairman
Most submissions indicate that a crucial factor in any case conference is the role of the conference chairman. This position calls for someone of ability, knowledge and experience, but this is not always fulfilled.

Location
Although participants noted greater flexibility, the study shows that the majority of case conferences are still being held in Social Service Departments. Whilst this may be best in some instances, experience indicates that medical personnel are more likely to attend if the meeting can be held in the hospital or the general practitioner's surgery.

Police involvement

This is obviously an area which has not been fully resolved. A number of social workers feel that police involvement in case conferences has led to role conflict situations. One quotation reads:

'When the police are present, they seem to be seeking evidence of injury for legal purposes, whilst the social workers are trying to assess the social situation in its entirety and this always leads to conflict'.

One area reported that a vote is taken at the initial case conference to decide whether or not the police should be involved.

Case conference decisions

The view has been expressed that, on a number of occasions, recommendations of case conferences with regard to Court proceedings have been frustrated by the Magistrate's refusal to consider Care Orders on technical grounds. A particular area of concern is that created when the members of the conference cannot reach a majority decision. It is felt there is a need for some form of Sub-Committee of the Area Review Committee to consider and advise on these cases.

General effectiveness

A large number of participants found the case conference procedures in their areas both effective and supportive. Typical comments follow:

'Procedures very clear - no unilateral action in last three years - differences of opinion stated and recorded - action implemented promptly - Divisional Review Committee meets every two months to examine cases of actual or high suspicion of injury - Area Review Committee meets every six months - Case Conferences well attended'.

'There is much closer liaison between all concerned - better pooling of information and the creation of a greater awareness and respect for each other's particular skills'

'Effective because they crystallise situations and utilise all the known information at time of conference'.

'Has had very positive effect in encouraging inter-agency communication and co-operation'.

However, there are a number of areas where problems continue to exist, as is illustrated by the following recorded remarks:

'There is a total lack of urgency and some departures from case conference recommendations. Generally, each agency reverts to "doing its own thing", thereby making the case conference irrelevant'.

'Case conferences normally held days after action taken. Medical members tend to assume "omnipotence".'

'Principal worker sometimes not in attendance; frequently there is indecision often affected by lack of resources'.

'Not yet proving very effective; still no set down procedures established'.

Conclusions

This study, whilst limited in its scope, nevertheless supports the view that there is a need for a more structured approach to case conferences. It also indicates that there are several areas of concern which remain to be dealt with by some Area Review Committees who appear still to be feeling their way. It is encouraging to note that, in the majority of areas, Area Review Committees have set up adequate procedures, which are felt to be of positive help in the provision of service to the families and in the mutual support of the primary worker by the multi-disciplinary team.

For specific recommendations see Chapter 28, p.192.

References

Carter, J. (1976) Co-ordination and child abuse. *Social Work Service,* **9**, pp.22-28.
DHSS (1974) Non-accidental injury to children. LASSL (74) CMO (74), London: HMSO.
Lancet (1975) Editorial, 'The Battered...', *Lancet,* **1**, 1228.
Tomlinson, T. (1976) *Violence in the Family.* Manchester University Press, pp.136-145.

Acknowledgements

The author would like to express his appreciation and gratitude to all colleagues working as fieldwork staff with the NSPCC who contributed material for this study. He would also like to thank Team members of the NSPCC National Advisory Centre who assisted in collating and editing the report and Angela Collier and Mrs Betty Dublins for preparing and typing the final manuscript.

Discussion

The first professional discussions between those directly concerned with a child and his family when abuse is suspected aims at reaching decisions about immediate action. Both medical and psycho-social information is essential. The presence of physical injury usually requires admission to hospital. Once the child's safety is assured, the case conference is called and all are invited who are concerned not only with diagnosis and preliminary planning, but also with contuning management and the provision of the services required.

Ray Castle's analysis of the work of and the problems created by case conferences coincided with the goup's general impressions gained from their own experiences. Particularly the time taken seemed too great a burden on busy professionals despite the importance of talking out the families' problems in great detail and of reaching a consensus about necessary management. Proper preparation for the meeting and experienced chairmanship should reduce the time taken. The fumbling through sheaves of case records would never occur if each member had prepared his report beforehand. Ideally, these resumes should be circulated for study before the meeting. For this preparation, adequate secretarial help is essential, as it is also for the circulation to all members afterwards of a confidential synopsis of what had occurred, what action had been taken, and what are the treatment objectives, including minority as well as majority opinions. The key worker's name should be stated.

Once the factual data have been reported at the conference, two stages of decisions are needed; first, what is the ideal solution and then, testing against availability of resources, what action should be taken. This is not a waste of time. When these are inadequate the provider of services may bias the decision against what is recognised as optimal management. Gaps in resources cannot be identified if the primary decision is taken only in terms of what is available. Such gaps should be notified to the appropriate authority as well as to the area/district review committee.

Too often a key person is absent. Greater flexibility of time and place should make attendance easier, especially for the general practitioner, although he could often be represented by the attached health visitor. An organiser or key-worker should be appointed, among whose tasks would be obtaining a written report from, or at the least holding a telephone conversation with, any key person who could not attend. In the follow-up case conference, one member should be designated to press the needs of the child both physical and emotional.

Some professionals involved still regard a case conference quite wrongly as a waste of time. Since friendly co-operation cannot be taken for granted, occasional meetings between the professionals likely to be involved in problems raised by child abuse, to supplement the business meetings at which swords might be crossed, should help mutual understanding.

When agreement cannot be reached, what should be done? One suggestion was resort to a sub-committee of the area review committee. In Bath (see Ch. 8) the members of the monitoring committee are available as advisers. In other areas disagreements seem rare, a situation which, it is hoped, does not reflect undue pressure by, for example, the chairman. When the question of court proceedings arises, the local authority solicitor should be called in for advice. Objection to applying to the court on the grounds that the case will not succeed needs careful scrutiny. To pre-judge the decision of the magistrates is unnecessary, and a good case that is properly presented should not fail. It is to be hoped that the justices will not frustrate on technical grounds applications which are in themselves sound and aimed at the protection from danger of the baby.

The DHSS might now circulate a fresh document giving advice about the conduct of case conferences as well as making clear that invitations to attend to those not directly concerned with the family are not commands. Some reconsideration of the functions and the structure of area review committees might also be timely. Both Speirs and Lupton had pointed out how difficult was the task of these committees because of the difference in status and in responsibility of the members. Now that the country is more or less completely covered by these committees, a study of local variations might help in the selection of the most practical procedures.

The group examined the functions of area review committees as listed in Appendix I of Concerning Child Abuse (p.165) and still supported them all except numbers 4 and 9 (see below, Ch. 27). The monitoring of a child's progress over the long term (No. 4) seems out of place and liable to misinterpretation. The committee should have a general responsibility, in collaboration with the area health authority, for seeing that facilities are adequate for care and supervision of abused children, whether with their parents or with foster parents or in residential accommodation. The Park Hospital for Children, Oxford, provides an excellent model of residential accommodation in which essential family treatment is carried out, besides giving opportunities for much needed research. An obvious need exists not only for continuing but also for extending this type of work to other areas.

PART 4

Legal aspects

23. Preparing the paediatrician's evidence in case proceedings

CHRISTINE COOPER

Doctors like some other professional workers, dislike giving evidence in Court about their patients, but in recent years most paediatricians have realised the importance during Care Proceedings of their evidence on the child's condition. Social Service Departments are increasingly involving the paediatrician, both in the assessment of the child and his family and in the Court Proceedings which follow. The social work and paediatric expertise complement each other and form a more complete case for the Local Authority.

Paediatricians and social workers are also being increasingly involved as expert witnesses acting for one or other of the parties in difficult cases in Care Proceedings, and by sitting in Court throughout the Hearing they can add to the lawyer's understanding of the case and suggest relevant questions which he can put to individual witnesses to bring out details of the evidence more clearly.

The paediatrician's contribution in court

The paediatrician may be needed to describe injuries and to give his opinion about possible causes of those injuries. Secondly, he will give evidence about the child's general physical state, including his earlier history, his growth and development, his general functioning compared with other children of his age, and the nature and effects of any physical or functional handicaps which may be present.

Thirdly, the Court should hear about the child's psychological well being including his intellectual and emotional state, his personality and his behaviour, and, if he is old enough, his educational progress. Fourthly, details about the quality of care he is receiving at home and about the parent-child and other family relationships are also most relevant in Care Proceedings.

It is normal practice to assess these details in a paediatric clinic, no matter what the condition for which the consultation takes place. Where psychological and family problems are particularly relevant to the child's condition, for example in psychosomatic disorders, learning or behavioural problems, the paediatrician will spend a good deal of time assessing the full psycho-social picture, often with help from the social worker, health visitor, teacher, psychologist or child psychiatrist. In no case is this more important than in the family problems of neglect, child abuse and parental inability to cope with a severely disturbed child, typically cases which may later come to Court for Care Proceedings.

The case conference

The Case Conference method of discussing and assessing or reassessing the child's and the family's problems has been in use for many years in hospitals, special clinics and schools, in order to collate all the known information about a child and his family and to make the best possible plans for treating and managing many different conditions of childhood. In child abuse and neglect the Case Conference has come into its own. Before Care Proceedings evidence should have been discussed by the Local Authority lawyer with all the individuals in the Case Conference in order to determine whether or not there is enough evidence for Care Proceedings to be initiated and who the witnesses in Court should be.

Preparing the medical evidence with the lawyer

Since the medical evidence on the child's physical and psychological state and on the parent-child problems is often the major part of the Local Authority's case, this must be prepared very carefully. The lawyer needs to understand the important deviations from normal, both physical and psychological, and their possible causes, and how all these are assessed. Growth charts on height, weight and skull circumference will often be useful evidence, as will a detailed chart of the injuries when these are present. X-ray findings and the results of blood tests are needed and photographs of the child and any injuries he may have. Psychological assessments too and relevant details on the other children in the family often help.

It is the common experience of paediatricians, especially when first attending Court, that through lack of adequate preparation with the lawyer of the evidence and a failure to reach a clear understanding of the various facets of the case, especially the psychological ones, the salient points are not brought out and the Magistrates do not receive the full facts.

It is important for the doctor to understand the law governing Care Proceedings and child protection, including the Sections of the Children Act, 1948, the Children and Young Persons Acts, 1963 and 1969, and the Children Act, 1975. He should also familiarise himself with the exact procedure which is followed in Court. Experience will reveal that this can vary from Court to Court and from area to area, and evidence which is allowed in one Court may be objected to in another by one or other lawyer or by the Magistrates' Clerk.

The Court may grant legal aid so that the child's case can be presented to the Court by a lawyer. In practice this lawyer usually takes his instruction from the parents, and the fact that their interests may conflict with those of the child is a source of real weakness in the present arrangements. If the parents contest the need for the Care Order, the doctor, whose evidence supports the granting of the order, may find himself being cross-examined by the lawyer, acting for the child but speaking on behalf of the parents rather than the child. The paediatrician then has the unpleasant task of emphasising to the Magistrates in front of the parents, their weaknesses and their defective care or management of their child, while their lawyer is trying to minimise these and excuse them.

At this stage the doctor may be asked rhetorical questions such as 'But surely, doctor, a baby of this age would sustain such bruising and the fractured skull by falling downstairs?' This may have been the parents' story. If the doctor replies, 'Well, it's just possible, I suppose,' he has lost the case! The writer is indebted to Professor Henry Kempe for much useful comment about giving evidence in Care Proceedings. In the above example, if the doctor is firmly of the opinion from all the evidence he has that in the case under discussion the child did *not* sustain his injuries by falling downstairs, his duty is to tell the Court so very clearly. It is not a hypothetical case, which is being discussed. Everyone knows that a baby *could* sustain bruises and a fractured skull by falling downstairs, but that is not the point at issue. What the Court needs to know is the doctor's opinion about the injuries in *this* case before them. Obviously, he would not be supporting the Local Authority case in Court if he thought that the injuries were due to falling downstairs. A proper reply to the question would be along the following lines, 'In my opinion, in the case of little Mary which we are discussing now, she could not possibly have sustained these injuries by falling downstairs'. It may be necessary, in cross-examination, to give his reasons for holding this opinion.

The doctor must also realise that the magistrates know nothing about the case or the family except what they hear from the witness box before they make their finding as to whether the case is proved. They then study the welfare reports before deciding what kind of order to make. If the evidence is not strong enough or if it is inadequately presented, the magistrates cannot grant the care order and a child who really needs the protection of the court will not get it. Not all the Local Authority lawyers have experience of care proceedings, nor do they all understand the subtleties of these cases. It is for the lawyer to discuss what is important with the doctor so that he can lead the doctor in examination. In these ways, the case for the granting of the order has the greatest chance of success.

The social work evidence is usually complementary and it may be as well for the doctor and social worker together to examine with the lawyer which aspects of the case each will be required to discuss in Court.

The doctor, in order to help the parents' feelings in Court, may also ask the lawyer to give him an opportunity in Court to say that the parents *have* tried in the past and how, in their way, they *are* fond of their child and anxious about his welfare, although they are unable to provide for his proper care in the immediate future.

Submitting a written report

Before the Court hearing it is very helpful if the doctor submits to the Local Authority lawyer a detailed medical report on the child. This should include his past history, the family details, a discussion of the immediate history and findings when the child is seen, and some observations about the child's growth, development and behaviour and the parent-child relationships. This detailed report can be the basis of the examination and cross-examination in the witness box and it is helpful to the lawyer acting for the child and parents, who usually receives a copy from the local authority lawyer. It greatly simplifies the giving of evidence, if everyone is clear what that evidence will be.

Discussing the evidence with the parents before the hearing

For the doctor to discuss with the parents what he proposes to say in evidence may
seem out of place and so the writer believed, ten years ago. Experience, since then,
has shown that to omit such a discussion is unfair to the parents as well as detrimental
to the total welfare and management of the family. The Court hearing should be
seen by all as a therapeutic step in the long term management of the family, although
it is not always easy to coax the parents to see it in this light.

In well managed cases the various facets of the child's problems, whether they
be injuries, stunting of growth, slow development, disturbed behaviour or mixtures
of these, will have been discussed with the parents by doctor and social worker as
the investigations proceed and the family problems unfold. Since nearly all parents
have been trying to care for their child well, it is important for the doctor to be
sensitive to their sense of failure and their anxiety about the Care Proceedings added
to the earlier family problems. Their own self-esteem has often been severely damaged
by the experiences of their own upbringing. It is further profoundly diminished by
the conclusions reached on completion of the investigations and by their need to face
the fact that they can no longer deny or hide severe problems and their inability to
cope with the child. Doctor and social worker can sometimes enable them to adjust
themselves to their problems by emphasising how much they *have* tried to cope,
despite the adverse circumstances over which they have had little or no control. Many
parents, given gentle explanations, much boosting of morale where possible, and repeated help to look facts in the face, can gradually come to terms with all this, so
that in the end they can view the Care Proceedings as a way of helping them with
overwhelming family problems. It is sometimes necessary to point out that their own
impulses to reject help when voluntarily offered is also a factor in the case.

What should be emphasised to the parents, perhaps on several occasions, is that
in Care Proceedings no-one is on trial. The parents should understand that the Court
is there to help the child gain the best care and protection in the future.

If the plan is to return the child to the family, gradually, after some weeks of
further treatment, but still under the Care Order, this should be fully discussed with
them too, and during the hearing it will usually be mentioned.

Some very damaged parents, in spite of all this help, are unable to see the doctor,
social worker or others as anything but condemning them, accusing them or being
unfair to them. This has been their experience throughout life of all other authority
figures from their own parents onwards. Angry outburst are often part of the behaviour
of such parents, who function for much of the time at a very immature level.

The doctor may find it painful to have to dwell on the parents' deficiencies in
Court. Experience may teach him how to emphasise their strengths and accept their
wish to improve their care for the child, while clearly stating to the magistrates that
at the moment they cannot manage to do it properly themselves.

It is important that in all matters before the Court everyone bears in mind
Section 3 of the Children Act, 1975, which states that the welfare of the child, both
now and in the future, must be the first consideration for all concerned.

24. Wardship jurisdiction

JEAN GRAHAM HALL

This contribution examines the use of wardship proceedings in the Family Division of the High Court as an alternative to the proceedings before the local juvenile court in cases of alleged non-accidental injury to children. It also evaluates the effectiveness of the two jurisdictions, showing where they overlap and sometimes complement one another. It explains the relationship between the High Court and the local authority. Finally, it makes suggestions for future reform.

Jurisdiction of the local juvenile court

Legal proceedings for the protection of a child, where non-accidental injury by the parents is alleged, are usually commenced by an application to a justice of the peace by the local authority, the police or the NSPCC under Section 28 of the *Children and Young Person Act 1969* for an order to be made so that a child in actual danger can be speedily and effectively put in a place of safety as a temporary measure. Section 1 of the Act sets out the conditions upon which the juvenile court must be satisfied when deciding the substantive case.

Criticism has been levelled at juvenile courts for making decisions of an inconsistent quality. Evidence acceptable in one court is frequently rejected by another. It is sometimes impossible to understand why apparently highly relevant evidence is excluded.* The local authority and the police who initiate these cases have no right of appeal to the Crown Court, by way of rehearing, against the refusal to make an order nor against the revocation of an order. Social workers and doctors often lose heart and conclude, rightly or wrongly, that all their efforts to protect the child are to no avail.

No alternative jurisdiction lies in the local county court.

Jurisdiction of the High Court

Infants have always been treated as specially under the protection of the Sovereign, who had the feudal obligation as *parens patriae* to protect the person and property of his subjects, particularly those not capable of looking after themselves. This obligation was delegated to the Lord Chancellor, passed to the Court of Chancery, then

---

* Regina v Lincoln Justice Ex p M.(D.C.) 1976 1 QB 957.

to the Chancery Division of the High Court and by the *Administration of Justice Act 1970,* to the Family Division of the High Court. There is no similar jurisdiction or concurrent remedy in any other court.

The jurisdiction is founded upon the necessity to look after individuals where it is clear that 'some care should be thrown around them*. Prior to 1949 a minor could become a ward of court in a number of ways usually by settling a small sum of money upon him and then commencing an action to administer the trust.

Since the passing of the *Law Reform (Miscellaneous Provisions) Act 1949,* the jurisdiction can only be invoked on an application to make the minor a ward of court.

With the transfer of jurisdiction from the Chancery Division to the newly created Family Division in 1970, it is possible for wardship applications to be issued in district registries, which have Family Division jurisdiction. Therefore a country or provincial solicitor can easily issue a wardship originating summons in the nearest district registry, although the hearing by a High Court judge has to be in a first tier court centre, or in London. There are only seventeen Family Division judges, all of whom go out of London on itineraries. All first tier court centres are visited once a year, and the larger centres, such as Birmingham and Cardiff, are visited twice a year. In 1975, a total of 1,203 wardship summonses were issued; 792 in the principal registry in London and 411 in district registries. A total of 556 orders were made confirming wardship and a total of 323 orders discharging wardship†. Approximately sixteen summonses are heard per week in London. Unfortunately, there are no known statistics for what happens in the provinces.

The usual order of the court today no longer keeps away an undesirable suitor from a rich young maiden. The jurisdiction is invoked in a much wider social setting.

Commencement of wardship proceedings

By the Rules of the Supreme Court, Order 90 Rule, 3, an application is made by issuing an originating summons in the principal registry, or a district registry. The minor becomes a ward of court upon the issue of the summons. He will cease to be one

1.   If an application for an appointment for the hearing of the summons is not made within 21 days thereafter, or
2.   Unless the court, hearing the application made within 21 days, orders that the minor be made a ward.

Virtually any person who has an interest in the minor may make an application. Most frequently it is made by one of the parents. The minor himself may apply. If no other suitable guardian *ad litem* is available, the Official Solicitor may be authorised to act in that capacity. He accepts responsibilities beyond the mere conduct of the proceedings, and is closely involved with the welfare of his wards.

* Wellesley v Duke Beaufort 1872. 2 Russ 1 at 20.
† Judical statistics 1975, HMSO

In a recent case * where B had been committed to the care of the local authority by a juvenile court and placed with foster parents, B's grand-mother issued wardship proceedings, and sought the transfer of the care of the child to herself. Lane J held that this court had jurisdiction, in the circumstances, to make a wardship order.

In another case † an educational psychologist attached to the education department of the local authority applied to the court to make D, a girl aged 10, a ward of court with the purpose of delaying and preventing an operation for sterilisation. Heilbron J held that this was the type of case in which the court should 'throw some care round the child', and confirmed the wardship.

Evidence on the application is given by way of sworn affidavits. The first application is before the registrar who gives directions dealing with the general conduct of the case, and if necessary, calls for a report by the court welfare officer. The substantive hearing is before the judge in chambers. The minor will remain a ward until he attains 18, or the court otherwise orders.

The local authority and the High Court

Section 1 of the Children Act 1948 imposes a duty on a local authority to receive into care any child in their area under 17 where it appears that their intervention is necessary in the child's interest. The authority of the High Court is not ousted where the local authority acts under this section. However, the wardship jurisdiction will only be exercised where it can be usefully employed without conflicting with the local authority's statutory sphere of discretion or where the case involves special circumstances.‡

The position is different where the local authority assumes parental control over the child by a resolution under Section 2 of the Act. M was received into care in 1956 and a year later the local authority resolved to vest the right and powers of the parents in themselves. In 1960 the local authority asked the foster parents to return M to them, whereupon the foster parents applied to the High Court to make M a ward of court§. The court held that although the power to make the child a ward was unaffected, 'the judge in whom prerogative power is vested will...not exercise control in relation to duties or discretions clearly vested by statute in the local authority'.

By Section 7 of the *Family Law Reform Act 1969* the High Court may itself in exceptional circumstances in wardship proceedings make a care order or a supervision order.

The juvenile court and the High Court

The powers exercised by juvenile courts in relation to children do not oust wardship jurisdiction although it is exercised more by way of supplement to the order of the juvenile court.||

* In Re B (a minor) 1974 3 AER 915
† Re D (a minor) 1976 1 AER 326
‡ Re C (A) (an infant) 1966 1 AER 560
§ Re M (an infant) Ch.328 at p.344
|| Re P (infant) 1976 2 AER 229

B, aged 14 months, was admitted to hospital suffering from a fractured skull and bruising to her face and buttocks. Twelve days later the hospital authorities discharged her into the care of her mother and stepfather. Four days later B was again admitted to hospital, suffering from cerebral haemorrhage and severe bruising over most of her body, limbs and face. Her stepfather pleaded guilty in the Crown Court to causing actual bodily harm and was sentenced to 18 months imprisonment suspended for two years. The juvenile court made a care order and placed B with foster parents. Thereafter the grandmother issued wardship proceedings, and sought transfer of the care of the child to her. As already reported the court held that it had jurisdiction to make a wardship order.*

The preferred jurisdiction

Where the possibility of choice has occurred to interested parties, and they have experience in battered children cases of both proceedings in juvenile court and of wardship proceedings, strong preference is voiced in favour of the latter. The judges are continually sitting to decide family matters, and bring a professional understanding of law and practice to the case. Facilities are available for dealing with preliminary issues, and expert reports and witnesses can be readily obtained.

Re Cullimore offers some illuminating lessons.† Sarah aged 16 months, had been picked up by her father, and her arm cracked. On the way to hospital, the parents decided, to avoid trouble with the mother's parents, that the mother would say that she had picked up the child. Sarah was found to have a fractured skull, and the parents were treated with suspicion. They were not polite, and their verbal aggression did not endear them to the social workers and the doctors. A case conference of three doctors and seven social workers was held, and as a result a place of safety order was obtained. Later an interim care order was made. Criminal proceedings against the mother were dismissed, and the father was acquitted by a jury of the charge of inflicting grievous bodily harm. The parents were allowed to have Sarah home, and later took her back to hospital, where an X-ray revealed a recent fracture of her left arm. After another case conference, a second place of safety order was obtained. The father then applied to make Sarah a ward of court. There was conflicting medical evidence as to whether Sarah was suffering from brittle bones or was a battered baby. The President of the Family Division, after a five day hearing, held that, on the balance of probabilities, the child was not a battered baby, but suffered from brittle bones. The President discharged the place of safety order, allowed Sarah to be in the care and control of her parents, and decided that Sarah would remain a ward of court and be joined as a party, so that the Official Solicitor would be able to act as guardian *ad litem.*

Can wardship jursidiction be extended?

As wardship proceedings become more popular, it seems a great pity that a local

* In re B (a minor) 1974 3 AER 915
† Re Cullimore (a minor) *The Times,* 23 March 1976

professional tribunal cannot be established.

It would seem logical to make the County Court the correct forum for the initiation of wardship proceedings in addition to the High Court. This would give local authorities and others interested in battered baby cases the same choice as now exists *vis-a-vis* the juvenile court in adoption proceedings. A circuit judge sits daily in the county court, many of which are designated as divorce county courts. The jurisdiction in that sphere is less and less in open court and more and more in chambers, dealing with urgent injunctions relating to family matters, and deciding cases of custody and access to children.

Without any legislation, it would be possible to make greater use of Section 24(1) of the *Courts Act 1971* by which a circuit judge can sit as a judge of the High Court for the hearing of such case or cases, and at such place and for such time as might be specified on behalf of the Lord Chancellor.

The following consequential matters still remain to be considered:

1. Whether the present exclusive use of the principal registry and the district registry should continue;

2. Whether one should employ the county court bailiffs in place of the High Court tipstaff to trace 'missing' wards;

3. Should all wardship cases commence in the county court and be transferred to the High Court only if there are international implications in a particular case;

4. Whether there can be local, extended use of the Official Solicitor as guardian *ad litem*. 161 new wardship references were made to the Official Solicitor in 1975.*

5. The necessity of continuing to use the procedure in Section 28 of the *Children and Young Persons Act 1969* so that, as a matter of urgency, a battered child can immediately be removed from danger and put in a place of safety.

---

* Judicial statistics 1975. HMSO

25. The Children Act 1975 and child abuse

R. A. H. WHITE

The effect of recent legislation on the prediction of child abuse or the prevention of abuse in its early stages is likely to be little or nothing. Legislation in child welfare matters is in very few instances preventive and invariably Courts are dealing with a child already damaged. Perhaps, inevitably, the criteria for removal from the parent has been the evidence that the child is suffering by not receiving adequate parenting. Maybe if we could establish to society's satisfaction by predictive methods acceptable as evidence in Court, that parenting will be inadequate, then what at the moment we can anticipate will occur in given situations, can be prevented.

The Children Act 1975

Where the 1975 Act ought to be effective is in increasing our ability to prevent the return of a child to conditions in which its welfare would suffer and to provide better legal bases for satisfactory placement. This paper explores three provisions of the Act with these considerations in mind.

Restriction of removal from care (Section 56)
One of the problems raised by the framework of child care legislation is that a child is often received into care on a voluntary basis under Section 1 of the Children Act, 1948, when he has been abused either because it is an easy way out or because care proceedings are not appropriate. Not infrequently parents are happy to get a child off their hands from time to time or minor abuses are dealt with by reception into care. The net result may be increasing damage to the child without consistent security. It also happens that a child remains in voluntary care for a substantial period of time during which the parents maintain inadequate contact and make to plans for the return of the child. The period can lengthen to such a degree that a child is established with substitute parents, but still no action is taken to protect that relationship.

Section 56 was implemented on 26 November 1976 and adds a further subsection to Section 1 of the 1948 Act. The relevant part states:

'Except in relation to an act done -
(a)   with the consent of the local authority, or
(b)   by a parent or guardian of the child who has given the local authority not less than 28 days' notice of his intention to do it.
Sub-section (8) (penalty for taking away a child in care) of section 3 of this Act shall apply to a child in the care of a local authority under this section (notwithstanding that no resolution is in force under section 2 of this Act with respect to the child) if he has been in the care of that local authority throughout the preceding six months; and for the purposes of the application of paragraph (b) of that subsection in such a case a parent or guardian of the child shall not be taken to have lawful authority to take him away'.

There are similar restrictions on removal of the child from the care of a voluntary agency, but periods with a local authority and a voluntary agency may not be aggregated.

The Houghton Committee gave as a reason for the amendment that a sudden move without preparation can be damaging to a child and have long term repercussions. It could also be said that a period of notice to the local authority before removal from care would give the authority an opportunity to consider whether any action should be taken to prevent removal from care. What the Section does is to make it an offence punishable by three months imprisonment or £400 fine or both for a child to be removed from care without local authority consent.

It would be rare for a caring authority to prosecute in such a situation, but at least it is established clearly that the authority has a right to retain the child to give an opportunity for consideration of its position.

What is not clear is what happens if a parent removes a child in defiance of the section. If the parent has no lawful authority to remove a child does that mean that the child is still in care? Even if it is, there is no means of enforcing the return of the child as Section 67 which concerns recovery of children in care under the 1948 Act applies only to children with respect to whom a resolution (see post) is in force. Nor would prosecution under S3 (8) enforce the return of the child. Possibly a resolution could be passed even though the authority does not have physical possession of the child, but grounds would still have to be established. The provisions therefore seem to be largely of persuasive value, and if the case is sufficiently serious, wardship may be the only solution.

The child that has been in care less than six months is even more vulnerable especially if the view of the law taken in B v B (Court of Appeal 1975) is correct. Dicta there suggest that if a parent makes a demand for a child to be handed over, the authority's powers are brought to an end. This raises difficulties of deciding when a child is in care. Is a simple demand sufficient or is physical removal with a stated intention of terminating care required? It is perhaps a pity that S56 has not been used as an opportunity to resolve this problem. Many problems will arise if it were to be sufficient for a parent simply to demand that a child be returned, because such demands are frequently made without real force by parents. Fraught situations can also be expected when a parent tries to remove a child at about the time that he has been in care for six months.

One effect of the Section could actually increase the dangers of abuse from the knowledgeable parent who perhaps would remove his child from care before the six month period is completed. The child may then return prematurely to a home which cannot cope with his care.

Section 2 Children Act 1948

Structure of section A number of important changes are introduced by Section 57 of the 1975 Act, which consolidates and amends previous legislation relating to the assumption by a local authority of the rights and duties of a parent in respect of a child under S2 of the Children Act 1948. Where the parent serves notice that he opposes the assumption of his rights and duties the local authority must apply to the juvenile court if it wishes to prevent the resolution assuming rights and duties from lapsing. The structure of this part of the section has been improved so that the court may confirm the resolution on any of the grounds which were open to the local authority.

At the same time the court's power has been made clearer than it was hitherto. Thus 'the court may...order that the resolution shall not lapse....
provided that the court shall not so order unless satisfied

1.   That the grounds mentioned in subsection (1) of thise section on which the local authority purported to pass the resolution were made out, and
2.   That at the time of the hearing there continued to be grounds on which a resolution under subsection (1) of this section could be founded, and
3.   That it is in the interests of the child to do so'.

The local authority therefore has a duty to prove that the specific grounds on which the resolution was passed existed at the time it was passed and that some grounds (though not necessarily the same) exist at the time of the hearing.

Technically it may be difficult to prove all this to the court's satisfaction, not least because there may be an extended period between the passing of the resolution and a hearing in court.

An example will illustrate the problems that may arise.

A local authority passes a resolution in respect of a child who has been in its care under Section 1 for eight months on the grounds that the only parent of the child suffers from a mental disorder which renders him unfit to have the care of the child. The parent objects and serves a Counter-Notice within 28 days and the local authority make a complaint within 14 days to the local juvenile court. The parent seeks legal aid and the earliest effective hearing date is six weeks after the complaint . has been issued. Delaying tactics such as seeking a further adjournment may prolong that period substantially. Thus three or four months after the resolution has been passed the local authority may have to try and prove its grounds. During that time the parent may, quite legitimately, have refused any psychiatric supervision.

How then is any evidence to be given to prove that the ground is well founded at the time of the hearing bearing in mind that the onus is on the local authority to satisfy the Court of this? Even if the parent is under psychiatric supervision and the psychiatrist is prepared to give evidence, it may be quite impossible to establish that the mental disorder still exists. By now the child may have been in care for well over a year and yet on the refusal of the Court to confirm the resolution, the parent could immediately demand the return of the child. Local authorities will be obliged to consider whether sufficient evidence exists at every stage of the proceedings and, it is suggested, will be forced to discontinue proceedings and return the child to its parents unless grounds can be established on the evidence. It may be yet another situation in which wardship will have to supplement powers under the Children Acts.

In this situation the fate of the child is clearly thrown in doubt for a lengthy period. Any well advised parent, who could even for a short time make sufficient effort to impress the Court, will be able to avoid the transfer of parental rights and duties to the local authority. This will add to the confusion which is experienced in planning for the future of the child of a grossly inadequate parent, especially in terms of the degree of access while the resolution is effective and in establishing the aims of that access. It should be noted that the court must also be satisfied that it is in the interests of the child to confirm the resolution. This is in keeping with a central principle of the Act that the first consideration in relation to a child in care is the need to safeguard and promote his welfare throughout his childhood. Local authorities will need to bear this in mind when dealing with the assumption of rights and duties.

Grounds The grounds set out in section 2(1) are:

1. That his parents are dead and he has no guardian or custodian; or
2. That a parent of his -
    (a) has abandoned him, or
    (b) suffers from some permanent disability rendering him incapable of caring for the child, or
    (c) while not falling within sub-paragraph (b) of this paragraph, suffers from a mental disorder (within the meaning of the Mental Health Act 1959) which renders him unfit to have the care of the child, or
    (d) is of such habits or mode of life as to be unfit to have the care of the child, or
    (e) has so consistently failed without reasonable cause to discharge the obligations of a parent as to be unfit to have the care of the child, or
3. That a resolution under paragraph (2) of this subsection is in force in relation to one parent of the child who is, or is likely to become, a member of the household comprising the child and his other parent; or
4. That throughout the three years preceding the passing of resolution the child has been in the care of a local authority under the foregoing section, or partly in the care of a local authority and partly in the care of a voluntary organisation.

The provisions in (3) and (4) are new. Since a reolution assuming a parent's rights and duties is passed in respect of one parent, it has been possible for the other parent, if no grounds exist in respect of him to demand that he be allowed to remove the child from care. The new clause may improve the situation where for example the local authority can show that a parent is likely to return with the child to the parent in respect of whom a resolution has already been passed. Again insufficient evidence may prove to be a stumbling block.

The local authority may now pass a resolution on the grounds that the child has been in care continuously for three years, which period may be partly with a voluntary agency, provided the child is in care under Section 1 of the 1948 Act at the time the resolution is passed. It is again necessary to prove that the resolution is in the interests of the child. One way in which this might be challenged is by looking at how the local authority has conducted its care. Hopefully, this will encourage local authorities to ensure that the welfare of the child is their first consideration and that regular reviews are maintained. In view of the difficulties which may be experienced with other grounds and the tendency for children to languish in voluntary care for years it may perhaps be anticipated that more will be protected by this means against removal by parents who had long since lost any real interest in the child's welfare.

Section 58 which amends section 4 of the 1948 Act should be noted because it introduces a general right of appeal to the High Court in cases concerning the assumption of parental rights and duties. The problem of delay in ascertaining what is in the child's interests will again arise. A close look will have to be taken at the allocation of court time to these matters.

Separate representation of child and parent

In proceedings under Section 1 of the Children and Young Persons Act 1969 (care proceedings) the child is the defendant to the proceedings and normally represented by his parent or guardians. The case develops between local authority and parent without either party necessarily taking up the child's position.

Section 64 introduces as an amendment to Section 32 of the 1969 Act appointment of a guardian *ad litem* to act on behalf of the child. For the time being the provisions relate only to unopposed applications to discharge supervision or care orders. Phased implementation is necessary because 'it will place extra demands on local authority resources and particularly on experienced social workers required for this work'. (DHSS Circular (75) 21)

The very small number of cases to which the provisions will initially apply will also give an opportunity to see how the procedures will work in practice. It does not seem likely that the resources will be available for full implementation for some considerable time.

The procedure in an unopposed application requires the Court to order that no parent or guardian shall be treated as representing the child or otherwise authorised to act on his behalf, unless satisfied that to do so is not necessary for safeguarding the interests of the child. Having made that order, the Court then has a further duty to appoint a guardian *ad litem* unless satisfied that to do so is not necessary for safeguarding the interests of the child. This will provide some protection against a local authority applying to discharge its statutory duties prematurely, or failing to oppose an application by a parent on behalf of a child, but cannot of course prevent the authority returning the child home under the Care Order. It is the vehicle by which the second opinion in care cases recommended by the Maria Colwell report may be obtained. Doubtless there will be minor difficulties which will hopefully be ironed out after experience of the workings, but two particular areas may provide sources of difficulty. Unless we are very careful these cases will be confused and inadequately dealt with. Perhaps one of the worst forms of child abuse would be created by the supposedly responsible adults surrounding the child being in a state of confusion and anger and thereby failing to create any secure basis for the child's development. Awareness of the difficulties may in some degree reduce the tensions which will arise.

Appointment and role of the guardian ad litem The guardian *ad litem* will be appointed by the Juvenile Court from a panel of nominated people most of whom will b drawn from local authorities or the probation service. When appointed the guardian will investigate the case, will consider whether the application for revocation should succeed and may conduct the case for the child.

The basis of the appointment is investigation and this inevitably includes investigation of the handling of the case by the local authority. Since the guardian cannot be from the authority involved in the case, adjacent authorities are most likely to provide a suitable person. There is some concern at the prospect of calling upon a social worker to question the work of a colleague in an adjacent authority. Considerable time will be consumed in some areas purely in travelling, and remembering also the seniority that will be essential to the proper execution of the duties it is important to ensure that adequate allowances are made both temporal and financial.

The local authority will be responsible for the professional competence of the guardian but the guardian will be answerable to the court and as such an independent person. The duties will be onerous and individuals will require support in carrying them out. Ideally panels functioning independently and providing internal support systems might have been the best solution but the financial implications would be too serious at the present time.

Legal advice and representation create further problems. It is anticipated that if there are legal difficulties, the guardian would instruct a solicitor on behalf of the child. If the child was old enough, the solicitor would then be obliged to take the child's view of the matter. The rules also envisage a situation where the guardian conducts the case on behalf of an infant not legally represented, unless he otherwise requests. The guardian might then need advice on the law before the case. DHSS Circular LAC (76) 20 suggestes that this support should come from the local authority, but it is questionable how valuable or accessible such advice would be in these circumstances.

Procedural difficulties will also need to be resolved. If the guardian is of the opinion that an application for revocation made on behalf of the child should fail, he must presumably seek to withdraw the application. Some provision should be made to ensure that the court can only agree to withdrawal after hearing evidence on which the parties have had an opportunity to cross-examine. Finally the rules specify that the Court can only receive any written report the guardian might wish to make 'after the applicant's case has been proved'. The initial report of the guardian must therefore be as evidence on oath and subject to the normal rules of evidence which will hamper the reporting role of the guardian. The effect of the provision is that the full report of the guardian will only become available to the court when they are considering whether to make a supervision order in place of a care order. It is doubtful whether a guardian will bother to write a report solely for that purpose, having given oral evidence on the question of revocation of the care order.

Status of parents in proceedings If the Court makes an Order that the parent shall not represent the child, the question then arises what part parents can play in the proceedings. Hitherto they have been able to appear before the Court 'acting on behalf of the child'.

The amended Court rules for care proceedings now entitle the parent or guardian:
1. To meet any allegations made against him in the course of the proceedings by calling evidence or otherwise: and
2. Where the Court has made an Order under Section 32A of the 1969 Act, to make representations to the Court after the close of the case for the applicant and the case for the respondent. Clearly many parents, and many of their advisers, are going to feel resentful that they cannot participate fully in the proceedings. Within the terms of these provisions they will be unable to call evidence as to why the Order should be discharged. This situation can only be adequately resolved by making the parents party to the proceedings.

Conclusion

Although there will be difficulties with the new legislation, it must be better to be optimistic that the provisions referred to will form the basis for continuing improvement in child protection.

The following suggestions are made for early detailed considerations of the workings in practice of the 1975 Act.

1.   When should a child be considered discharged from care?
2.   How far do the Children's Acts as now amended provide grounds by which satisfactory protection for the child can be achieved?
3.   The provisions for separate representation of the child must be closely supervised and researched and quickly amended if necessary, insofar as they relate both to the functions of the guardian *ad litem* and to the part that may be played in the proceedings by the parents.

Child abuse : the implications for lawyers

There are a number of reasons why child abuse has become a matter of concern for lawyers as much as for other professions in the past few years. The Children and Young Persons Act 1969 required social workers to participate more with the courts than before when they were geared to preventive work and voluntary care. Almost simultaneously with its implementation the social services departments underwent reorganisation so that those experienced as children's officers also undertook work with geriatrics and mental health and similarly officers working in those fields became involved with child care. Inevitably the professional experience and knowledge of child care became diffused.

The Maria Colwell inquiry (DHSS 1974) also produce a greater awareness of the problems of child abuse and examination of the relevant legislation. Since court proceedings and the interpretation of various complex acts are sometimes necessary for the resolution of these problems, it is natural that legal assistance should be sought to meet the difficulties.

Lawyers had not previously been noted for their involvement in such matters, but these events did coincide with increased interest in welfare law. Children's rights were also receiving greater emphasis and the spread of legal aid enables those rights to be protected. Since child protection cases are dealt with in a court setting and require proof by evidence, it is desirable that they should be presented by an advocate familiar with this arena. It is equally desirable that early advice on problems should be sought and that the evidence necessary to support or oppose a case should be collected by a person who knows what he is looking for and is accustomed to interviewing witnesses. Although improvements are being made, these are areas in which lawyers have so far largely failed to provide an adequate service. There are insufficient people familiar with the legislation or the ethos of cases in which children are involved.

It can be seen that the lawyer has a place in a multi-disciplinary team dealing with abuse. He can advise on problems presented by abusing families; he can advise at case conferences; he can prepare and present cases where court proceedings are necessary; and incidentally he should bring to the team an objectivity which workers closely involved with a family may have difficulty in maintaining.

However to be helpful to the team he must have a reasonable practical knowledge of the legal problems together with an understanding of the attitudes and roles of the other participating professionals. Hopefully he will also be able to develop the understanding of his own role and discipline by the other professionals. His contribution should be positive by providing the best legal solutions, but too often it is negative because he is only called in when there is a bitter fight in court complicated by earlier decisions taken without regard for legal difficulties.

With our present organisation the lawyer in a child abuse team will be working in local government, usually inexperienced, and with no formal legal education in the subject. There are a few postgraduate courses which contain some welfare law but it is most unlikely that a local government lawyer will have studied on any of them. He will therefore be learning while advising his colleagues, assuming that he is willing and able to devote sufficient time to acquiring the knowledge and experience. Similar problems exist for lawyers working on their own account and representing children or their parents. The juvenile court is too frequently a place where young and inexperienced advocates learn their skills.

Overall there are too few lawyers in the field and much could be done to remedy this through education both before qualification and in practice. Qualifying exams could include at least one subject relating to welfare law, and psychology would be useful in this and incidentally in many other matters with which lawyers get involved.

Post qualification training should be expanded and the possibilities of inter-disciplinary study be more widely explored. Understanding and being understood by colleagues and providing a suitable remedy for their problem must be as important to the lawyer as presenting a case in court, in the matter of child abuse as in any other. A good method of attaining this is to set up mock discussions and mock hearings so that difficulties are sorted out before the real event.

The lawyer will inevitably play an increasingly important role in child abuse as the emphasis on children's rights develops. It is incumbent on all concerned to ensure that it is a positive and creative role.

Discussion

A two way process of mutual education between lawyers and professionals is still needed and has been high-lighted by the increasing demands for child abuse decisions. Ignorance of child legislation is not all on the side of the professionals. The group hopes that the new Children Act 1975 will ease certain situations, in particular by the use of Section 12, subsection 2(f)2 and subsection 5. This enables their consent to adoption to be dispensed with in the case of parents deemed impossible to rehabilitate. The appointment and the functioning of guardians *ad litem* will be watched with critical interest. If the guardian *ad litem* is to be called upon to conduct the child's case in court he will need special instruction in carrying out what will be, for him or her, a new duty. The group expressed unease about the adequacy of his powers of investigation.

The group was interested in the possible extension of the use of Wardship pro-ceedings and invited Judge Graham Hall to prepare a paper which she has most kindly done (see Ch.24) Comment on variations in procedure between juvenile courts, especially about admissibility of evidence, led to a hope that a standard code of practice might be introduced and a basic instruction manual produced by a lawyer for the other professionals.

The hope was also expressed that care proceedings would be heard in time in County Family Courts. Meanwhile in-service training in family problems concerning children is needed, and some appointments might be created where family and child development can be learned. Lawyers working in local authorities should be closely involved in child abuse work.

Legal problems, it was agreed, go much further than decisions about court orders.

26. Statutory removal of a newborn baby

ANTHONY C. FAIRBURN

Summary

Four families are contrasted:
A. - (1969) First child manslaughter / 4th - late removal.
B. - (1975) Child abuse / 7th - removed at birth.
C. - (1975) Gross neglect / 2nd - removed at birth.
D. - (1976) Psychopathic couple / 1st - not removed yet.
Three aspects are discussed:
1.   The professionals' changing credibility,
2.   The 'immediate-rather-than-later' argument,
3.   Wide preparatory briefing, and the hospital link-job.
        Last year in Bath we removed two babies at birth and from this limited experience
we learned a great deal about close working and communication. As background, we
had for four years been operating a tight, over inclusive child-abuse monitoring scheme
in this small city (Population 90,000), and had helpted prepare the way with some in-
service training seminars with the Bath magistrates, discussing Child Care principles
and professional concepts.

Family A
Family A had moved to Bath from another city in 1967 with two small children while
the neurotic and immature step-father was under probation for manslaughter of the
first child (proven and admitted multiple violence, including intracranial haemorrhages).
        Mrs A cooperated closely in the fieldwork monitoring (health visitor and social
worker) and an automatic cross-check every month continued until her fourth pregnancy - to be their first natural child, very much a wanted baby.
        In 1969 it was considered in good faith by all of us that no case could be made
for a removal at birth, but preparations were made to try to get the mother to remain
for an extra week in hospital after delivery, so that an urgent interim care order could,
if necessary, be made to take all three children into protective custody, the strain of
a new baby being the trigger, in our view, for breakdown. The trouble was that the
criteria thought acceptable at that time were that things had to be seen to be going
wrong, whereas in the event we had to report quite honestly that Mrs A started
'bonding' closely and normally to the newborn child, despite her severe neuroticism
and shallow, deprived personality.

It took many months of care crises and the invocation of the Children and Young Persons' Act (violence was avoided), arguing against parental competence '... without which he would not fulfil his full emotional and psychological potential', to achieve long-term care for this fourth child. The instability and difficulties of the fostering and access arrangements undoubtedly contributed to his developmental delay, as also to the mother's extra problem in demonstrating her competence. At the subsequent long drawn-out legal proceedings (and an appeal which failed but was borderline), much was made of this factor.

One encouraging note in our dealings with this sad and bereft couple is that they still accept the social worker's support, and recently consulted the Department about whether a further pregnancy would simply result in a fifth child being removed at birth. This has yet to be worked out with them, but at least a democratic element is visible.

Family B
Family B was already in our close monitoring scheme from 1970. Two years later, by means of obsessional recording (of 'clusters' of bruises, mostly minor) it had proved possible to take the fourth, fifth and sixth children into long-term foster care, but we knew that, being childless again, they keenly wanted (and intended) to conceive a seventh. So, quite late in the pregnancy, in the summer of 1975, the Area Social Services Officer and his committee made the tough decision to attempt removal-at-birth. Paediatric and local authority medical officer evidence on the previous injuries had been solid (first child serious and repeated, second a cot death, fourth to sixth minor but repeated).

For this to be possible for the seventh child, convincing evidence on child-care principles and parental incompetence would have to be equally solid. Prior consult-ations with the local authority's solicitor had to contain an assurance that factual and convincing evidence of Mrs B's serious lack of mothering skills could be presented, with the firm opinion that she would not learn or progress further to become an able mother. The father's aggressiveness and restrictively authoritarian attitudes were clearly known.

To avoid forewarning the parents, who would simply have disappeared to have the baby elsewhere, and in case the intention leaked out via hospital employees who might know the family, policy remained 'top secret'. Only the two consultants and their senior administrative nursing officers (midwifery and paediatrics) could be briefed. The newborn baby would have to travel immediately across the city to the other unit, a plan disliked by all. Precautions against its discovery and removal by the father, as well as possible aggression by him to maternity or paediatric nurses, had to be planned for, as had Press headlines.

Mrs B's mental state after losing this baby, her need for sedation and comfort, return to her husband early and good general practitioner support had to be carefully worked out.

The constraints involved in having so little time to plan and in the need for extreme confidentiality, and ignorance of when labour would start, made for possible loopholes.

In the event all went smoothly, but everyone was sad to see that a final nail was unintentionally hammered into this wretched and desperate couple when the local press reported their later eviction from their home, referring also to the removal of all their children.

Miss C

In Miss C's case, we were more concerned that suicide could result from our actions.

Aged 19 and dull (ESN), she lived resentfully with her parents in a muddy smallholding in deepest Wiltshire. Of her eight brothers and sisters, the first four had been ill-treated and/or neglected, and the last four had produced major problems requiring intervention by many agencies.

Her own mother was shallow, specious and egotistical, lived erratically and, what might have been crucial to the case, had demonstrated her own lack of parenting qualities only too clearly. Miss C had already neglected and twice abandoned (in a farm lane) her first baby and had twice changed her mind about adoption. By then 13 months old and with long-term foster parents, he had become withdrawn and disturbed. This precedent seemed to justify a care order on a preventive basis, although it would need all the ground-work to be done in case of later appeal. Her mothering knowledge at the time needed recording in detail, for she might claim that she had learned new skills and matured by 19, and would do better with a second child. One had also to establish that the baby's maternal grandmother could not offer adequate substitute mothering, as the couple would obviously have to depend on the parental home for a long time yet. None of this proved in fact to have been necessary (though it had to be done well) for there was no legal challenge to the action.

The greatest practical need was clearly going to be for therapy, as Miss C had made two suicide attempts and still had an immature, histrionic side to her. The obstetric registrar had a worrying weekend during the puerperium and needed frequent support in dealing with a deeply grieving and distressed mother, who pocketed all the medication given to relieve her after-pains and her sleeplessness, and stood out on the fire-escape. It was a difficult decision to advise that she should stay with the staff whom she knew and liked, and not go over to the psychiatric ward for her own safety. Fortunately she decided to keep herself intact for her daughter's return, and our main job was to get some surprisingly reluctant transport out from a distant country town so that she could return to grieve effectively with her mother's support.

Family D

Lastly come the D's who had met in Rampton. The young man is a voluble, unstable, deprived, and inadequate psychopath, with a low irritability threshold. His younger, duller wife is equally deprived. Neither has ever made an enduring relationship with any adult, each achieved temporary stability only in institutional settings, and the three-year marriage has taken them over several counties, moved on and rejected by landlords. Their personal relationship is like that of two hunted children, immaturely interdependent.

Mrs. D. aged 22, obese and insecure, had a low threshold for violence, absconded as a teenager, had *no* mothering skills and little patience. This third pregnancy, the only one not aborted, was intended, and had set off intense nest-building and over-acquisition of baby gear.

At the large and senior case-conference before the birth, the legal advice was that action for removal could only be justified after the care of an actual baby had broken down, even though nearly everybody agreed that this couple could not raise a child. The 'preventive removal' case put forward had the weakness that it depended on opinions only, and these, however expert, were not regarded as strong enough.

As had been felt possible, strong 'bonding' occurred during the puerperium, and immediate baby-care skills were being learned fast. Daily visiting by a 'key worker', who is getting regular support, and by the special problem-families health visitor, is continuing.

The young couple know the meaning of this intensive scrutiny and are able to discuss it with us. Mr D has not yet built it into his repertoire of mildly paranoid thinking: '... everybody-turns-against-us-sooner-or-later'.

Commentary

Carrying conviction with the magistrates
Apart from the earlier help with child-care seminars, two things may have influenced our credibility with our Juvenile Court colleagues:
1. Over ten years, whenever citing maternal incompetence as a reason for care proceedings, we gave the parents credit, when possible, for trying to cope within their limits. Our magistrates are usually anguished at having to remove a child or to block the return of children to a pleading mother, whose solicitor may well suggest that the services 'had it in for them' all along, a suggestion that must be firmly countered.
2. Two years ago, in a narrowly borderline decision, strong medical evidence had helped persuade them to disallow the return of a ten year old girl to live with her incestuous father again. Three weeks later, in the course of an agreed Sunday afternoon access visit to the home, with the wife chaperoning, the father raped his daughter on the kitchen table, his wife assisting in removing her pants.

The need for prior preparation of an ample case, to be made available to the local authority's solicitor in time for case-conference decisions, has proved its worth. So also has the solicitor's professional confidence and experience in handling child care cases.

Presenting an expert opinion on parental incompetence carries conviction only after a lot of obsessional work, recording replies and opinions on child-rearing, noting actual mother/father-and-child interactions, and being able to give examples of progress as well as the lack of it. Cross-examination in front of parents, who may well have put their trust in oneself, can involve tricky interpretations, taking account of their morale and feelings. We are, as Carolyn Okell Jones has said elsewhere, coming to think of this court experience as an extension of our management and guidance of the parents for the future.

The removal-at-birth argument
It is necessary here to know whether the mother went through the 'bonding' process with her previous child. We knew that Mrs B and Miss C had done so quickly and

easily, for each liked very small babies, although they could not sustain the relationship beyond this. Documenting 'bonding' is best done at the time, questioning maternity staff who were on the postnatal wards at various shifts, and if possible observing the mother reacting to her baby after the first day or so. She will almost certainly also be able to give pretty clear instances of this intense and vivid process if it did in fact happen.

The cruelty, however, short-lived, of removal-at-birth has to be set against the much greater and lasting bereavement effect on a mother who has been relating to her child for weeks or months.

The other half of the argument is necessarily theoretical, in spelling out the child's need for a consistent, long-term mother ('caretaker') figure and the avoidance of broken fosterings from the earliest weeks. Professional opinion is, as a result of the new research into babies' perception, moving back to the concept of early traumatic distruption again, while the stronger and generally accepted arguments against removal of a child from six months onwards still stand.

Magistrates standing by to grant an emergency interim care order at an hour's notice may well ask for a personal briefing beforehand, when these two aspects can be presented to relieve their minds.

The health and social services link

A hospital-based consultant who knows the senior obstetric and paediatric staff is really the best person to see this through. The obstetric consultant, having given full permission, is then unlikely to be on the spot but will help with interpretation of the mother's ante-natal state and with the phenomenon I call the 'shifting EDD' (estimated date of delivery).

The briefing of senior nursing colleagues, who also have day and night shifts to allow for, and obtaining their agreement to procedures, has to be water-tight. The ASSO is of course a stranger to them and it helps very much if he has had a chance to talk direct to them remembering that they know little about the background to the decision. The link across to the other nursery has to be made, and phone numbers left with crucial people, so that they will have immediate access in the night and at weekends. Anxiety will be felt at several points, requiring immediate support, with sometimes a decision to be modified, about, for instance the timing and management of the bereft mother's return to her spouse or parents. This requires the general practitioner's knowledge.

The distasteful thought: 'Has 1984 now arrived?' is hanging like a thought-balloon over everyone's heads, and this requires bringing out, with careful, supportive discussion.

Discussion

Fairburn's paper was given and discussed at Farnham in its logical place, namely after the papers concerned with the care of the pregnant woman and of the mother and her newborn baby (Ch. 11 and 12). The paper has been relegated to its present position at the end, chiefly because some members of the group felt that what he was describing was indefensible, that the paper should not have been given and that it should be omitted from the book altogether. When it is considered and discussed openly, as the author legitimately requests, the paper and the philosophy behind its subject matter bring into dramatic focus some important ideas, not to mention some deep feelings, about the whole subject of child abuse.

A woman, known to be violent, to have damaged earlier children to have been unable to provide a safe environment so that at least one of them has died and others have been removed from her care, becomes pregnant once more. Nothing that she can do can rehabilitate her and restore our confidence except caring successfully for this latest baby. Should she be given this chance or is this too dangerous for the baby and indeed for her herself?

If the answer is no, and the baby must be removed, here are the data for Fairburn's equation. All of us have sometimes faced this problem. To 'creep up on the mother', as described, may be considered necessary, for otherwise she may simply disappear to a hospital which knows her not. Fairburn claimed that the chief requirements were immense courage and superb organisation on the part of all concerned. Others felt that knowledge was still lacking over some vital matters and that, without this knowledge, to remove a baby at birth can never be justified.

What we are trying to avoid on behalf of the baby, apart from physical damage, is the emotional damage that we believe to be done when a young baby is left in a loveless limbo. What we do not know is whether biologically a baby needs to have an immediate opportunity for bonding. If denied this opportunity, is the bonding process irreparably damaged and if so, is that damage greater than the timely formation of the bond with the mother which is then soon broken? And for the mother, is she more or less likely to wish to be pregnant again and to have another baby if she has never seen and handled the baby of whose presence in her womb she has been for long aware?

The only ways to counter the compulsion to have a baby felt by many abusing mothers are to resolve the underlying basic psychological difficulties or to legalise obligatory sterilisation. The latter practice would contain too many dangers.

The majority opinon was that the mother should handle her baby while in the maternity department, but that a care order should be sought so that the baby would not go home. A period in residential care for mother and baby might sometimes be suitable, but only under the closest supervision.

PART 5

Proposals and resolutions

27. The Tunbridge Wells Resolutions reviewed

The original point of departure for the Study Group was the management of families in which there had been physical injury known to be or suspected of being non-accidental. The group's main concern, apart from the improvement of diagnosis and of the identification of abusing families, was with techniques for ensuring the maximum support for families, caught up in the problems of non-accidental injury to their own children, so as to limit or to prevent further harm both physical and emotional. The first ten resolutions therefore dealt with prevention only in relation to repetition of the injury and to countering the effects of deprivation. This does not mean that the Study Group failed to recognise the supreme importance of preventing the abuse in the first place. Indeed discussion of prevention and its necessary pre-requisite, prediction, was left explicitly for a future meeting.

One of the tasks was to look again at the original resolutions to determine whether they need modification in the light of the experience of the last three years. These sixteen resolutions were printed and circulated by the DHSS as 'Report and Resolutions' of the Tunbridge Wells Study Group' (1973). They were not reprinted in 'Concerning Child Abuse'. Fourteen are reproduced here. Two (O and P), of internal interest only, are omitted.

Resolution A
That for children damaged by non-accidental injury or when this is suspected, immediate hospital admission of the child is the essential first step.

This resolution had two purposes, the establishment of a diagnosis following careful and complete screening of the child and the family, and the protection of the child from further injury. For the former purpose an immediate hospital referral for examination and consultation is the essential first step. The group now believes that admission into the hospital may not always be absolutely necessary. The latter purpose, protection, can be ensured in other ways, perhaps by removing the child from the parents to previously known foster parents or even rarely by leaving the child at home with suitable help for the family. The possibilities should be explored for admitting mother and child to avoid interference with bonding but with the most careful supervision.

Since the meeting in 1973, the Study Group, while in no way regarding as less important the gross physical effects, the stunting of bodily growth or a coeliac-like syndrome or, indeed, the physical injuries, has paid greater attention to the emotional stress resulting from cruelty, neglect, rejection and deprivation.

Resolution B
That close links should always be established between the hospital children's department and the accident and emergency department.

A number of papers have been published which show beyond doubt that the possibility of abuse should be borne in mind whenever there appears to be an accidental happening to a young child. Drowning, poisoning, sudden infant death (cot-death) as well as burns and scalds must all be brought within the range of possible abuse in order that the same kind of enquiry is made into all aspects of family life as is now made when non-accidental injury is suspected on account of fractures and bruises.

Resolution C
That health visitors should be informed directly of all young children involved in accidents, including poisoning (particularly those under the age of 2 years) so that they may visit the home. The general practitioner should always be informed.

This plan is being followed in many general practices for all childhood accidents. The group stresses the special importance of studying all accidents to children of 3 years old and less. The information should come from accident and emergency departments to the general practitioner and so to the health visitor. When there is no general practitioner or when he has no attached health visitor, the information should be passed to the Area Nursing Officer (Child Health).

Resolution D
That the Social Service Department should be informed immediately whenever there is suspicion of non-accidental injury.

Resolution E
That when non-accidental injury is suspected or known to have occurred, the NSPCC, the RSSPCC, or other voluntary Society, when already concerned, should continue to be involved in management and included in all professional discussions.

These two resolutions are supported and no comment is offered.

Resolution F
That the Police should be involved in the early discussion of these cases even when there is only a suspicion of non-accidental injury. The Study Group is aware that at present this involvement is often inhibited by fear of the effects on the family of some police investigations and therefore agrees that approaches be made to the Home Office, the DHSS and the Association of Chief Police Officers to explore the ways of promoting increasing mutual understanding between the police and the other professions concerned.

The reference to the Association of Chief Police Officers is out of place.

There are still problems of co-operation and collaboration between the Police and the other professions involved in the management of child abuse. The Home Office and the DHSS have circulated a memorandum*which is designed to ease this situation. Nevertheless whatever the guide lines, the only satisfactory solution in areas, where mutual suspicion does still exist, is the acceptance of a common policy of early notification and honest communication. The nettle has to be grasped. The wider recognition of the existence of child abuse has increased the proportion of families under suspicion in relation to those where the child has been subjected to gross physical abuse. But deprived and neglected children have as much right to the protection of the law as those criminally assaulted, and the group stands, hopefully, by Resolution F.

Resolution G

That representatives in the Study Group of each of the parties likely to be involved with a family, while reserving their professional rights, strongly deprecate unilateral action. When such action seems necessary, all the other parties involved expect to know what action is being taken and the reasons for it so that mutual trust and confidence can be preserved.

The Study Group has always recognised that professions with statutory duties and responsibilities have the right to take unilateral action. What has been and remains their hope is that consensus views will be reached or, if not, then the party taking unilateral action will feel a responsibility towards the other professionals for explaining carefully the view taken. The question of consensus is discussed on page 143. Although attention is often focused on unilateral police action, it is as well to remember that strong differences of opinion may and do exist between the other professionals.

Resolution H

That the Study Group strongly supports the establishment throughout the United Kingdom of the case conferences and the area review committees as suggested by the DHSS (ref CMOs letter 10/72, with enclosure 'analysis' of reports submitted by medical officers of health and children's officers) but recommends that the functions of these bodies be more clearly stated and that their composition be modified.

Resolution I

That review committees should be set up at Area Health Authority and Local Authority level and should hold quarterly meetings. That case conferences should supervise the management of families involved and that review committees and case conferences should have the functions and the composition set out in detail in paragraph 24 and 14 and 15 respectively of the Report and Resolutions.

---

* Joint DHSS/Home Office Circular (LASSL(76)26,HC(76)50) Home Office Circular 179/76 of 18 November 1976 - Non-Accidental Injury to Children: the Police and Case Conferences.

These two resolutions (H and I) recorded the Study Group's strong support for the case conferences and area review committees that had been suggested by the DHSS and asked for clear statements of composition and functions. The Group's present views were aired in the lengthy and detailed interchanges which followed the papers printed in Chapter 19, 21 and 22 and are summarised in the discussion on pages 6. See also Resolution 1, p. 153-4. 192.

Resolution J
That specialised groups are also needed, such as those now being established by the NSPCC, to act as the focus for consultation, research and training as well as to provide treatment facilities in their immediate area.

Fortunately the NSPCC has continued its work and is able to provide valuable information for all those who are concerned with child abuse. In addition to the National Advisory Centre (originally the Battered Child Research Department, established nine years ago) there are seven NSPCC Special Units, the details of which are printed as Appendix IV.

There is need also for other specialised workers, such as are already found in some local authorities

Resolution K
That a direct approach be made to the Secretary of the Criminal Law Revision Committee about the law and about legal procedure in cases of non-accidental trauma to children

The group is not at present pressing for any changes in the law.

Resolution L
That the Casualty Surgeons Association be asked to make, with the assistance of the DHSS, a census by age groups and diagnosis of all children treated in accident and emergency departments.

Unfortunately no progress has been possible (but see Resolution 2, p.196)

Resolution M
That a small working party be set up to collect information on reporting, registering and notification in the United Kingdom and in other countries and to make a report on advantages, difficulties and disadvantages.

No decision has been reached and no further views are recorded on the subject of reporting, registering and notification.

Resolution N
That since child abuse is reported to be associated in a sizeable proportion with low birth-weight, representation be made to paediatricians, obstetricians, midwives, nurses, health visitors and social workers about methods which can promote very early intimate mother-child interaction, and about the need for informed follow-up.

This resolution is concerned with further studies of mother/child interaction in maternity departments. Many observations have been made since 1973 which have a bearing on bonding between mother and child, and this subject forms a basis for much work on prediction as well as on prevention. During the same period the many changes in attitude in maternity units have been followed by changes in practice, all tending towards a more sympathetic and understanding approach. The group gives so much importance to the subject that a new resolution (Resolution, 3, p.196) is proposed.

28. Some fresh proposals

During the meeting as well as the set resolutions that follow in Chapter 29, some proposals were made, which received general support. They included much detail and were rather too complex for expression in the form of resolutions. Their appearance in this separate chapter means neither that they had less support nor that they are considered less important. Indeed they may prove to be of greater practical use than the broader matters embodied in the resolutions.

The social worker

The responsibilities of social workers extend from their contributions to diagnosis through the provision of social reports and through all stages of decision-making and management to the eventual evaluation of the success of the treatment plan. The group's attention was drawn by Sally Beer to their special training needs and by Carolyn Okell Jones to some of the management and evaluation problems. Throughout ran the theme of the social workers' own dependence on support from colleagues and on their need for protection from being made scapegoats when things go wrong.

The following recommendations, made by Sally Beer (see also Ch. 16 pp. 117-120) were supported by the group.

All teaching must include experiential methods.

1. Basic courses for professional qualifications should include:
    a) greater concentration on normal child development leading up to identification of the abnormal;
    b) review of teaching methods including
        i) placements, giving contact with children
        ii) case studies following a child through its first year of life;
        iii) joint training sessions for social workers, nursery nurses, health visitors and others for whom a knowledge of the needs of growing children is essential;
    e) information about what resources are available and what they can achieve with the child who has difficulties, for example, specialist units, play therapy etc.
2. Post-qualification courses for workers who, after a minimum of two years experience, should have consolidated the basic training. They should be given the opportunity to:
    a) develop further ability to communicate with children;

b)   understand and recognise special situations likely to stress children, for example on:

    i)   reception into care,

    ii)   admission to hospital,

    iii)   separation from parents,

    iv)   and on receiving divided care from different caretakers, and professional workers;

c)   improve therapeutic skills in working with children with specific problems.

Carolyn Okell Jones stressed the importance of 2(a) which would come best through experience of working directly with children.

Carolyn Okell Jones' recommendations, which also met with general support, centred round the needs of abused children and their siblings in their own right. One member of a reviewing case conference should be designated advocate for the child. Any review of a child's progress should include not only the question of re-injury, but also assessment of development and of emotional state. The numbers of both day and residential centres for multi-faceted family treatment and for research, with the Park Hospital for Children, Oxford, as one excellent model, must be increased She urged the need for a research project on the relative merits of different kinds of protective placements in comparison with the home environment. The use of foster placements as a long-term therapeutic experience for abused children rather than for temporary safeguard should be explored, and foster parents, who should be paid for their services, should form part of the management team.

We must never lose sight of the importance of realising and studying the consequences of professional intervention.

The health visitor

The discussions on Health Visitors revealed a general anxiety that since the change-over from working in a geographical area to attachment to general practice, those families who are not registered with a general practitioner and who may be the most in need of the health visitor service may be 'lost'. A possible solution, proposed in the Court Report, would follow the territorial planning of child health work for the proposed Child Health Visitor and a return to a geographical responsibility in addition to her general practice attachment. The implications of this proposal were, of course, not discussed at Farnham. Meanwhile Resolution 4 (p.196) aims to diminish the risk of losing sight of vulnerable families, since there must be few pregnant women now who do not reveal their identity, at some stage, at booking clinics.

The 'change of address' mobility of abusing families is recognised as a further cause of anxiety. Jean Davies' suggestion that Area Health Authorities should be notified of any changes of address of families applying for the family allowance, was not supported by the Group. Well-intentioned and efficient as it might be, such notification smacked of infringement of liberty.

The midwife

The emphasis of the meeting being on prediction and prevention, the midwife could, it was felt, make an extremely important contribution to both. What she could do by trained observation in the maternity department is described by Pamela Howat in Chapter 3 and forms an important part of the lessons of Henry Kempe's film (see Ch. 9). She had a unique opportunity to give preventive support to vulnerable mothers in the perinatal period.

That she could play an earlier part was generally agreed and Dr Stone's suggestion was strongly supported that some ante-natal examinations should be carried out by Community Midwives in the home (see Resolution 5, p.196). The advantages are spelled out in Chapter 14 on page 109. Observations on the family at home during these visits should aid prediction. The midwife could contact the health visitor so that together they could give extra support during the pregnancy to families considered vulnerable.

The training of midwives should include experience of taking group discussions. This skill would increase their ability to help not only mothers liable to abuse their children but also normal mothers.

The general practitioner

After the publication of the Report and Resolutions of the Tunbridge Wells Study Group in 1973, a few general practitioners voiced the complaint that they had not been represented in the group. The reason was plain enough. The organisers did not know of a general practitioner who was in a position to read a paper on the subject. Since then, many general practitioners have become involved.

The two present at Farnham took their full share in the discussions and made practical proposals for increasing the numbers of family doctors so involved as well as suggesting how they would help. Dr Stone particularly made useful proposals about recruiting the interest of the others. Dr Beswick describes in Chapter 13 how a primary health care team can assist under the present arrangements in prediction and prevention (see p.102-105). The practical difficulty remains of finding time to attend case conferences, and Ray Castle has made some suggestions which could avoid or overcome the resulting difficulties (see p.192).

While the accent is on helping the child, Beswick's proposals of necessity include help for the whole family (see p.102). It is the general practitioner's knowlege of the family as a unit that could provide one of the most useful contributions towards the decisions of case conferences.

The family oriented general practitioner can learn by organised studies of family life, the difficulties of adjusting to its needs by those with distorted personalities, its pathology and especially its psychopathology. This knowledge could be of the greatest possible value in prediction and prevention of child abuse.

Meanwhile Dr Stone, with his heartfelt cry, 'Remember the general practitioner', made six proposals all of which met with the support of the Study Group:

1. Remember the general practitioner. Look for every opportunity to include him in. This is a message for all trainers in this field and should be included in any manual for trainers.
2. Remind clinical tutors to include the subject in their syllabuses at least once every two years. The responsibility for this reminder must rest somewhere, perhaps with the Advisory Centre for the Battered Child.

3.   Remind those responsible for courses always to think of applying for S.63 approval, and of circularising the general practitioners, which is best done through their local Family Practitioner Committees. This should also be part of any manual for trainers.

4.   Press for changes in S.63. Multi-disciplinary courses organised not necessarily by doctors should be readily eligible for full recognition. This Study Group would be one of many bodies which could approach the DHSS.

5.   Senior social workers should explore the idea of discharge summaries to be sent to general practitioners.

6.   Encourage community midwives to carry out some ante-natal examinations in the home (see Resolution 4 and 5, p.196).

The obstetrician

The group welcomed Dr Anderson as a harbinger of a future interest by obstetricians who have a real part to play in the prevention of child abuse. Ideas and methods are presented in detail in Chapters 11 and 12 and in the report of the discussions that followed. Without the active support of obstetricians, theory will not be translated into practice in the matter of the importance now attached to bonding or to early contact, physical and visual, between mother and baby, and to the mother's need for security, reassurance, confidence and sympathetic understanding.

If much of the ante-natal supervision can be delegated to the community midwives, as proposed in Resolution 5 (see p.196), the obstetrician will have more time to discuss problems with mothers identified as vulnerable.

The Royal College of Obstetricians and Gynaecologists will, it is hoped, join with the Central Midwives Board and the British Paediatric Association in fulfilling Resolution 3 (see p.196). The study group believes that only good could result should the College, perhaps through its President, bring the subject of child abuse to the special notice of its Fellows, Members and Diplomates.

The paediatrician

As a matter of history, the paediatrician has taken the lead over non-accidental injury to children. That he is finding that this work occupies an inordinate amount of his time should add zest to the search for preventive treatment. His main roles must always be in diagnosis and in teaching child development, and it is to the paediatricians that other doctors, especially doctors in training, should look for methodology. Some social workers have experience of maladroit handling of abused children and their parents in both paediatric and accident departments. To be avoided is any accusatory implications in history-taking, too readily felt by parents who are guilty, unwilling to face up to what they have done and all too ready to hate authority and to dislike co-operation. The child who has suffered physical abuse at home may still fear separation from its cruel parents. Removal of clothes, which are a protection, and a clinical examination may be from the child's point of view assault in yet another form. The child's panic may easily be met by the doctor with annoyance if not anger and the whole incident may seriously stress the child. A suggestion was made that such first examination should usually be made only by experienced or senior paediatricians. This was considered by the group to make the unwarranted assumptions that sensitivity to the patient's feelings was a quality always found in seniors and never in juniors. The British Paediatric Association and the British Association of Paediatric Surgeons are to be invited to comment on these observations.

The conduct of the case conference

Chapter 22 contains the report on the NSPCC's case conference study and reveals some disquietening features. As the result Ray Castle, the Director of the NSPCC National Advisory Centre, made the following recommendations:

1. Case conferences should be structured with an experienced Chairperson.
2. Each member should provide a short resume of his/her involvement with the family.
3. Involved personnel who cannot attend should, when possible, submit a report.
4. Time limits should be set.
5. There needs to be more flexibility of location to enable better attendance of medical personnel.
6. It would be helpful to consider the setting up of special Sub-Committees of Area Review Committees to advise on those cases where the conference members are unable to agree on a decision.

These proposals received the support of the meeting after a discussion, the details of which are recorded on pages 153 to 154. The group deplored the wastage of expensive professional time resulting partly from inadequate preparation but partly from the paucity of secretarial help. The case conference, when it finds that the choice of the best management plan is impracticable through lack of services, must inform the area review committee. This is of the utmost importance if gaps are to be identified and ever filled.

The area/district review committee

Both Geoffrey Lupton in Chapter 21 and R.W. Speirs in Chapter 19 describe the difficulties inherent in review committees. Practice seems to vary considerably in almost every detail of structure, function and procedure. The group believe that these committees form an essential element in the management of child abuse and neglect and that the collection of the details of the various patterns by the DHSS and their study could form the basis for another advistory circular. Each committee could then examine itself, and by comparing its own methods with those of others could learn useful lessons. The question of consensus in case conference decisions was also discussed and over this, too, experience and practice varied. The feeling was generally expressed that the review committee has the responsibility for hearing about and discussing those difficulties and of devising methods by which they might be resolved. Anthony Fairburn recommended the Bath monitoring scheme (see Ch. 9) which, it was thought, might be useful in some other areas. Such arrangements would contain both 'follow-up' and 'register' implications. Each area needs to devise its own system in line with local circumstances.

On registers

Dr Chambers felt that the collation of the numbers of chilren on the local registers and of the numbers who have died with the cause of death should, ideally, provide a measure of prevalence of non-accidental injury to children. The Study Group did not believe that the present registers could be used in this way. They do accept the need for a more realistic knowledge of prevalence and for this reason urge DHSS to establish the confidential enquiry outlined in Resolution 2 (see p.196). Meanwhile the examination of the different methods used in compiling and using local registers on a countrywide basis should be informative and could be helpful. If registers are to do more than assist in local management, some standardisation of the records is urgently needed.

Apart from the general register to include families suspected as well known to be abusive to children, some form of follow-up register is essential. Anthony Fairburn, using the Bath monitoring system, categorised families as 'high risk' or 'low risk', preferring this to 'known, suspected or potential' abusers. Concentration on the high risk families could save work by possibly overloaded workers.

The highest risk families are those believed to be beyond the possibility of rehabilitation and reliable criteria are badly needed for their identification. Opinion was divided as to the procedure to be adopted when a new baby is considered to be in real danger in the parents' care and the parents are considered not be amenable to treatment (see Ch. 26 and the discussion following).

On confidentiality

Opinion was also divided on the question of confidentiality when a family's name is entered on a register. Ideally the family should know about it and also should know about the discussions in the case conference as well as the outcome. On the other hand considerable maturity of outlook, insight and the ability 'to think out rather than act out', are required by men and women before they can cope with this knowledge. Unfortunately these qualities are not well developed in abusing families. The group recognises that a return to this subject in the future is desirable.

The group heard with great interest the description by Dr J.J. Pietersee of Rotterdam of the so-called 'confidential doctor' in Holland, which does overcome some of the problems of confidentiality. The paper will be published in the Proceeding of the First International Congress on Child Abuse and Neglect, Geneva (*International Journal of Child Abuse and Neglect*, 1977. **No. 1**, Oxford: Pergamon).

On assessment of progress

The group throughout its discussions stressed the importance of proper assessment of progress of families. The abused child needs direct help and the success or failure of that help can only be judged if comprehensive data are collected. The absence of further physical injuries, although highly desirable, is totally inadequate by itself. Growth in height and weight over a period gives a sensitive guide. Educational progress for the older child and developmental progress for the younger one, especially of language skills, as well as evidence of emotional adjustment must all be taken into account. But it is not only the abused child whose progress needs assessment. The siblings may, without actual physical abuse, be suffering from neglect and emotional abuse. The parents, too, should be responding to treatment and Harold Martin indiscussion (see p.69) described the criteria on which judgement can be based.

On education

Considerable time was spent on education at all levels and this is dealt with in specific Resolutions (8 and 9, see Ch. 29).

On the law and legal procedure

The Study group remains uneasy, as a result of the experience of its members in Court, about the importance given to the child's welfare. One proposal discussed was that in future legislation concerning custody, care or control, the best interests of the child shall be the first *and* paramount consideration.

Richard White pointed out that the matter is not as simple as that. Where statutory intervention by a local authority under the Children Acts is considered, specific grounds are needed for the removal of care from the parents. This is one reason for the present interest in wardship which avoids such restriction. The welfare of the child is then the first and paramount consideration, as in other proceedings relating to the custody and upbringing of children which are governed by the Guardianship of Minors Act 1971.

Her Honour Judge Graham Hall has provided the following informative note.

'By Section 44(1) of the Children and Young Persons Act 1933 "every court dealing with a child or young person brought before it, either as an offender or otherwise, shall have regard to the welfare of the child or young person and shall, in a proper case, take steps for removing him from undesirable surroundings and for securing that proper provision is made for his education and training".

'Professor H.K. Bevan (in *The Law Relating to Children,* Butterworth, 1973), submits that it is with regard to criminal jurisdiction that uncertainty surrounds Section 44 owing to differing opinions as to how far criminality should involve the interests of the public as well as those of the juvenile. He points out that, in their criminal jurisdiction, juvenile courts are divided between the view that the effect of the section is to make the juvenile's welfare the paramount, even the sole factor irrespective of the nature of his delinquency, and that which relates his welfare to the delinquency and to the public interest.

'In civil cases the juvenile courts are statutorily directed by Section 1 of the Guardianship of Minors Act 1971 which states that "where in any proceedings before any court the custody or upbringing of a minor is in question the court in deciding the question shall regard the welfare of the minor as the first and paramount consideration". Where custody and care and control was in issue, the Court of Appeal has so held in a number of recent cases. In S.(B.l.) v. S.(J.J.) Infants Care and Consent 1977 1 AER 656 C.A. Lord Justice Ormrod explained that the law was quite plain and the statute perfectly clear that it was the best interests of the children which predominated.

'With regard to Adoption in the Children Act 1975 Section 3 states "In reaching any decision relating to the adoption of a child a court or adoption agency shall have regard to all the circumstances, first consideration being given to the need to safeguard and promote the welfare of the child throughout his childhood". These words are repeated verbatim in Section 6 of the Adoption Act 1976. In Re B 1972 2 WLR 755 Cumming Bruce J, explained that the effect of Section 3 of the Children Act was to impose upon a court responsible for making an objective appraisal of the reasonableness of the parent in witholding consent, a duty to regard the welfare of the child as the first consideration in the process of weighing several conflicting considerations which have to be taken into account.

'Although these two Acts do not go as far as some people wished, they are a further step in the direction away from the attitude of protecting parents' rights towards that of protecting the child's rights. In summary in Adoption the child's welfare is now the first consideration, but not the sole consideration.

'Even "first and paramount" does not mean "exclusive" and the court should consider and weigh all the circumstances that are of relevance, giving absolute priority to the child's interests.

The Study Group does not feel able, having clarified the issue, to make any proposals or resolutions.

One Tunbridge Wells Resolution (K) and three, 6, 7 and 9, at Farnham directly concern the law. The many problems both of law and of court procedure were discussed at both meetings, one evening at Farnham being devoted to discussions with Judge Graham Hall.

One problem, easily identified, is the weakness of the supervision order, and Sally Beer presented the views of her association in the following terms.

'Supervision orders: Under Section 68 of Schedule 3 of the Children Act 1975 the Secretary of State may make regulations regarding supervision orders whereby conditions might be imposed. The British Association of Social Workers supports the proposal and would like to suggest three possible conditions:

'a)   A right of access to the child
'b)   A right to require a medical examination
'c)   A right to require that the child attends some designated facility (e.g. day nursery or play group).'

The group, while approving in general the proposed conditions, considered that to establish them as rights in any effective and legally sanctioned terms would be difficult. They rest at present on the wording of Resolution 6 (see p.197).

The new Resolutions 6 and 7 deal respectively with the strengthening of the supervision order and the presence of legal advisers at case conferences. The need for continuing education of magistrates and clerks to juvenile courts is catered for in Resolution 9. The Study Group expressed concern that at present there shall be a guardian *ad litem* and the child shall be legally represented only in uncontested suits for revocation of care orders. In contested cases the child's point of view is not always put to the court by the solicitor who is supposed to be representing the child on whose behalf legal aid is granted.

29. Resolutions from the Farnham meeting

The previous chapter sets out and brings into focus many of the proposals made by participants in the discussions and by authors in their papers. The Tunbridge Wells Study Group hopes that Chapter 28 as well as Chapter 29 will prove helpful to the wide variety of professional and lay people who are concerned with the management of the problems of child abuse and with the provision of services. In a study group gathered by this common interest but coming from many professions, some members in a sense representing those professions or institutions, others representing only themselves, the formulation of specific resolutions presents almost insuperable difficulties.

The Editor, who must take responsibility for the final version of such resolutions, has tried to reflect the general views of the members. He must make it absolutely clear that not every member agrees with every resolution and that no profession, institution or government department is committed to accept the views, proposals or resolutions expressed in this book, even when made by its representative.

That having been said, nine specific resolutions seem worth presenting.

1. That the DHSS be asked to prepare and circulate a further paper on Child Abuse giving procedural advice on the conduct and the responsibilities of area and district review committees and of the case conference (see Ch. 21 and 22).

2. That the DHSS and the Scottish and Welsh Offices be urged to establish a confidential enquiry lasting for one year into all childhood deaths up to the third birthday. Among important questions to be studied are marital status, the conditions of siblings and the social indices of families.

3. That the DHSS should make recommendations, aimed at limiting to the minimum the separation of newly delivered women from their new babies, with the co-operation of the Central Midwives Board, the Royal College of Obstetricians and Gynaecologists and the British Paediatric Association.

4. That every booking at an ante-natal clinic should be notified through the Area Nursing Officer (Child Health) to the appropriate Health Visitor so that she can visit the home before the baby is born.

5. That, especially in families judged to be at risk, greater use should be made of community midwives in the ante-natal supervision of women either in their homes or in health centres.

6. That the supervision order should be strengthened and that the progress of every child under such an order should be adequately assessed on the basis of regular examination.

7. That the local social services department should make available experienced legal advice at every case conference at which the legal position of any of the parties is to be considered. This is of special importance when a decision may be made that legal action is required to protect the child.

8. That the DES, the DHSS, the Scottish Home and Health and Education Department, and the Welsh Office be asked to look into the provision and the content of existing courses in parenting, family care and child development. In the opinion of the Study Group, these courses could play an important part in the prevention of child abuse. They could also improve the care of children generally. Their effectiveness would be increased by treating them as important elements in the school curriculum, by making them available to all pupils of both sexes and by inviting experts from outside the teaching profession to make some contribution to the teaching programme.

9. That there is need for common courses in child development, child needs and child care for teachers, social workers including probation officers, doctors and medical students as well as nurses, midwives and advocates. These courses should be open to magistrates and clerks to juvenile courts and in Scotland to sheriffs, reporters and panel members. The need should be recognised for continuing education in these subjects by all those whose work puts them in a position for making decisions about the care, protection and custody of children.

10. That in all care cases, psychiatric reports on parents and caretakers should be regarded as essential. Of particular importance are the parents' attitude towards family life and children and their response to crisis.

Note

The presence of an adviser to the Scottish Office has ensured the mention of that body in some resolutions. It is our hope that neither the Welsh Office nor the Northern Ireland Office will take exception to the singling out of the Scottish Office, but that they will regard themselves as included in the appropriate places.

Appendix 1. A suggested syllabus for a course in child development and the family

A suggested Syllabus for a Course in Child Development and the Family reproduced by kind permission of the Inner London Education Authority and the Metropolitan Regional Examinations Board.

Aims

1. To provide for the pupils a course in which, by studying family life and the pre-school child, they themselves may be helped to grow towards maturity and become responsible parents.
2. To encourage a greater awareness of the needs of young children through learning about environmental and other circumstances which may affect their development.

The syllabus is designed to cover two years but could be taken in one year by fifth or sixth year pupils provided sufficient time is allocated on the time table. If the course is taken in one year, *at least* one session (a.m. or p.m.) plus one period per week is required. An essential part of the course is practical experience with the under-fives in play groups, nursery classes, etc.

Use should be made of films, slides, loops, tape recordings, books and other media which will stimulate interest. Visits out and invited speakers should be used where possible. Practical sessions relating to food, clothing and toy making etc., for young children should also be included.

Contents of the course

Family and kinship
1. Social structure; extended and nuclear families here and in other cultures
2. Social services

Marriage and parenthood
1. Relationships and responsibilities within and beyond the family
2. Planning a family

Growth and development from conception
1. Heredity; physical and tempermental characteristics
2. Nutrition and its effects on the mother and unborn child
3. Health during pregnancy
4. Physiology of pregnancy and childbirth

5.   Preparation for the new baby
6.   Infant welfare services
7.   Clinics and immunisation

Family adjustment to the new baby
1.   Mother's health and reaction, physical and emotional
2.   Adjustment to new routine for both parents
3.   Father's role

Needs of baby and young child
1.   Physical needs
   a)   Food: importance of balanced diet: Preparation of nutritious meals
   b)   Health: Fresh air, exercise, sleep, clothing, dental care
2.   Emotional needs
   a)   Love, security, warmth, companionship
   b)   Training for independence; short separations from mother
   c)   Formation of good habits

Communication and language development
1.   Vital importance of talking to, reading to and listening to children
2.   Satisfactory language development dependent on communication

Stimulating environment
1.   Curiosity leading to discovery: need for play in the home and outside
2.   Nursery schools or classes
3.   Play Groups, 1 o'clock Clubs
4.   Preparing for school

Personality development
1.   Emotions: love, jealousy, hate, fear, grief: learning to cope with emotions;
   problems associated with them, e.g. insecurity, aggression

Social training
1.   Learning to live with others; truthfulness; rewards and deterrents

The sick child
1.   In the home; common ailments and simple home nursing
2.   In the hospital; stress

Safety of the child
1.   Home safety
2.   Road safety
3.   Hazards outside the home

First aid
1.   Simple First Aid including mouth to mouth resuscitation

The handicapped child
1.   Physical and mental

Children in special circumstances
1.   Adoption, fostering, one parent families, children in care, children and
   neglect

Appendix 2. The 1976 survey by the probation and after-care service

An inquiry about the number of cases arising out of offences involving non-accidental injury to children under the age of 17 years, for which the Service had a responsibility on 1 October 1973, showed that at that time probation officers were concerned with such cases in about 350 families. In some 250 of these families, one or both parents were in consequence subject to probation orders. That inquiry formed the background to the more detailed study undertaken for the Probation & After-Care Department by Janet Sturgess and Kevin Heal of the Home Office Research Unit on the subject of 'Non-Accidental Injury to Children under the age of 17', the report of which was produced in May 1975 (RES 663/2/65). Guidance given to the Probation Service in an Annex to Home Office Circular No 4/1975 about children at risk advocated that positive steps should be taken to identify and to maintain a special register for families in which a child may be at risk of injury or neglect. Internal registration by the Probation and After-Care Service is not intended as a substitute or an alternative to registration with the responsible authority under Area Review Committee arrangements. It is however intended to bring into operation certain safeguards covering assignment of work, regular and specific review by a senior officer to provide an objective check to judgement, professional support to the probation officer, and to sustain effective agency and inter-agency practices. The internal register is not confined to cases in which children are at risk of non-accidental injury but includes those who are at risk of other kinds of child abuse, including neglect and other forms of ill-treatment. It may therefore be broader in scope than registers established under Area Review Committee arrangements.

In April 1976 chief probation officers were asked to provide information on a wider front than was reported as at 1 October 1973, about the extent to which the Service is now concerned with children at risk of abuse. This inquiry focused upon cases which had been registered as at risk of abuse in accordance with the guidance given in the Annex to Home Office Circular 4/1975. It was intended to clarify additionally whether the cases so registered were also registered with the responsible authority under Area Review Committee arrangements and, if not, the reasons for differentiation.

All chief probation officers responded to the inquiry which produced the information given in the Annex to this paper concerning registration of cases at at 1 April 1976. There was a discrepancy in the returns from areas in that the total

* Reproduced by kind permission of the Probation and After-Care Service of the Home Office

number of internal registrations was not entirely matched by the detailed breakdown of categories of case. There were 33 fewer cases in the detailed breakdown than in the total registrations, but this was too small a discrepancy at less than 1.5 per cent to justify going back to areas for fresh information. In the summary information contained in the Annex, we have therefore resorted to the device of expressing the total in each category as a percentage of the total cases reported in the detailed breakdown since this accurately reflects the distribution within the total for which information was given.

Reference has been made to the possibility that a probation area internal register may be broader in scope than the register established by Area Review Committee arrangements. To a large extent, however, the difference of 414 between cases registered internally and under Area Review Committee auspices represents a difference of criteria in assessing risk. Internal registration by the Probation Service more universally reflects perceived risk, which may fall short of actual known injury. This is consistent with the purposes of early identification and prevention. By contrast, in a number of cases it is stated that some Area Review Committee arrangements exclude registration in the absence of pre-existing known injury. In some such cases for which central registration is not agreed by the responsible authority, a note is nevertheless made by social services department against the possibility of other referrals or enquiries.

In general, probation areas are satisfied that due consideration is given in the great majority of cases notified for registration and are not aggrieved at refusal to register. There are however some grounds for thinking that in a few cases such refusal is believed to be misguided and short sighted, particularly if the effective decision is taken not by case conference but by a single agency. These are exceptional, and by and large the Probation Service is content that it should maintain its own safeguarding procedures pending more certain identification of risk. There may however be a case for questioning whether refusal to register centrally in the absence of known injury could be counter-productive to early recognition of risk, sharpened alertness of workers to precipitating factors, and the ready mobilisation and co-ordination of agency and inter-agency preventive measures. A register which is too narrowly conceived might be in danger of becoming a register of children at risk of further injury rather that one of children at risk who may be prevented from actually experiencing serious injury.

That 18 per cent of Probation Service internal registrations are not also registered under Area Review Committee arrangements seems understandable in view of the explanations given by areas. It may be said that probation areas are tending to be fairly cautious and rightly are concerned to ensure so far as possible that they respond appropriately to the risks which they perceive.

In another sense, namely that over 81 per cent of cases identified by the Probation Service as at risk are similarly acknowledged by others concerned with registration under Area Review Committee arrangements, it may be considered that the numbers registered by the Service are a fairly realistic measure of the extent of its involvement with children at risk of abuse.

The information gleaned from this inquiry about the distribution of related Probation Service responsibilities is of interest. In as many as 58 per cent of cases registered the responsibility arises from an adult offence other than child abuse. This confirms what we have believed from such evidence as has been available to us, that child risk in a very substantial proportion of cases is not the natural focus for the probation officer arising from the nature of the offence by virtue of which he has been given a supervisory responsibility. This finding adds point to the view which has been expressed that in such cases, in which non-accidental injury is not central to the purpose of Probation Service intervention, there may be the greatest professional demand in terms of awareness and recognition of risk.

Other features of note are the low involvement arising from juvenile offence and care proceedings and the negligible involvement arising from domestic work (other than matrimonial and wardship supervision) and voluntary supervision.

Table A2.1 Registration by the Probation and After-Care Service of children at risk as at 1 April 1976

				Numbers	Percentages
1.	Total cases (i.e. households or family units) registered by the Service			2,267	n = 2234 (98.5%) 100.0
2.	Cases registered by the Service which were not also registered with the responsible authority under the Area Review Committee[arrangements			414	18.3
3.	Probation Service responsibility arose out of:				
	(a)	An adult committing offences involving:			
		(i)	Non-accidental injury to a child	386	17.3
		(ii)	Other forms of abuse to a child	205	9.2
		(iii)	Other crimes	1,309	58.6
	(b)	Juvenile offences or care proceedings		80	3.6
	(c)	Civil matters			
		(i)	Matrimonial and wardship supervision	179	8.0
		(ii)	Other domestic work, e.g. conciliation casework	25	1.1
	(d)	Voluntary supervision		50	2.2

Appendix 3. The NSPCC questionnaire

Full Name

Title

Group

1. State number of case conferences attended between 1st March 1976 and 30th May 1976.
2. How many case conferences attended during this period were the first held on the family concerned?
3. How many first case conferences involved non-accidental injury?
4. How many case conferences attended during the period were called because of re-battering following previous conference on the same child?
5. How many case conferences attended during the period concerned first time non-accidental injury to a sibling of a child on whom a previous case conference had been held?
6. Who initiated?
   (a) Social Services
   (b) NSPCC
   (c) Hospital
   (d) Area Health Authority
   (e) Probation Service
   (f) Other
7. Who chaired the conference?
   (a) Senior Member Social Services
   (b) Senior Member NSPCC
   (c) Hospital Consultant
   (d) Senior Member Area Health Authority
   (e) Senior Member Probation Service
   (f) Other

8.   Where was conference held?
    (a)   Hospital
    (b)   Social Services Department
    (c)   General Practitioner's Surgery
    (d)   Probation Department
    (e)   NSPCC Group Office
    (f)   Other
9.   Time element: how many of these conferences took
    (a)   Up to one hour?
    (b)   One hour — two hours?
    (c)   Over two hours?
10.   Involvement of medical personnel: In how many instances did general
    practitioners attend?
11.   In how many instances was hospital consultant present?
12.   In how many instances was a member of the police present?
13.   Whereabouts of child: where was child or children concerned at
    time of case conference?
    (a)   At home
    (b)   Hospital
    (c)   Residential Nursery
    (d)   Foster Home
    (e)   In the care of relatives
    (f)   Other (state where)
14.   Legal Proceedings: initial case conferences
    In those cases where this was an initial case conference
    how many recommended court proceedings?
    (a)   Juvenile court
    (b)   Adult court
    (c)   None
15.   Follow up case conferences: how many children in these cases
    were already the subjects of care orders or supervision orders?
16.   Initiation of court proceedings: if juvenile court proceedings
    were recommended, who initiated proceedings?
    (a)   NSPCC
    (b)   Social Services
    (c)   Police
    (d)   Probation Service
    (e)   Other
    If other state 'who'
17.   Adult court proceedings: if adult court proceedings were
    recommended, who initiated proceedings?
    (a)   NSPCC
    (b)   Social Services
    (c)   Police
    (d)   Other
    If other state 'who'

18. Indicate ages of children concerned:
   Number   Age
             Under 5 yr
             6 - 11 yr
             12 - 16 yr
19. Write brief comments giving your opinion about the
    effectiveness of case conference procedures in your area.

Appendix 4. The NSPCC special units

National Advisory Centre on the Battered Child, Denver House, The Drive, Bounds Green Road, London N.11; Executive Head: Mr. Raymond L. Castle; Tele: 01-361-1181

The NSPCC Special Units are as follows:

MANCHESTER: 5 Wynnstay Grove, Fallowfield, M14 6XG (Tele: 061-248-6060
 Team Leader: A.E. Maton

LEEDS: 1st Floor, 10 Woodhouse Square, LS3 1AD (Tele: 444198)
 Team Leader: D. Turner

NEWCASTLE: 2nd Floor, MEA House, Ellison Place, NE1 8XS (Tele: 611719)
 Team Leader: D. Hall

COVENTRY: 34 Smithford Way, CV1 1FX (Tele: 22456)
 Team Leader: P.P. Tudor

NORTHAMPTONSHIRE: Orchard House, Wellingborough, Northants (Tele: 0933-223920)
 Team Leader: P.W. Griffiths

GOLDTHORPE: Dearne Town Hall, Nr. Barnsley, S. Yorks, S63 9EJ (Tele: Rotherham 894299 & 893847)
 Team Leader: S.J. Mitson

NOTTINGHAM: Gordon Road, NG3 2LE (Tele: 57189 & 57176)
 Team Leader: Mrs. K.P. Hill

Index

207